LANDFALL AT SUNSET

By the same author

THE BRASSBOUNDER, 1910
BROKEN STOWAGE, 1915
MERCHANTMEN-AT-ARMS, 1919
THE LOOKOUTMAN, 1923
CAPSTAN BARS, 1931
MERCHANTMAN REARMED 1949
THE QUEERFELLA, 1952

The Author

LANDFALL AT SUNSET

The Life of a Contented Sailor

by

DAVID BONE

GERALD DUCKWORTH & CO LTD
3 Henrietta Street, London, W.C.2

First published November 1955
Reprinted January 1956
Reprinted March 1956

Printed in Great Britain by
Richard Clay and Company, Ltd., Bungay, Suffolk

TO THE MEMORY OF
MY BROTHER
MUIRHEAD

CONTENTS

CONTENTS

ILLUSTRATIONS

'You are a man washed up from the sea and you should know of these things. You weren't so long in the sea, you'd say in your foolishness. I tell you now, you were long enough. You were in it, rolled in it, lost in it, found in it, and the tide left you, so you are a son of the sea. . . . You will never think of the sea again but as a friend. If you were in a dismasted ship alone, rolling in the troughs of the waves, and hopeless in the minds of men, you would not hate the sea. The man who has never been handled fully by the tide of the sea is always in fear, not so much of his body, but of his spirit. He thinks the sea will try and get a piece of it anyway, though he believes perhaps he can resist the sea. . . . But a man such as yourself knows that the spirit of the sea will never touch your spirit any more . . . and you will always have your secret understanding.'

Silvanus, in *The Charmed Life*, by J. B. Yeats

ACKNOWLEDGEMENTS

The author is grateful to many kind people for permission to include in this volume a number of quotations from copyright works: to Mr Jack Butler Yeats, R.H.A., for the short text from *The Charmed Life*; to Mr John Conrad for permission to quote from his father's letters to the author; to the Literary Executors of the late Rear-Admiral Sir Douglas Brownrigg for the use of excerpts from *The Indiscretions of the Naval Censor*. To the Anchor Line of Glasgow (whose centenary of oversea operations occurs at about this date) the author is indebted for access to its files and the use of illustrations from official sources; to Lady (Gertrude) Bone and my nephew Stephen I am grateful for permission to reproduce my brother Muirhead's drawing of our father in his writing days.

Chapter I

STORM IN THE NIGHT

TO establish a far-back link in the chain of early memories there should be a significant experience connected with it. Mine is the recollection of a tempest that swept across Scotland when I was about five. I remember that, lying in bed, I thought I could hear a voice in the wind as it sang through some faulty jointing in the attic skylight. But that night there was nothing like a song in the scream of the fierce gale as I lay for long awake listening and in dread of it.

The day had broken on a moderate storm of wind and rain, in no way unusual on Clydeside at that turn of the year, and my two elder brothers had set off for school; but with Muirhead, who was two years younger, I was held indoors. For a time we played together, but something sinister in the weather cast a shadow on our childish pastimes. How the wind rose and an incessant deluge of slanting rain and sleet battered and sluiced the window-panes! There was thunder too, and the lightning had a greenish glare amid the racing storm-clouds. But before the short December day had darkened down, some change in the wind took place, and except for furious squalls the rain ceased. Soon, but for the racing and ragged storm-cloud as the gale increased, the sky lightened and a freezing period came to pattern the windows with a crust of ice or snow. As darkness fell it became bitterly cold, and even the blazing fire in the kitchen, around which we children huddled, seemed to have lost all warmth, despite the abundance of coal so frequently piled on. We were all put early to bed, and found comfort in the warmth of the blankets. . . . But not for long. I suppose we must have drowsed or slept for a while, but if sleep did come to us in such a Viking roar of wind and rain, we were alarmingly aroused from it. At some time in the early morning, and at the height of the gale, a large piece of

13

masonry broke away from the chimney-head and crashed through the sodden roof to hurtle down the attic stairway to the lower flat. I cannot remember what was done to deal with the situation, recalling only the cries of frightened children, the sudden inrush of the furious icy wind, the falling of slates and debris from the roof, and the gaping black wound in the ceiling overhead. My father was on night duty at his newspaper office in the city, and only my mother and a frightened maid were in the house; but soon kindly neighbours came to aid my distracted mother and we were taken from the attic flat, now open to the thundering riot of the elements. ... The date was Saturday, 28th December, 1879. The black night of the Tay Bridge disaster!

It may well have been as a result of that experience that our household was removed shortly after to a less exposed dwelling in Laurelbank. Although well within the boundaries of the busily industrial burgh of Partick, our new address had good grounds for such a sylvan street-name. It was not on a main thoroughfare, as our former noisy dwelling in Dumbarton Road had been, but situated in a short and almost rural cul-de-sac branching from the traffic-laden Crow Road, ending in a wide expanse of green fields where the local dairymen pastured their herds. In Laurelbank there were modest villa dwellings, each with its neat flower-garden in the front and a sizeable vegetable area in the rear, but it is not in one of these my memory lingers. Ours was again a flat in a tenement building almost on the summit of Partickhill. Our parents had ever their fondness for a good view—a far outlook—above all else in selection of a dwelling, and Glenavon Terrace met their wishes without hazard of a vulnerable rooftree. There may, too, have been an economy in this lofty preference, for lifts were then unknown and the lower flats were more greatly in demand by the prosperous elderly house-hunters.

From this new eminence the windings of the Clyde could be followed from down-stream at Clydebank to the shipyards at Meadowside and Govan, a view that was obscured by factories and workshops from our lodging in Dumbarton Road, and we quickly found fresh excitements in watching the passage of ships in the river. There was education in that arresting panorama, and before long we had learned about the tidal periods in which the inward and outward-bound traffic was at its height; we could often name the busy

The Author's Father
From a drawing by Muirhead Bone, about 1897

'Outward Bound in square rig'
Drawn by the author

coastal steamers by their multi-coloured house-flags or by some peculiarity of deck erections. The river steamers, with their foam-crushing and resounding paddles, were specially our favourites when we crowded to the windows to watch them weave a passage upstream or down. They were the harbingers of summer holiday, when, after wintering at Bowling or in the quiet of the Greenock quays, they reappeared in the river spruced up in brave new coats of paint to meet our needs for sea-travel on the Firth of Clyde.

It was in keeping with that inspiring maritime prospect from our windows on Partickhill that most of our nearby friends and neighbours were in some way occupied with the building of the ships or the construction of the engines for them, and when the launching of a new vessel was in prospect we could always learn of it in time to gather for the stirring sight. The great shipyards at Govan and Linthouse lay plainly under our eyes, and we could see the construction of a ship from a gaunt iron skeleton on the stocks to the magnificence of a fully-plated liner standing beflagged and erect on the river's bank to await her formal baptism. A launching at the Govan shipyards could best be seen from the pasture-fields at the western end of Laurelbank, and it was there the children of the district assembled to enjoy the spectacle. There was no appearance of haste in the ceremonial. Let the day be fair, we were there to see the peopling of the decorated platform erected at the bows or the gradual encroachment of the shipyard crowds on nearby points of vantage. How the great new ship with her canopy of gay flags seemed solidly immovable, highly perched over there on the river's bank . . . and how long the waiting before high water came. Then would come the shrilling of steam whistles from the tugs in the river and the engine-shops on its banks to give us word of her release. Movement, impatiently looked for, was painfully slow until the ship herself took charge and gathered way to back majestically into the river, brimming its banks with the foam of her displacement.

But even on Clydeside not all ship launchings go smoothly and according to plan. I remember returning from school on a summer afternoon in early July of 1883 and seeing my mother's serving-maid rushing frantically down the Crow Road towards the river, shrieking wild cries and from time to time throwing her apron over her head to veil her grief, in the way Highland people do. I learned later that the newly-built *Daphne*, in which her father was employed, on being launched at Linthouse, had overturned in the river and that many workmen—our Mirren's father among them—were believed drowned.

Chapter II

THE NAUTICAL CAP

MY father, who began his adult life as a journeyman compositor, had come from his native town of Ayr to follow the printing trade in the town of greater opportunities. In time, employment in the case-room led to preferment on the reporting staff of the *North British Daily Mail*, a strongly Liberal newspaper published in Glasgow. He remained in its service throughout his working life. He had good ancestral warrant for the radical opinions he so often supported, for a Chartist grandfather (incidentally a farm schoolmate of Robert Burns when under the teaching of John Murdoch), who, when not bewailing the confiscation of his printing press or in jail for some libellous misuse of it, edited a broadsheet named *The Mustard Blister*, to the scandal of the County.

I remember my father as a tall man of lithe build and active movement. His was a distinguished appearance, to which an oversized beard added a patriarchal solemnity, somewhat belied by the humour of observant eyes. He was notably explosive of speech and had his way of dramatizing the most ordinary remonstrance or reproof, so often called forth by the destructive or messy habits of his young. 'In the name of God,' he might declaim—'in the name of God . . . look at your boots!' pointing to evidence of the casual impact of sharp causey stones. Or, gazing in disgust at sticky fingers that had left their impress on chairs or clothing—'The curr-rse of this house is jam!' Except when engaged upon such 'weatherly' journalistic assignments as the sea-trials of a new Atlantic liner—when a 'nautical' cap was thought the appropriate headgear—he always wore a tall silk hat. It may be thought that an expensive silk topper was overly extravagant for a modest newsman, but it may well be that he had his own sources of supply in the wagers that he so often won, when in argument concerning the tonnage of the new

liners or the indicated horse-power of Tod and Macgregor's marvellous triple expansions.

In his coverage of events for the *North British Daily Mail* he
specialized in shipping news, and particularly in writing of the
amazing developments in steamship construction and marine
engineering, nowhere more actively and triumphantly pursued than
on the Clyde. In the years between 1880 and 1900 there were few
ship launches or trial trips he was not invited to attend, and his informed reports on them were widely quoted. It was he who coined
the phrase 'greyhound of the Atlantic' as descriptive of the long,
lean, and swift *Alaska* of the Guion Line, in which he had made a
voyage to the United States as a passenger in 1882.

When the needs of a growing family could not always be met by
the modest salary he earned from daily journalism, he was sometimes able to augment it by occasional outside contributions. A
special feature of the *North British Daily Mail* was his expert survey
and summary of Scottish shipbuilding and engineering throughout
the year, and from his copious notes on the subject he often placed
an article with journals and newspapers across the border. On
occasion his authoritative surveys of Clydeside shipping and shipbuilding obtained even more distant publication. In 1880 Bret
Harte was appointed United States Consul in Glasgow. Not im-
probably, the busy rounds of his office, that entailed reportage of the
commerce and industry of a great city, proved irksome to this genial
bookman and novelist. In the upshot, he sought expert local assist-
ance, and it was for a period my father's informative reports he put
before his superiors in Washington, to the admiration of Congress
consultants.

Another special assignment, and one that afforded him an exercise
to his particular liking, was sport. In the years that I remember him
he was in charge of the sporting page in the columns of the Monday's
North British Daily Mail and on Scottish events he was also the
correspondent of 'Bell's Life in London'. While association football
was the most popular game that, in its season, took many columns of
description in the Press, cricket was the sport for which he had the
greatest aptitude and enthusiasm. As a young man he had played
the game when it was a newish form of athletics in Scotland, and
his love of it he carried with him almost to his deathbed. His book
Fifty Years of Scottish Cricket was published in 1898.

The weekly production of copy for the sporting page was almost a family affair. We elder children, now reaching an upper school age, were brought in to help with it. In the winter season, with the pressure of football games demanding unorthodox methods of reportage, we could be useful with scissors and paste in cutting strips from the Saturday's evening newspapers; or, did the importance of a fixture call for a brief paragraph, we could at least translate the jargon of the 'finals' to a less sporty English and render it suitable for staid reading on the Monday morning. That was not difficult. 'Quin made his effort to score' would do for 'Jeemy belted the sphere towards the enemy's citadel.' . . . An odd exercise for a Scottish Sunday afternoon! But it had its merits.

In the summer we were rewarded for our labours by a form of free admission to the cricket matches at Hamilton Crescent or Titwood or, on rare events, at Drumpelier. On these occasions we had no editorial duties. It was our father's privilege to attend to that. Our *modus operandi* was to prepare a special envelope marked in black printed letters—PRESS. URGENT.—and address it to 'Mr D. D. Bone, On the Ground'. When this was shown to the custodian at the turnstiles he would wave one on, to hurry towards an agreed position out of his sight where the open sesame could be passed through the high palings to an awaiting brother.

My early memories of conventional education in Partick are a compound of schooling at an old building in Church Street and later at a completely new and sightly edifice fronting on the cricket ground at Hamilton Crescent. I have only vague recollection of the progress, or the lack of it, I registered at either of these establishments. I suppose I must sometimes have appeared to have intelligence of a sort, else how did I manage to pass from one class to another? My best memory of the Hamilton Crescent Public School is of a teacher of English named John Main, who interested himself in unusual methods of arousing a pupil's latent capabilities. A friendly man, having none of the airs of masterdom and contempt for puerile stupidity, he brightened his classes by extra-mural excursions on Saturday afternoons to points of interest in the district. A visit to the underground of a nearby coal-mine or an hour of his company at the newly excavated fossil grove at Whiteinch might awaken an interest in a pupil that would not otherwise have been aroused. While eloquent on almost any subject, Mr Main had made physiography his own preferred study. Not the least of my many grateful memories of him is of being encouraged—with my class-mates—to submit a coloured sketch of geological strata that had been the subject of a talk by him. Knowing of my feeling for the sea and its affairs, and recognizing my ignorance of the stratum of old red sandstone, he was at pains to find something to commend in my drawing of the lighthouse and its flags that I had worked in a-top my wrongly variegated cliff formations.

In the bookcases at home were many volumes concerning ships, but these were mainly devoted to their construction, dimensions, propulsion, speeds—the technical data that my father used in his compilations. Few were of adventures on far seas, and it was for these I hankered. Mr Main set my foot on surer ground than the *Dick Deadeye* type of 'twopenny bloods' I favoured. He procured and lent to me the stirring novels of Marryat, Fenimore Cooper, Clark Russell, and Morley Roberts. Upon these I fastened, to read and re-read them until I could almost recite them by heart. Oddly, it was in Clark Russell's romances I gained a specious knowledge of sailoring in square sail. In much of his writing he exulted in relating incidents of single-handed prowess; so lucid was his detail of how this or that was done in his disabled ships, I took to childish experiment in the broad-beamed punt with hand-sewn sails of sacking that was my joy on holidays in Loch Goil, where our parents rented a summer cottage at Carrick Castle. On return to school when the glorious summer days were gone, it was Mr Main's custom to inquire of us where we had been and what we had done. Upon my mention of Clark Russell's devices and my endeavour, feeble as it was, to emulate his feats in the family punt, he said he thought that a most surprising effort. He added that real sailors were very proud of their skill in seamanship and quoted a sailor's poem to emphasize that view. (I have since learned that it was a line or two of Falconer's *Shipwreck* he recited.) It ran:

> Man the clew garnets! Let th' main sheet fly!
> It rends in thousand shivering fragments high.
> For he who strives the tempest to disarm
> Will never first embrail the lee yardarm.

A grand man, John Main! He taught me much that I could never have gathered from any more learned but less understanding dominie.

In 1887 my mother died. I have only vague memories of a loving lady who cried, with me, at my misdeeds. All I can learn of her ancestry is that her maiden name was Crawford and that her father, a tailoring contractor on the south side of Glasgow, supplied uniforms for the City of Glasgow police force. But if these particulars are indeterminate, I can testify to the sweet voice I knew that made her a favoured singer with the Glasgow Choral Union in about 1865. I think that was the mutual interest that brought my father to his knees, for he, too, had a fine voice and was a member of the Choral Union. All I can contribute to the memory of that lovely lady who, a little while before, had taken me in her arms, hiding my bloodstained face in her bosom—for I had as usual been fighting—is of her standing beside our jangling piano to sing 'Oh how can a poor gipsy mai-iden like me, ever hope the proud bride of a noble to be', and my father, fingering his well-macassared beard, joining in with baritone endearments as his part in the duet. That is a fanciful picture, perhaps, but it has warrant: we were six sons and two daughters born of that harmonious union.

Not long after our mother died we removed from Partick to the city and found a home in Jane Street off Blythswood Square. It was from there I set out on my first sea voyage, and 'Greek' Thomson's belfry on the Church of St Jude's across the way, now defiled by brick disfigurements, was my point of departure for ports abroad.

I suppose the pattern of my introduction to a life at sea was the not uncommon one of frequent truancies from school to wander by the riverside and the docks and indulge romantic fancy that someday I, too, would do such manly deeds as to climb the rigging and work cunningly with ropes, for it was always of seafaring in a sailing-ship that I dreamt. Certainly there was much of interest to be drawn from the sight of steamers propelling themselves with so little apparent effort up-river or down, but it was the tall square-rigger I sought; and in 1885 I did not have far to seek.

My resort on these illicit wanderings was at the south-east corner of the Queen's Dock, where the fine ships of the Loch Line of Australian clippers loaded their cargoes and prepared for sea. At first I was content to sit on a quayside bollard and do no more than observe the activities of the crew as they went about their business aloft and on the decks; but I may have become a familiar figure there at my watching post, with my father's 'nautical' cap on my head to avert the attention of the truancy officer. There were occasions when one or other of the heroes might pass a word with me. I learned that a full crew was not employed in the ship whilst she was in dock and that the lads I had so greatly envied were the apprentices, the 'brassbounders' who drew no pay. From such a casual contact to a closer association did not take long. There came a day when, prompted by them, if uninvited by any higher authority, I joined a working party employed in transferring deck stores from a lorry on the quayside to the ship, and I spent a happy hour of the late afternoon helping to carry drums of lamp-oil, coils of rope and cordage, bolts of canvas and hanks of tarry marlin, bags of nails and other sundries on board the *Loch Vennachar*. I must have been without guile in those days, for I did not consider it significant that the ship's mate, after seeing me thus busily occupied, waited until the lorry was emptied and the job completed before counting me out with a gruff inquiry as to what I thought I was doing? 'Get th' hell out of it,' was what he said. I did.

It was quite a long time before my visits to the dockside were resumed, for my delinquency had been discovered at home. One can't lump drums of colza oil or shoulder bundles of tarry spun-yarn without blemish and odours remaining on clothes and person. My one disguise, the nautical cap, was taken from me to be cleaned and securely locked up. But my bent for seafaring—that had been thought a passing fancy—was recognized and there was tacit understanding that when I had left school I would be apprenticed to the sea.

Chapter III

'SIGNING ON'

'*M-mmm!* He might have the makings o' a sailor,' was the doubtful opinion of the rugged old ship's husband when, with my father, I attended at the City Line offices in Glasgow to be bound apprentice to the sea. But the faint shade of approval contained in it was perhaps intended only to set my parent at ease, for there was little sign of a good impression in the glance that Captain Francis Brown cast at the new recruit before him. It is unlikely that I appeared a seemly applicant for sea service. A family photograph of the date portrays an undersized youth, strongly and stockily built, perhaps, but with slightly bent legs—a not uncommon blemish in a native of the Gorbals. But in that now faded photograph there is some promise revealed in the posture. It is aggressive. My inturned feet are sturdily planted, my fists tightly clenched, and my mouth pursed in a manner that shows no concession to the patient photographer's pleadings and admonitions. Perhaps it was in a pose like that I stood on the carpet in his office when I came under the critical eyes of the old sea captain. Sizing me up, he may have seen something in me, in my look, my stance, that he recognized as not unsuited to the hard sea trade he had known in his day.

That was in 1890, and I was rising sixteen—of an age to be put to work. It was a day to which I had long looked forward with enthusiasm and expectation. I had just signed my indentures and had the happy prospect of sailing out in the full-rigged ship *City of Florence* on far voyages; but my excitement and my joy in the thought of it were dampened by the grave bearing of my elders in the Captain's office room. My father was in sober mood and pondering the promise of the path I had elected to follow. His kind face betrayed a concern that was not there when, one by one, my elder brothers had set off to their first jobs. For them there was the

23

surety of steady progress and useful earnings, but not for me. I was then the odd man of the family, to whom an opening in counting-house or workshop or shipyard made no appeal. It was the sea that called me. I had no ear for any other voice.

Although the Clyde shipyards at that date were building steam-ships of great dimensions and power and speed (in 1889 the Atlantic was crossed in six days by the S.S. *City of Paris*), it was still considered that only on the reeling decks of a sailing-ship could the arts of seamanship be acquired. The City Line of Glasgow (George Smith and Sons) owned both sailing and steam ships, but only in the sailing vessels were apprentices indentured. The parents or guardians of these eager brassbounders were called upon to pay a premium for their instruction in 'the duties of a seaman' which was all the obligation the owners incurred. A premium of twenty-five pounds, return-able on completion of the contract, was the customary figure; an outfit, too, would have to be provided. It may have been these expenses that weighed with my father and caused him to hesitate while I fidgeted to be off and away. To a struggling journalist with a large family, twenty-five pounds was a considerable sum to be risked on the good behaviour of a wayward lad. Had he not heard of apprentices to the sea quickly tiring of it and leaving their ships in ports abroad, while others, equally perverse, had disobeyed the master's orders and broken the contract, to the forfeiture of the premium? He would have his doubts as his eyes turned from me to scan again the Articles of Indenture to which we were both committed.

Already they had been read over to us by the owners' managing clerk. There were many disciplinary clauses binding on the appren-tice. These were worded in traditional phrase and some were not very clearly applicable to the seafaring of the day. Certainly I could be diligent and obey the orders of the master, but what was all this about not attending fairs or conventicles, nor to gamble or play at unlawful games? Barratry, too! The clerk had looked fixedly at me when he spoke out—he knew his lines by heart—'. . . faithfully to attend to his duties and not to be party to the theft of the Owners' goods or the tackle and furniture of the ship, or the barratry of the mariners in respect of the cargo, but to report to the Owners any plot or plan of which he had gained knowledge'.

That my father was equally interested in the listing of deeds and misdeeds laid down in the document could be guessed at from his expression as he read it for himself. Relief was there; relief that he could not find my many faults and failings described as venial. Even the very major interdiction did not seemingly cause him anxiety. The apprentice was to be of sober habit, he read, 'and not to frequent taverns or alehouses—except upon the master's business'. . . . He was a clever journalist, and I can still imagine him chuckling at that apt exception. While some might take it to refer to the running of an important message, he thought—as phrased—it could point the duty of the industrious apprentice to bear his master safely from the tainted premises at closing hours. . . . Curiously and only once, that happened.

On leaving the office of the City Line, then in West Nile Street, my splendid father was in good spirits. His wayward offspring— the third of the series—had been settled in a trade. All might be well if only the lad applied himself to the business he had chosen. But still there was the matter of the substantial premium. 'Why,' he said reflectively, as though talking with himself, when we left the office and took our homeward way—'why should we spend all that money on making a sailor of the lad, when Willie made a good sailor of himself and cost his father nothing?'

The comparison that occupied his thoughts was not inept. Cousin William Hall was often spoken of at home in family dis-cussion of our kin. A forthright lad of twelve years, he had run away from his home at Irvine in about 1865, trudged on foot to the new port of Ardrossan, and sailed, a ship's boy, in the fo'c'sle of an American brig. His journal, which I have and cherish, relates his adventures. In it he wrote bravely:

> 'I had no reason for running away to sea. I had kind parents
> and a good home. But I was young then and thought that all
> the best things were far away.'

Perhaps I, too, thought that, as I trod the rainy streets of Glasgow. Now, after nearly sixty years of happiness in seafaring—meeting its trials and sharing the secrets of a not unkindly sea—I wonder if I did not find them.

Chapter IV

THE BRASSBOUNDER

THERE were three of us in the steerage of the Rotterdam boat. One was a Jew who beetled his brows and asked himself fierce questions in Low German; the other was a young little Fleming with strong arms and a hard head, who told me he had been a fireman on a "vickly" boat. (He explained that a vickly boat was one on which vickly wages were paid.) I was going to join my ship at Antwerp—going to sea on my very first voyage.

'The regular steamer for Antwerp had had a mishap and would not sail for some days. For me there could be no going back home after I had set out in my bravery of brass buttons and had made my bold good-byes. So I came in the Rotterdam boat and trusted to find a train.

'We left Leith Docks about midnight—a black, bitter midnight, with the wind strong east outside and a big sea rolling up the Firth and shattering on the pier-heads. I lingered to see the town lights vanish into the mist astern and, feeling ill, went below. How the *Britannia* plunged into it! How sick I was! I lay on my back in a low bunk and tried to court sleep, while the vickly man, in bad English and worse voice, sang "Leedle Fischer Ma-aiden".'

In these words I described my setting out in an article that appeared in print many years ago. What transpired after the vickly man's effort in song is of no interest now, save that I found him a kindly man who, upon our arrival in Antwerp—his home town—insisted on seeing me safely at the dockside where my ship lay. When, after many devious turnings and the crossing of canal bridges, we arrived alongside and he had helped me to mount the ramshackle gangway with my luggage, he did not stay for long. He gazed, almost in fright, at the masts and spars and the lonely decks of what seemed a forlorn and deserted ship. It was a bitterly cold day in November. It may have been the chill of the weather that made him shiver a little as he wished me well and hurried off to visit his friends in sailor-town. He would take nothing. I was 'for de sea out', he said.

It was long after the vickly man had gone before I found anyone to take notice of me. Cargo work in the ship had finished for the day and everyone was gone. Dusk had fallen—a gloomy dusk and cold—when the Mate, returning from some business ashore, finding me seated on my sea-chest at the lip of the gangway, vented sharp surprise in sailor fashion. 'What th' hell you doing here?' he asked. Recalling my experience in the *Loch Vennachar*, I hastened to explain myself, and was relieved to be told that I could stay. Mr Baird was not as angry as his challenge implied. He had had no word of anyone joining the ship, nor did he think the Captain had heard anything about me. There was no crew on board and all the ship's apprentices had been sent on leave while the cargo was being discharged. The half-deck, in which the brassbounders were berthed, was cold and empty. No food either. He had just been to a beer-house for a bite of supper, he said. Captain Leask was not on board. He was living in a hotel on shore. But there was a stove in the cabin where his room was. He said that I could stay there until some other arrangement was made. It may well be that I spent my first night in the *City of Florence* sleeping in the Captain's bunk.

It was early in November when I joined the ship in Antwerp: it was February of the next year when we sailed outbound for San Francisco. Hoary old Father Frost reigned without challenge in Europe in the winter of 1890–91. . . . Weatherly events are of sudden intensity. On the night of the 4th December, being fully loaded, manned, and prepared for sea, we warped the ship towards the lock gates of the Afrika Dock in expectation of being towed out into the Scheldt on our way to sea. We did not sail.

For some days the wind had remained steadily at E.N.E. and a hard frost prevailed. In the great dock where we lay, tugs and heavy Rhine barges had been moved about to break up the ice as it formed in the still waters there. But there was no apprehension; icy conditions in the port and river were nothing new. When we warped out towards the river gates we had every difficulty that could be imagined in a ship—a weak and drunken crew, frozen ropes and moorings, ice on the decks to aid King Alcohol in down-pinning our men at the capstan. In the river, huge masses of hard ice churned and groaned on their way downstream. With our bows almost entered into the lock, we were arrested by loud and worried commands. '*Vast heaving!*' In some way the big caisson of the sea-ward gate had become jammed by the pressure of the shelving ice and could not be operated. Quickly recognizing the gravity of the situation, the dockmaster ordered all further movement within the docks to cease. It was not until February that ship traffic in and out of the port was restored. We were 'ice bound', and so reported at Lloyds.

While the ice in the dock was still friable, we hauled the ship back to the buoys in the water area and tied her up. Later, when by day and night the huge ice-pack in the river showed no sign of lessening as it groaned and ground its way to sea, we unbent the sails from the yards, unrove the running gear, and put the ship in Arctic trim. In these skilled sailor operations I took no part; but, as the ice thickened and held us firmly, a new requirement posed a problem to the busy Mate, one that brought me and my inaction to his attention. It had become possible to walk safely anywhere on the ice out there at the buoys, and as I was the youngest apprentice—the glow-worm of the half-deck, he called me—it became my duty to get out on the ice at some distance from the ship and dig a sizeable crater in it, to which I had then to transport the ship's garbage for timely refrigeration. As these refuse dumps froze up quickly, a new pinnacle became a daily addition. Fifty paces from the ship, Mr Baird had said; but I could choose my points of attack, and had a sense of pattern in doing that.

One other casual incident remains impressed, in recollection of the great European freeze-over of 1890–91. It is of the Captain coming up on deck of a morning to consider the sadly immobile state of his once active and buoyant ship. How briskly, in sailor manner, he would pace fore and aft the poop, doubtless pondering the commitments of the day! And pause at the shoreward turn of his gangway to make a single protest against the misfortunes of his long detention! For it was there, as his eyes took sight of it, that the office of the dockmaster stood up beside the deserted and silent water-gates. It was not at stout, rosy Mynheer Willems that his morning's anger was directed, but at a frozen bird which symbolized all hope deferred. Above the structure of the Dock House a sub-

stantial signal flagstaff was crowned by a weather-vane, its gilded
cockerel frozen stiff on a heading of east-nor'east! . . . It became *the*
sight of the day with us, watching from the shaded doorway of the
half-deck, to see the Captain stiffen up when nearing the next turn of
his tramp. He would always pause then, his hands held up to high
heaven, fists tightly clenched, to be shaken in anathema at the frozen
symbol of his distress. We thought it likely that he might then be
reconstructing in his mind the scene in the Owners' office in Glasgow when, at his desk with the morning's correspondence in hand,
old George Smith would ponder the unchanging report that his ship
was still ice-bound and the crew in her still eating the bread of
idleness.

But it does not freeze for ever. In mid February the sky over
Antwerp, that had been brightly calm and placid for so long,
clouded up and quickly became heavily overcast. Rain fell. A mild
southerly wind prevailed. Hastily and in hope we set about the
preening of our sea-wings and, in the business of bending sail, I was
encouraged to lay aloft and bear a prentice hand with my mates.
Ice-bound and all, I had found my first tottering sea legs. From high
aloft I could look down on my labours, my curious pattern of
refuse-mounds and pinnacles, and rejoice to see them all washed
out in the swirl of slush and turgid flood-water that came to set us
free to prosecute the voyage.

Chapter V

SEA DIARY

BY a recent and timely happening—the finding of an old and long mislaid diary—I am enabled to see myself mirrored, reflected as I was in 1891, when I sailed out from Antwerp in the *City of Florence*. The book is a stoutly bound one of post octavo size which, probably by barter, I had acquired from a better-equipped shipmate early in the voyage. In it there is quite a volume of USEFUL INFORMATION as preface to the dated pages. The well-worn state of the book suggests that it was often consulted, doubtless to settle the not infrequent arguments of the half-deck . . . Queen Victoria reigned when we set sail, Lord Salisbury was Premier, and Mr Gladstone thundered in opposition. Income Tax was sixpence in the pound then, and Inland Postage was one penny the ounce:

And no one quite remembered what Mister Gladstone said,
When the penny stamp was purple and the hap'ny stamp was red.

This youthful effort to write a summary of life on shipboard reads oddly to me as now I scan its pages and recall the many acts and incidents it puts on record. Its text, too, reflects moods and interests I had not thought were mine when I sweated at brace and sheet and halyard to sail a ship. Not infrequently, I read on as a stranger making first acquaintance with a new writer. Was I ever like this?

This other self of mine seems suddenly to have become an able hand and appears to be learning his trade at uncommon speed. In comment upon the taking of a cast of the deep-sea lead on the Little Sole Bank, he tells of 'hag's teeth' being brought up in the tallow arming of the sinker. Hag's teeth? How did a green apprentice, only a day or two at sea, come to know of such bottom being obtained in the pitch of the Channel? (My elder self confesses that he has now to consult a dictionary to learn that hag's teeth are the dental remains of departed dogfish, often found in a depth of about thirty fathoms.) Again, a few pages later, this young 'know-all' criticizes the sluggish sailing of the ship. He puts the slow progress down to the long imprisonment in the ice at Antwerp Docks. Right enough! That could be a reasonable explanation, but how is such an expert conclusion reached after no more than a few days at sea? A presumptuous fellow, this! His sailor talk, too. He lays aft to heave the log; he does not start work—he 'turns to'; he 'bears a hand' at this or that. Right again. . . . But how is he informed?

That speculation seems answered by a new note which creeps into his writing farther on. There he reveals an admiring interest in his shipmates, not only in the deeds of his fellows in the half-deck, but in the competence of his watchmates before the mast as well. By hearing the talk of shipwork and by observing their varying skills in seamanship he is accepting the lessons of an old calling.

While, in 1891, a few sailing-ships in the colonial trade gave special attention to the training of apprentices—and that at fairly high cost to parents and guardians—not many of the hard-working windjammers engaged in other trades had such scheduled instruction to offer. Competition with the steamship—enormously grown since the opening of the Suez Canal in 1869—had effected a big reduction in the crews of sailing vessels, and under such short-handed conditions neither Mate nor Master had leisure to spare on the voyage for regular lessons in seamanship or navigation. The 'duty of a seaman' could be acquired in a rough-and-ready system of picking up the threads of it, and the youngster was encouraged to shift for himself. Haphazard as that system—or the lack of it—might be, it often turned out the better hand in sailor-work, for, quite early embarked, he was spurred on to acquire a helpful turn of seamanship by those who had most to benefit from his competence. The dependency of one seaman upon another was nowhere more clearly demonstrated than in the grossly undermanned windjammers of the nineties.

In keeping with this established reliance between shipmates, a sterling fellowship, unknown in steamships, was fostered. Of course there was not always amity in square rig. Recrimination and critic-ism, directed not so much at mood or manner or even speech, but rather at ability in shipwork, was common, and a bout of fisticuffs could easily arise from a shipmate's complaint about a job ill done.

A life might be at stake, but, despite passing contentions, the lasting bond of teamwork so constantly engaged, held sailing shipmates together in a way that was rarely possible in steamships. The close companionship of a night watch, pacing the deck in expectation of a call to sudden action, was never the part of sea life in steam that, necessarily, it was in sail.

We were five in the half-deck at the time I wrote in that old Diary, and, while all are mentioned from time to time, it is the name of Hans Petersen that screams at me from the written page. He, the leading hand in the Mate's watch, was the eldest apprentice and I the youngest: Mr Baird had dubbed me the 'glow-worm of the half-deck', and even at this late date I glow with warmth in thought of one whom I had long committed to the shades. I recall him now, a sizeable and understanding lad of incredible courage and resource, when I took my allotted place beside him at the picking of the watches after we had got under way from an anchorage in the Downs. I think he had Danish blood in him, but whatever the admixture may have been, it was of sterling stream and it was he who led me in my duty. . . . Hero-worship? Yes! It was the look of Hans when seas were running high that put heart in me. . . . In many pages of the old diary I read that Hans did this or Petersen said that. One's fortune turns on little things. It was the impossibility of evenly dividing five boys into the two watches that let me share the skills of a superb seaman like Petersen in my impressionable years.

As the voyage progressed, an effort to enliven my entries becomes apparent. I do not give only detail of the weather and the routine of the night watches. There are still callow descriptions of the sailor-work in the ship, or the bending of sail, and the overhaul of the rigging, but these become fewer. I make note of the rarer incidents: the sighting of another ship on the lonely sea route, the days in the trades when flying-fish slatted aboard and schools of dolphin or bonito gambolled under our forefoot and tested the skill of our champion harpooner, braced under the bowsprit for a throw of the grains. As the ship bore away south, seeking to round Cape Horn, and darkling skies and high seas prevailed, the seabirds of the region, that included albatross and mollymawks, flocked upon us and provided Captain Leask (of Stromness in the Orkneys) with specimens for his collection of stuffed seabirds. He did not shoot his albatross, for that would not have delivered a specimen in good plumage into his clever hands, but, undeterred by gales and mountainous seas—and the penance of Coleridge's Ancient Mariner—he would tow his lines to ensnare the birds. He was a very skilful taxidermist.

In the long-continued bitter weather, when beating against the prevailing westerly gales to round the Horn, illness and accident reduced our numbers, and we became a pitifully small sailor group to pit against such a hurricane succession. Since crossing the line and in the fine weather of the south-east trades, I had been allowed to take a turn at the wheel on calm occasions—with the regular helmsman standing by to correct my many faults. I cannot remember that I took special pride in these dictated efforts, the helmsman being often a crabbed teacher and always too near at hand for my liking. I came away from them without feeling any particular elation, although the sight of the towering canvas above me—all sail being set—remains a grateful memory to this day. . . . It was quite different in the strong winds and high testing seas down south, and it was only as a labouring assistant at the lee-helm I was told off at times to bear a hand. But one day an accident put the governing weather-spokes of the wheel into my eager hands. My preferment came when James Mason, an A.B. in our watch, was thrown from his post at the helm and injured his wrist and forearm. In the Mate's watch we were short-handed through illness and injury, else there would have been some alternative to the employment of a first voyager; but I was ordered aft to take the wheel at the changing of the watch.

In the diary I make much of my advancement. Vaingloriously, I write of it as a red-letter day for me and, as such, the entry is suitably embellished. 'First regular trick at the wheel' is the simple way the phrase goes, but it is boxed in by a flourish of graphic curlicues expressive of its importance. Let it not be thought that I proved myself on that first attempt, for I had as yet everything to learn of this great personal art in seamanship. But I did my best; I was proud of my preferment. I recall that we were then southward of Diego Ramirez, the ship hove to in face of a roaring westerly gale and a heavy head sea running. Of course we would be under small canvas and, in such a circumstance, there would be little for the helmsman to do except to hold her to the wind by small adjustments.

But the ship was labouring and pitching violently, and sudden combers crashed on the weather bow to seek me out. Many times anxious Mr Baird staggered from his post at the fore end of the poop to see what helm I carried. In that titanic pitch and toss I came quickly to learn that when the ship's stern, having risen high in it, was again settling in the trough, then was the moment to look out for the 'kick' of the jarring rudder that had thrown James Mason across the wheel. Mine was not an over-long spell at the helm, for one-hour periods were the rule in the bitterly cold weather that prevailed down south; in the frequent hard squalls, the driving sleet cut at the eyes like the lash of a whip. Warmed by my personal elation, I had no thought of physical distress. It was a big and inspiring occasion for me.

In this revealing looking-glass that reflects my actions of so long ago, I see myself outgrowing the role of a greenhorn at sea. In the pages that follow upon my first real seamanlike achievement I appear no longer the wide-eyed neophyte in a quiet corner of the half-deck when there is talk of far ports and sailor doings. Whether accepted or not, I offer myself as a new inhabitant, a compeer, even if of minor sort, ready on occasion to enter into argument with my elders—often, alas, with chastening effect. But I can stand my watch. I can steer now.

The old diary is still far from being discarded in this personal reminiscence of the year 1891. There is still an essence to be distilled from its yellowed pages—the essence of arrival in port after long and hard voyaging. Than that, there can be few more thrilling moments, and these I savoured to the full when, entering by the Golden Gates (which Drake on his circumnavigation had missed) we anchored off Alcatraz Island, 183 days out from the Downs. That was no passage of which to be proud, but the Old Man, fearing that the delay might have caused him to lose a homeward charter, called for the gig to be lowered and manned to hurry him ashore to visit his agents. It was the duty of the half-deck to supply the gig's crew, and in some way I found myself in the bows, as we rowed him ashore to the steps of Mission Wharf.

For a lad of sixteen, I counted myself a passable boatman and had no great fatigue with the short bow oar, but wondered how the others managed to make such apparent light work of their longer oars, that were of heavy, straight-grained ash. It had not occurred to me that in our six months voyaging on sparse rations and more than ample exercise, we had been in constant and strenuous training for almost any athletic event. As we rowed away from the ship's side in the morning's bright sunshine, she lay fairly in view—a sea-stained ocean wanderer with the red-rusty scars of lengthy sea-keeping disfiguring the long, checkered strake of her painted ports. But not even the dingy paintwork of the hull could detract from the grace of her lovely lines; only the topsails, clewed up in the gear but as yet unfurled, struck a lubberly note as they thrashed, for so long untended, in the breeze.

It was evident that the Old Man, seated in the stern-sheets, had his own thoughts about the unfurled topsails, although perhaps from no æsthetic distaste like mine. His frowns were for the shore-boats clustered under the bows, and it was their being there that gave him the reason for delay in furling all sail. As I was to learn later, the crimps from the waterfront were holding session in the fo'c'sle. Emboldened by routh of potent grog brought off by the boarding-masters' runners, our men had suspended, if not abandoned ship-work, and sat in their quarters to listen to the lying tales of wondrous well-paid jobs awaiting them on shore. Before we had brought up at the steps on Mission Wharf more than one of the shore-boats had cast off from the bows of the ship, the fore-sheets loaded high with sailors' sea-bags, the owners of which lay out of sight on the stern gratings, already drunk to the guards and ripe for reshipment on one or other of the out-bound ships now anchored in the Bay. The 'blood money' for that service would be fifty dollars! The Captain sighed as he mounted the steps. It would be an old story to him. He had no recourse to law and order, as well he knew, in a port where the infamous 'Shanghai Brown' was said to have the attentive ear of every waterfront magistrate. It was not without reason it was known by sailors as 'the Barbary Coast'.

Chapter VI

THE CAPTAIN'S BATH

IN this age of preserved ship stores, of ice-boxes and mechanical refrigeration in ships at sea, it is with difficulty that one remembers the queer little world of a sailing-ship such as the *City of Florence* and considers the limits of her self-containment in a long voyage. Of 1,199 tons register, and measuring only 227 feet in length, with 35 feet breath, she would have no great storage space for even the scanty rations on which her crew subsisted. But it was the inadequacy of her fresh-water supply that chiefly I remember. On the third voyage I made in her, and when homeward bound from Portland, Oregon, a mishap—simple in itself—brought us to a thirsty pass.

The poop—the post of command in the ship—was always a reserved enclosure. No one but the Old Man and the mates stepped briskly, sauntered, or loitered on its planks—according to their several habits. Occasionally an apprentice would be posted to leeward to stand in one place immobile as a punishment for some delinquency. But the wheel stood on the poop, and that had to be manned. At two hours' interval an alien from the main deck appeared, mounted the leeward ladder, buttoned his jacket, and relieved the steersman. Sometimes there were moments of hurried action. The shrouds of the mizen rigging led to the chains at the fore-part, and when sail had to be made or reduced there was a rush of men laying aloft. But the normal state of the poop was one of quiet movement, for it was the Old Man's rooftree, and he slept lightly, as a commanding sailor should. In the early morning hours, though, there was a minor activity. It was the duty of the apprentices on watch to fill the Captain's bath. For this, a spar and a canvas bucket had to be rigged, the blue salt water drawn from overside and poured through a pipe inlet in the deck above his quarters. Close to this inlet, and not dissimilar to it, there was another 'flushhead' through which the carpenter could lower his sounding-rod to determine the content of precious fresh water in the tank far below. Both had brass screw caps, fitted to close the pipes when not in use. These were lettered to distinguish them one from the other.

On a day of calms and light airs in the South Atlantic advantage was taken of the dry weather to shift canvas. From the first sign of daybreak the watch had been hard at work unbending the heavy sails of oo Storm that had brought us round the Horn, and setting in their place the older light canvas suit that could still serve its turn in the settled trade winds. The second mate was ambitious to do well before handing over to his senior at eight bells, and the routine of a normal morning watch was perhaps disrupted. Somewhat late, he realized that the Captain's bath was not yet drawn and both apprentices were aloft. He ordered two men of the small deck party to attend to it, then resumed his supervision of what he may have thought the more important work. . . . Unfamiliar with the job, the Belgian lamp-trimmer, who could not read, unscrewed the wrong pipe-head and poured the statutory twenty full buckets of Neptune's salty best into the fresh-water tank!

Had that tank been nearly full the saline content would not have mattered very much, for we were hardy, but we were long out from Portland and its level was low. Except for a small emergency container of about ten days' normal supply and the *barrecas* in the lifeboats, it was our last reserve. Its water was now heavily brackish and just barely potable: the end of the voyage was still far distant.

But the 'sweet little Cherub' who sends wind to fill the sails has his own way of watering a sailing-ship at sea, and it would be in the hope of torrential rains in the 'doldrums' that the Captain stood on northward through the south-east trades, dismissing any thought he may have had of putting in to Montevideo to replenish. As the days wore on, preparations were made. The spare tank, already exhausted, was cleaned and lime-washed; the poop was scrubbed as never before; the brine tubs, charred by fire and scraped anew, were held in readiness; old sails were patched and fitted as catch-waters. We were all ready. . . . But the rains did not come as we worked ship from the petering south-east trades to the 'Line'. This was sufficiently unusual to arouse disquiet. If we had no rains, what then? The ration, now reduced to one half-pint per man per day, that had been drawn from the emergency container, was now exhausted, and we had no recourse but to the salted tank. Curiously, it did not taste as vile as when the Belgian's error was first discovered. Had we grown 'case-hardened', or was the rusty floor of the tank effecting some chemical reaction? The few sips that could be saved from cooking were red-rusty and thick like syrup. Maybe old iron had its merit. But there was not enough of the 'tincture'.

What Captain Leask thought of it we did not know. As he strode briskly on the poop there seemed no special anxiety in the eyes as he turned to windward at each end of his thirty paces. Was he confident that the rains would come, as so often he had found them there; or had he the hope of 'speaking' other ships at the known 'Line crossing' in 28 West Longitude? We could not know.

'Doldrums'—the zone of baffling weather that lies between the influence of the constant trades, was not in character with its description in the pages of Findlay's *Atlantic*: it was not the seaman's purgatory so often doggedly endured. Calms there were, and light, wayward airs, but not the black nights of incessant downpour, the thunder of weeping skies, or the interludes of brazen, breathless heat broken by sudden fierce squalls of wind and rain. Nor was the watch, now enfeebled and distressed, called upon to haul yards and trim sail incessantly to meet each capful of a furthering wind. The days stayed fair. Infrequently and at night there was vivid lightning and the rumble of distant thunder; a few light showers fell, but did no more than wet the canvas and the decks. The tubs stood empty when the drizzle had cleared. . . . But we made progress. The *Florence*—built for the tea trade—had the quality of ghosting in light airs. By what seemed little more than the *thr-r-rap* of her canvas she carried some trifle of steerage way, and we reached the parallel of two degrees North.

There we sighted the first ship we had seen since Vootgert's adventure with the Captain's bath. Only from high aloft was the stranger seen, and it was late afternoon then. Almost a flat calm prevailed, and we spent an anxious night wondering whether she would still be there at daybreak. She was, and appeared even to have drawn nearer. We guessed that she was outward bound. A day later the ships had closed perceptibly and signals were exchanged. She was the *Mermerus*, outward bound, right enough, for Melbourne. The business of flag-signalling—that had started with such uncommon ardour—became a long and exhausting task as we made known our plight. The flags hung limp in the windless air and had to be jiggled and flaunted in the effort to secure recognition. It was nearly dark when we were fully understood, and the ships were then more than five miles distant. . . . Darkness or no, we were thirsty, and when the *Mermerus* showed a light in her rigging we lowered and manned the longboat and pushed off to get our drink. The Mate was in charge, and we were six oarsmen, but the heavy and leaky old craft—she had been used for loading guano at the Chincha Islands and stank of it—taxed all our powers. It was ill-sitting on the thwarts, too, for we had encumbered the boat with the awkward tubs and could find no proper purchase for foot-grip as we layed back at the oars. But the Mate was understanding and did not press us. At frequent intervals we lay-to—gazing ahead at the lamp, that seemed no brighter for all the effort we had made.

We were in poor shape when, just before midnight, we paddled wearily alongside the good Samaritan. Captain Cole was he indeed. Our Mate, always to the fore, had his programme to advance; but the Captain of the *Mermerus* would have none of it when, in his cosy cabin, he took one look at us. There was no sign of wind, he said: if it did come, well, he could then work nearer to our ship. No. *His* 'people' would bale out the longboat, and they would also attend to the watering during the night. It would be time enough at daybreak for us to return. Meantime——

By all the standards, we should have slept and rested in anticipation of the greater labour on the return journey, with the longboat deeper and heavier under the load of fresh water the Captain had promised; but there was little sleep when, after a good meal and water—*water*—we snuggled down on the main hatch-covers under the stars. The activity and excitements of the day, the realization that our plight was at length relieved, promoted a state of wakeful well-being, and that was encouraged by the sound of new voices as the crew of the *Mermerus* gathered around to 'pass a word' with us. There were many words. Although hailing from Greenock, on the Clyde, the ship was engaged in the lordly trade between London and

Melbourne and was manned largely from Ratchcliffe Highway—
and we of the *Florence* were mainly Scots. But we found at least one
compatriot: her carpenter was from Port Glasgow. He was our first
visitor, and with him as occasional interpreter we got on famously
with the London men. Three of our boatmen were foreigners,
shipped under duress at San Francisco. These slept heavily throughout the night, undisturbed by the talk and the laughter, the knocking
out of pipes, the striking of matches, that went on from time to
time; but with Grainger and me and a 'bluenose' sailor from Lunen-
berg the 'people' of the *Mermerus* could not find enough to say, to
discuss, to inquire. A ship visit in mid-ocean is sufficiently unusual
to arouse interest in any event, and rumour had spread to enlarge
our sufferings far beyond the real truth of scarcity and discomfort—
but not quite the stress and agony they presumed. Curiously, there
was little argument and no controversy in the babble of talk, which
was mostly reminiscent. Statements that would have been hotly
challenged in a tavern on shore were calmly accepted on the main
hatch in two degrees North Latitude. We all lied famously concerning the respective merits of our ships, the fast passages they had
made, the gales they had encountered. There was little said of the
news of the day and happenings ashore. In 1893 Britain stood out
peaceful and serene, the embodiment of unchallenged strength
and power. It was that way when the ships put to sea, it would
be that way when they returned. Of what use to talk about
it when there was so much to be said of ships and passages,
of landfalls and departures—with ever and anon the big Scots
carpenter breaking in to ask again what ships were building on the
Clyde?

That night on the main hatch of a friendly ship had all the
elements of a pleasant dream. I suppose we must have slept at
intervals, for I was strangely refreshed. At times orders sounded
out from the poop to haul yards or trim sail to meet some wayward
breath of wind and I found myself, sheepish and but half awake,
tailing on with the 'people' of the *Mermerus* at brace or halyard in
the darkness, then going quickly back again to my nest on the
hatch-cover, to court another cat-nap while gazing up at the masthead and the stars they pointed. It was a pleasant night, for all the
distractions and fitful slumbers. Nor was the awakening, when the
grey of day came flooding from the eastward, any portent of the

hard task we had so lightly forgotten in the concert of the night. By some miraculous agency, the ships had closed to a distance of about three miles, and the sea was still calm.

Under broad of day we sailors so strangely met at sea took stock of one another. In contrast with the cleanly appearance of the London men, we of the *Florence*, tanned and ragged, stood no comparison at all as we lined the starboard bulwarks to gaze outboard at our ship before spitting on our hands to reach her. It was over a month since we had had fresh water to indulge even a cat-wash; our beards in the interval had grown to Biblical proportions. Only twenty-five days from the Downs, the 'people' of the *Mermerus* had not lost the landward habit of washing. Ample water was available in their ship, and she had even a machine to make more. But despite our grimy appearance we seemed the harder in the grain, and when it was clear that Captain Cole was on the point of enlarging his benefaction by sending away his cutter laden with brimful water *barrecas*, there seemed the prospect of a test in that convoy. As with the men, so with the ships. Around her decks the *Mermerus* was immaculate in fresh paint and well-stoned planking; even the brace-coils were flemished down in readiness for any sudden call to trim the yards: she had an order and formality about her that would not have disgraced a frigate. I could see that our Mate, talking with Captain Cole on the poop, had eyes for all this. He would be thinking of our sorry state and the effort he would have to make to remedy it before the Shore Captain of the City Line, the arbiter of promotion, met the ship at a homeward port. . . . Looking outboard, I could see the dingy, red-rusted hull of our ship as she lay, windless and heading southerly in the calm. There was movement on the sea—a long and gentle swell from eastward that swayed her to expose the slimy growth on her underbody. There and on her weather-beaten top-sides she showed the scars of long voyaging, but she swayed buoyant and seaworthy as we viewed her when shoving off from the smooth, unblemished plating of the out-bound *Mermerus*.

Any thought we might have had of making a match of the distance was quickly dispelled as we got under way. The longboat was deepened like a dumb barge, and the fulcrum of such a low gun'le productive of many mis-strokes and feeble puffets. Had she been fitted with outboard crutches, we could have stood upright and faced forward, the way the Latins do, and have made better progress by digging our blades deep for purchase. But these had been unshipped long ago and left as jetsam on some Chincha Island beach. Our hands, too, that we had thought hardened by ship labour, proved flabby at the unaccustomed frictions, and painful broken blisters bloodied our palms. It was no occasion for friendly competition as the cutter of the *Mermerus* forged ahead. But she, too, was burdened, and the flashy stroke at which she passed us was not long maintained. At intervals, growing more frequent as we laboured on, a halt was called and we lay within hearing, shouting out catchwords for mutual encouragement. It took over two hours to make the distance, and we were barely able to mount the pilot ladder when we blundered alongside.

The transfer of our precious cargo, completed without haste, was not a task for exhausted boatmen, and we were left at liberty to further the friendships we had formed with the men from the *Mermerus*. Foremost among them, the Scots carpenter strove to make the most of his visit. Quickly he discovered a fellow towns-man in our young sailmaker, and nothing could exceed the native dialectics—with the 'r's' rolling like thunder-bursts between them. Although 'sails' was eighteen months from home, he could remember the state of activity in the Scottish shipyards and even the names of ships then under construction. But it was of steamships he spoke, for few if any sailing-ships were being built. . . . Such talk led in-evitably to condemnation of the new steam seafaring and of those who engaged in it. We had our fine conceit, but more than one looked at his bloodied and blistered hands with private reservations. The signal of recall was hoisted in their distant ship all too soon, and we cheered them away with hearty thanks. The calm still held, but the slight easterly swell I had remarked at daybreak seemed more pronounced as the cutter left us—bowing to it with a slight upsurge of broken water. The wind could not be far away.

It came in late afternoon, perhaps conjured by the westing sun. Its rising was not the dramatic glooming of squalls, or even an over-cast of the unclouded sky. It grew out of thin air, and in both ships there was much hauling of yards and trim of sail to capture it. Being to windward, *Mermerus* was the first to start afoot when there appeared the shadow line on the eastern horizon—the darkling that seamen pray for in light weather. We watched it creep towards her, saw her canvas lift and flutter, then blow a-taut as she backed fore-

yards to pay off on her southerly course. Soon we, too, were
working ship (bemoaning our blistered hands) as the breeze carried
down to us, and it was no time for sight-seeing. . . . When next I
saw her the *Mermerus* was leaning away before a fine quarterly wind
while we stood 'full and by' towards home.

Chapter VII

SMOKE ON THE HORIZON

MY first intimate view of a steamship was when I visited Hans Petersen in the *Turret Belle* at Glasgow. But for my desire to see my old shipmate (who was third mate in her) I would not have gone on board, for there was little about the gaunt iron decks of this 'tramp' steamer of 1894 to invite the interest of such as myself, serving indentures in square sail. I admit prejudice. In the half-deck where I had now spent over three years of my time one was considered a poor sailor if one showed the least regard or sympathy for steamboat men. We had no shade of tolerance for those weaklings who preferred to 'knock off the sea and go in steam'. But still . . . a shipmate must be visited, even in jail. So I stepped across the tongue of the Queen's Dock to where she lay.

The *Belle* was of the very early turret type, an ungainly and grotesque vessel measuring about 3,000 tons. Even in a day when most cargo steamships presented immature and strange outlines, she stood out as the oddest creation of them all. In his effort to depart from the usual lines of a ship (possibly to emphasize an intolerance of seamanlike convention) the designer seemed to have made her purposely forbidding in appearance. She had no masts—only upstanding poles. Saving the gross swollen round of her huge sides, there was not an honest curve or bend in her. Rigid angles met the eye everywhere; she seemed to have been hewn out of a solid, rather than built plate by plate. I ventured on to a deal plank, stretched precariously from the turn of her whale-back to the copestone of the quay, and clambered aboard. The dockers had stopped work for the day and there was no one about the decks. The great hatchways, hastily and inadequately covered, roused a new feeling in me, a sense of insecurity in a ship that made me step warily. The litter of cargo operations (in our old windjammer it would have been swept up and the ropes coiled down) lay as the workmen had left it in the rain, and made slippery the narrow passages of the deck. I found no one to direct me, and wandered round looking for the officers' quarters.

Accustomed to a sailing-ship in which most doors opened directly on to the deck, I was confused by the entries and passage-ways that led to the living-rooms of the vessel. Stepping into a recessed doorway, I looked down at the engines, and it was here that a vague mental questioning that had troubled me since I boarded her became distinct. I realized suddenly that she did not *smell* like a ship. There was no proper sea-tang in the odour of heated oils and iron and coal-dust that prevailed. I missed the indefinable air of a clean-living ocean sailing-ship, the understandable whiff of tar and cordage, tinctured by faint essences of pine-spars and woodwork.

Petersen had changed in the short term of his steamship experience. Certainly he was friendly and joyous enough at our meeting, but the old things that used to be so near to him did not seem to excite him greatly. When I set out to tell him of that big gale off the Plate—'the time we split the fore tops'l and sprung the yard and the weather boats were stove in the chocks'—he did not appear to be interested. His animation came when it was his turn to recite all the ports he had been in since he left us, of great doings ashore at Genoa and New York and Bremerhaven. Then he had much to say about the new *Turret Whim* that was building in an East Coast ship-yard and was due to be completed very soon. She was sixty feet longer than the *Belle*; there was a prospect that he would be pro-moted second mate in her; he would have his Mate's certificate by that time: a command was not so far away, if only he could get his qualifying time in quickly enough. I had little to say. I felt that all this steamship talk was boastful and ambitious, but perhaps there was a shade of envy in my reflections as I contrasted my prospects with those of one whose feet were already so well set on the ladder.

I was curious to learn how things were done in the *Belle*. What kind of 'work' was carried on? How many knots could she go? Who set the jobs for the hands? What did they do on a voyage at sea with no sailor-like business to employ them? Hans was some-what vague. 'Oh, work and enough,' he said. 'We don't muck around with yards an' canvas, like you do in a crazy old wind-jammer, but there's plenty to do with cleanin' th' winches an' chippin' decks an' settin' out th' gear for the next port.' I realized the gulf that now lay between us.

When speaking of his own work—watch-keeping on the bridge at sea—Petersen became much more voluble and communicative. He was enthusiastic in praise of the system that ensured him eight hours' rest to four of active duty. His watch was always the same—from eight to twelve. There was plenty for him to do. While he had no immediate charge of the men on deck (the Mate looked after that), he was busy with the navigation and other matters. Of course, he kept a good look-out; one had to alter the course from time to time to keep clear of other ships—or watch the other vessel's change of course when, by the Rule of the Road, it was her duty to keep clear; there were bearings to be taken of the land; the steersman had to be watched; the speed of the ship was another matter to be attended to. He showed me his navigation books. One was a record of the errors of the compass as determined by the sun's bearing in his watch—columns of figures in a neat hand.

This was all very puzzling to me. To talk of the land as if it were always above the horizon! And the steersman having to be watched, as though one could not tell when she was off her course by a squint at the sails—but no, of course there were no sails. Then, this business of keeping clear of other ships when there was need. I had never thought of that. A strange sail on the horizon when far out at sea would be a day's event with us. The Captain would be on deck to see her; he and the Mate would talk for hours about the cut and set of her sails; in our ship, the second mate (we carried no third) would only have a look at the stranger from over the pinrail as he went about his business of keeping his watch hard at work. A compass book? Of course I knew that such records were kept, but had thought that was the affair of the Captain, or perhaps the Mate. With us, the second mate held no high official position. He was but slightly senior to the carpenter or the ship's steward. While the Captain might address the Mate as *Mr* Baird or *Mr* Stainger, he would never use the surname of the second mate. 'Mister' was the word: it was not considered good for the master of a ship to remember the second mate's name. That the 'Mister' of the *Turret Belle* should himself alter the course, watch the steersman, assist in the mysteries of navigation, and keep the compass records, struck me as odd; but I was to have a further revelation of the strange order of things in steamships.

As we sat talking, someone called from the deck above, and

Petersen went out. He returned accompanied by a pleasant-faced young man not much older than himself. I was prepared to meet the Mate, but this was the Captain, and I returned his friendly greeting not without embarrassment. There was some talk about charts, and Petersen produced another book in which the names and numbers of the charts on board were entered. A point was settled, and the two then fell to talking of music-halls and comedians and programmes. There was Hans (who, not so very long ago, would jump at every bull-roar from the poop) lounging at his ease against the polished boarding of his bunk—and there, the young 'Old Man' of the *Turret Belle* talking to him as though to an intimate friend. To me, the structure of seniority that I had thought so solidly established seemed to crumble in that little six-foot cabin while these two talked of Empires and Alhambras.

I had much to ponder on my way back to my old ship. I reviewed all Petersen's vaunts and advices: that one was completely out of the world in a windjammer; that he had been into more ports in a month than I had visited in years; that there was fresh mess and plenty of it in a steamer, while we had to live on hard tack and 'salt' horse for our rationed fare. Who but a fool, he asked, would stand for watch and watch—four hours on and four hours off duty—often in bad weather, on deck for days on end? I could see for myself what a fine job he had in the *Turret Belle*. For the very life of him, he couldn't understand how anyone would ever look sideways at a rotten old barge of a sailing-ship that could hardly get out of her own way!

Naturally, I was shocked to hear my old shipmate talking in this way of a real ship, but there was much in his argument that could not be casually dismissed as idle abuse of old ways and old days. 'Who but a fool would stand for this watch-and-watch business,' he had exclaimed! As I left the *Turret Belle* and passed along the breast of the quay, I pondered that testy exclamation. Who but a fool! Still, there was another side to it. I thought of the joys of spirited action under sail in high winds, the ship leaning over under the press, and compared them with the puny business of turning the handle of a contraption on the bridge to oblige the engineer far down in the bowels of the steamer to do something. I recalled, too, the affairs of navigation old Hans was now engaged with—the compass book and the charts and all that. A clerking job—the kind of thing one runs

off to sea to get away from. No proper seafaring for a bold fellow!
. . . Still, one would indeed be blind to ignore the trends of occupation in great waters. Pausing in my steps to survey the shipping in
the Queen's Dock, I saw much to favour the views of my old shipmate. . . . True, in 1894 sailing-ships were still being built—huge
four-posters, full-lined to carry a great cargo, but guaranteed to
chill the heart of any seaman, master or man, who had known the
fine-lined clippers of the past. One of the newly-designed four-
posters, lately launched at Port Glasgow and towed up to the big
crane for masting, lay just across the dock from where I stood.
Stark of line and broad of bow, her naked hull held out no invitation
for an able seaman to seek a 'sight' in her. . . . As though in contrast,
the Loch Line loading berth was occupied by the *Loch Garry*—one
of the most beautiful of the many fine ships the Clyde had fashioned
for the long colonial voyage. These were the ships, thought I!
Other than these, the vessels that lined the quays were steamships,
and it required no far vision to see approaching the years when the
sailing-ship would be only a memory. I hurried on.

So, this precious *Turret Belle* and her kind were to be the ships
of the future! I was depressed at thought of it. She did not smell
like a ship.

It was nearly the turn of the century before the local Education
Authority discovered the merchant sailor and recognized his needs.
Before that date small schools of navigation were operated by retired shipmasters in the seaports, often in partnership with the
established business of a nautical optician or ship-chandler. . . .
When I had served my four years apprenticeship to the sea and
could consider myself a certified 'able-bodied seaman', I had still
much to learn before presenting myself as a candidate for a first
certificate of competency. I had heard that Captain Knight of Macgregor's Nautical School was thought a good tutor, and enrolled
with him.

His was a curious establishment, having formerly been a dwelling-
house situated above the shop premises of D. Macgregor and Co.,
Nautical Instrument Makers and Compass Adjusters, in Clyde Place
at Glasgow. Some alteration had been made to provide two long
rooms and a smaller one for the classes, but all the signs of former
domestic occupation were still apparent, the wallpapers of varied

patterns showing where the dividing walls had been removed. It was a 'come and go' classroom in which old Captain Knight and his assistant strove patiently to instil the principles of navigation into a somewhat rough-and-ready group of hard-fisted but often bookless candidates. There seemed no particular rules for attendance. The system of fees for tuition was perhaps responsible for the casual attendances. A standard sum was charged for each grade of certificate; no time limit was set for the course of instruction; no one but the candidate seemed to bother very much when, having been failed by the Board of Trade examiner and sent back to sea for a further qualifying period, a desk in the second mate's corner was abruptly vacated. It was not long before another came in from sea to occupy the empty chair. . . . In time, the unfortunate wanderer would return to try again.

A feature of Macgregor's Nautical School was the splendid effigy of a naval officer in knee-breeches, white stockings, and skirted uniform dress-coat and epaulettes—a sword, too, as I remember—who stood out firmly projected before the central window. Whether or not the little mannikin was the fixture of the commercial establishment below or a property of the old Captain we never learned, but the fact that the carver had designed him using a sextant, in the act of taking an observation of some celestial body, could support both suppositions. As the front at Clyde Place faced due north, it could only be the altitude of Polaris he was seeking, and the line of his visible horizon would be vexed by the serrations of the building line across the river. Among these the tower above the Sailor's Home, in which also the examination rooms of the local Marine Board were situated, stood up—a landmark for vessels in the harbour because of its Greenwich Time signal at high noon. This odd circumstance—the little figure's concentration on the northern horizon, where our fortunes lay—was often canvassed when the fortnightly examinations were being held. By the visibility across the river, did we seek definition, over the shoulder of the effigy. My horizon was none too good.

Young sailors in from the sea are inclined to be vain of their achievements. Often they think there is something specially meritorious in having endured the rigours of the sea, and that by it they have earned a priority of some kind in their association with the people who prefer to live on shore. It was possibly in this pretentious spirit that I presented myself for examination when my four-years apprenticeship was completed and I sought the junior certificate of competency necessary for me to serve as second mate of a ship. Properly and promptly, the examiner—a former ship-master of high attainments—chastened my brash assumptions. He 'failed' me, and sent me back to sea again for a six months period to mend my manners.

Coming down from my clouds, I could find no job in a sailing-ship for a voyage as short as six months and, anxious to repair my imperfection as quickly as possible, I had the good sense to seek employment in the steamships I had tried to despise. I had been taught the duties of a seaman and was rated able-bodied: I could sail before the mast with anyone. I found a berth without difficulty.

The S.S. *City of Agra* differed greatly from the then new-fangled turret-steamship (of which Petersen was now second mate); she had almost the appearance of a tall clipper ship with an auxiliary engine installed. Built at a time when the ship designer had still a whole-some respect for the coefficients that made the graceful lines of the sailing-ship seem 'the bright reflection of her strength and sea-worthiness', she had three tall masts and was barque rigged—that is, square sail was still carried on the yards of the fore and main for use in favourable circumstance or in emergency (that was not greatly feared when men were still sailing who knew how to harness the wind.) . . . As I looked her over in sailor manner from the quayside before mounting the gangway to seek employment in her, it was the tapering 'man-o'-war' fashion in which her sails were furled that took my admiring eye. Rolled on the yards with a taut exactitude I had never known before and nestled under snowy pipeclayed sail-covers with jet-black ties or gaskets, I thought them expressive of a precision of seamanship I had yet to learn.

I signed as a quartermaster in her, a rating that had its own peculiar shade of minor authority, for the ship was largely manned by Indian lascars, respectful of their white associates. The officers were British, mostly recruited from the Company's apprentices in the sailing-ships. We were four in the quartermaster's fo'c'sle, and our main employment was to steer the ship. The *City of Agra* carried a limited number of passengers on her voyages to Calcutta. I remember thinking how strange it was to see people on the decks of a vessel who had no duties to perform. Of my two voyages in her only one incident remains stamped on my memory, the case of fire on the mainyard. It was then I discovered that the splendidly furled mainsail I had so greatly admired at Glasgow was a dummy, cleverly made up of strips of old canvas and topped by a skin-tight sail-cover to catch the eye of old 'Francey' Brown, the Company's Marine Superintendent who was the active agent of all promotion. Some sparks from the funnel immediately below the yard had set fire to it. By the way the lascar serang and his men tackled that blaze in the middle of the night and beat out the flames, I surmised that it was not an uncommon occurrence.

St Elmo's fire I had known in sail, but this was a burning of more material significance. One of the junior engineers stood beside me on deck, watching the lascars beating out this remarkable blaze over our heads. We did not know that we were witnessing the funeral pyre of a brave tradition.

Chapter VIII

LOCH NESS

AS I passed along the breast of the quay in the Queen's Dock at Glasgow, heading for the Loch Line sheds where so often, as a truant schoolboy, I had watched the fine colonial clippers being loaded and prepared for sea, I had every reason to think that the day was going well with me, for I had the Captain's letter in my pocket and was on my way to report on board the ship *Loch Ness* as her new second mate.

My steamship experience had served its corrective purpose. In the S.S. *City of Agra* I had used my leisure hours to good effect in reading up the subjects in which I had been found wanting six months before, and I thought that there was now no need for me to wait until I returned to Glasgow before again presenting myself for examination. So, at London, where we docked to disembark passengers and unload part cargo, I sought the Captain's permission to 'go up to pass'. He was helpful, and I had no difficulty in obtaining a certificate. . . . But, to get a post at sea that fell in with my ideas was not as easily contrived, and I had been idle over long. Vacancies in steamers were numerous. At Macgregor's Nautical School—a centre for exchange of shipping information amongst the unemployed brassbounders—the 'come and go' atmosphere was amazingly stimulated by the demand for young officers to sign in steam. A normal course would have been for them to serve further periods in sailing-ships in order to qualify for a full-grade certificate, valid in both sail and steam, but many preferred to abandon further sail training and elect for steamship service alone.

My experience in the S.S. *City of Agra*, while pleasantly convenient, had troubled me in a curious way. From her high decks the sea appeared different. One looked over it in quick and casual glances, not in the long, expectant, and lateral survey one exercises from the lower freeboard of a sailing-ship. The sea seemed far, but it was perhaps the manner of the steamboatman's look-out over it that disquieted me. It seemed almost that in steam no sailor need look overhead any more for sign of promise or threat of adversity, that the new outlook at sea was averted from the sky and the trend of cloud and now concentrated on the line of the horizon from whence alone danger might threaten.

These views concerning service in steam were laughed at in the schoolroom. I was thought to be slightly 'touched'. Only old Captain Knight approved them, though not openly, for it might well be that the new trends were proving profitable to him. He had held command in both sail and steam before retirement from active sea service, and thought the merit of a thorough training in sail outweighed the convenience of steam. But the sailing-ship to meet this preferment was not one of the new 'four-posters' that, as a last despairing effort on the part of sailing-ship owners, were still being launched on the lower reaches of the Clyde. The old Captain shared my distaste for them and counselled me to wait until the fine ships of the Loch Line were fitting out for the Australian wool season. It was he who sent me up to Aitken Lilburn's office with a note to Captain Martin, who, as he had heard, was sailing out in the *Loch Ness* and might have a vacancy for a second mate.

I had heard much of Captain William Martin, a famous shipmaster who had made many records in the fast wool-clippers of the Loch Line. On Clydeside and in many ships at sea he was known as 'Bully' Martin, and many tales were told on the waterfront of his hard driving under sail and his harsh treatment of the sailormen and the mates who signed under him. In sailor song—in the chanties that were roared out to concert united effort at sheet or halyard—he was often mentioned, curiously enough, in the prideful idiom that made a hero of a notorious 'hard-case' seaman. Long before I met him in the flesh, I had joined shout at the halyards to the rousing tune of 'Blow the man down'—

> Ses I who's th' skipper o' that little witch?
> *Way, hey-ee! Blow th' man down!*
> Ses he Bully Martin, th' son of a b——h!
> *Give us th' time an' we'll blow th' man down!*

When I first saw him, at the Loch Line office in Buchanan Street, he was far from appearing the sour old sea tyrant, full of bile and bitterness, that rumour had made him out to be. A big man, whose height was deceptively offset by remarkable breadth of shoulder, he carried himself well for a man of his years. His massive head was crowned by a shock of tawny hair; a full beard was neatly trimmed. Strongly featured, his complexion was rubicund with traces of lingering sunburn remaining to temper the wrinkles that the years of wind and sea had brought about. A Viking of a man. He was then nearing seventy, and doubtless much of the old storm had blown out in him, but he still had the look of one dangerous to cross or counter. But he was kind and even genial towards me, scrutinized my papers and appeared satisfied. He did not question me about ship manoeuvres or sailor-work, as I had expected, but conversed amiably on casual matters. In the upshot, I was taken on as second mate to sail with him in the *Loch Ness* on a voyage to Port Adelaide and Melbourne and return to the United Kingdom. He said that I should join at once and get acquainted with the ship before she sailed. There would be much to do now that she was about to load cargo in the Queen's Dock.

'No time like the present,' he said, concluding the interview and reaching for a pen to write his letter of appointment. 'I'll have ye know that the voyage is made or marred long before we set out on it. Good sailing begins with careful stowage. You'll take this note down to the Mate right away. He'll need somebody now for the count of the deadweight.'

Out of earshot, I repeated to myself the Old Man's last few words. 'The count of the deadweight!' . . . Deadweight? Certainly I knew that deadweight was the sailor term for heavy cargo that took up but little space . . . but why the 'count'? Whatever——?

When I asked him, Mr Nicholson studied me reflectively. We were seated in his cabin in the *Loch Ness*, where I had come to present the Captain's note. The Mate was an elderly man of quiet manner, and although his reception of me was friendly enough, I had the feeling that he was sizing me up as I sat there, forming his opinion of a new shipmate. 'Count of the deadweight,' he repeated. 'That means the tally of the weights. You'll know all about that soon enough. Ever stowed cargo in a fine-lined ship like this?'

I said I had seen cargo stowed in the *City of Florence*. Cement and coke out of Antwerp for San Francisco; wheat and bags of flour for the homeward passage; coal out to Montevideo, and from there we were in ballast to Portland, Oregon. Yes, I had seen the cargo being loaded. I had worked at it myself too. I recalled hard labours I had known.

He smiled tolerantly at my flood of reminiscence. 'Yes, yes,' he said, 'but these were bulk cargoes, not general, such as we will be loading out of the Clyde for the Colonies. Did you have a squint at the goods in the shed as you came through?'

I remembered the heaps and stacks of merchandise already piled up at the dockside for shipment and realized the complexity of its stowage in the holds of the ship. I had thought that the loading of a ship was the business of the stevedores and the longshore labourers of the docks, for cargo problems formed no important part of a second mate's examination at that date. Loading a cargo, as I had known it in the *City of Florence*, was a straight go-ahead kind of business. I could remember no instance of goods being weighed up by the ship's officers before shipment. I must have replied to the Mate's inquiry with some stupid hint of such a belief, for he studied me with something akin to pity for my ignorance.

'You have a lot to learn, young fellow,' he said. 'It's time you learned that you can't load general the way you dump coal in a ship—or cement, or bags of wheat or flour. Properly placed, the deadweight is what will hold her to the wind. It will be your job, starting at six to-morrow, to weigh up that shipment in fifty ton lots.' He picked out a paper from a file on his desk and passed it over to me. It was a 'shippers note' for a consignment of Gartsherrie pig iron. Not fully comprehending, I read it aloud. Three hundred and twenty tons. Rough pig-iron bars. And I was to start in on the morrow to weigh all that amount of heavy stuff! How——?

Mr Nicholson smiled at my appearance of dismay. 'No, no,' he assured me, '. . . you won't have to parcel it out by the pound yourself. The shippers will have it all carted down to the dock roadway outbye, and Spencer's men will do the actual weighing under your eyes. You'll see how easy it is, using heavy turn-around beam scales. They do it quickly, but you will have to check every hundredweight. The Old Man won't have anybody but an officer

who is sailing with him in the ship to check the weights, and he
has his way of talking out loud about it when we get to sea and
meet a spell of head winds. He'll make it all your fault, your
errors at the scales, if the ship doesn't work t' windward the way
he wants.'

'My fault? How can he make that out? What——'

'We-ell! Yours or mine. What's it matter? . . . He has to have
something to say about it.'

I remembered Captain Martin's remark, strange to me at the time,
when he was writing the letter in the owners' office. 'Good sailing
begins with careful stowage,' he had said. I spoke of it.

'Exactly! And maybe he's right, too. He needs her tightly
stowed and stable—the way he always seeks wind and wind and
more wind when he's running his easting down in high latitudes.
He will have her draught at five inches by the stern, too, and
there will be all hell to pay if we can't trim her to just that.' Mr
Nicholson sighed as he turned again to his shipping lists, seeking out some sovereign distribution of the commodities there
detailed, to obtain a sailing draught of five important inches by the
stern.

When I took post on the quayside in the morning, my duty at the
scales seemed trivial and out of all proportion to the importance my
seniors appeared to attach to it. A mechanical performance. *Stroke
. . . stroke . . . stroke . . . stroke . . .* and a fifth, made gatewise on the
lines of the tally book, was the pattern of the count I marked down.
From where I stood, I could see the mooring bollard on which as a
boy five years before I had sat to watch the loading of another Loch
Line wool-clipper. A truant schoolboy from Garnethill dreaming his
dreams . . . and he could have kept account as well as I was doing
now! What had I learned in all that five years of apprenticeship.
Certainly a little of the trade of sailoring. I could hand, reef, and
steer with anyone. I could keep a good watch. But was that
enough?

Spencer's men worked steadily and well as the shipper's carts
rumbled down to the quayside to deliver the loads, but the traffic
of the dockside increased with the passage of the day, and there
were often stoppages. At these intervals I had opportunity to reflect upon this business of stowing cargo to the master's exacting
demands. 'Always an officer to check the weights,' the Old Man

had decreed. To me, it then seemed unnecessary, though I now remember one revealing incident. Across the dock roadway, and inset with the sheds, I could see the official weighing box of the Clyde Navigation Trust that rules the operations of the Port. To it the carts and lorries hauling goods within the docks drew in to have their weights and tare established. Why could not our 'count of the deadweight' be made in such a way? I spoke of this to the leading hand at the scales. He didn't know. Only he said—'All them carts that pulls in t' th' Wee-in' Boax across th' road is for the steamers on th' berths doon bye. Mabbe there's a difference wi' th' windjammers. The Lochs aye put th' deadweight on the scales this wye . . . gey particular!'

Unconscious of the emphasis his act conveyed, he let fall the bar of pig-iron he had just lifted, obviously to make it break in two in a certain and special way. He then picked up the smaller piece to add it to the burden on the scales and called out *tally* to the accurate skip of five true hundredweights that were to hold us to the wind when out at sea. . . . I had been taught another lesson by the stevedore.

When we unmoored and towed down-river on a bright morning in July, I was brimful of confidence and felt able to do everything that was required of me. A month had gone since the day I joined, and I had become well acquainted with my duties in the ship. The crew we had signed in Glasgow differed from the world wanderers that had sailed with me in the *City of Florence*. Nearly all were local men whom the Mate had known on former voyages. While the ship was loading in the Queen's Dock, they had come on board, singly or in pairs, looking for a 'sight', as the word goes. It was the sight of the former discharges they had earned that was meant, and the Mate was able to select his men in advance of 'signing on' for the voyage. This was markedly in contrast with the practice I had known before, where boarding-house crimps were the agency through which a sailing-ship's crew was recruited.

All our men were not paragons, and the passage down the river was not remarkable for sober action. We anchored off Kilcreggan to embark a small consignment of explosives and lay there overnight —an opportunity of which Mr Nicholson took advantage to send all hands below both as a safety measure and an opportunity to clear their heads. The Captain, who did not sail down-river in the ship, came off from Greenock on the following day, together with the passengers who were to sail with us.

In the morning, and with the hands reasonably clear-headed, we rigged out the jib-boom and set up all gear in preparation for weighing anchor. Captain Martin came off from Greenock in the tug that was to tow us to a position below the Cumbraes. I remarked that, before coming alongside, the *Flying Coot* took up a position at bow and stern from which Captain Martin could study the exactitude of the ship's trim. Apparently satisfied with the five inches by the stern that Mr Nicholson had been at such pains to achieve, he waved to the tugmaster to haul along-side.

When he had discussed with the Mate, who met him at the gang-way, the state of the loading, and had passed orders to heave up and get under way as soon as the passengers and their baggage were embarked, he went below and did not come on deck again until we had towed to sea. The hard-voiced, snarling, and choleric old tyrant who then reappeared to stride the face of the poop, barking out orders and passing bitter comment upon the manner of their execu-tion, had no resemblance to the amiably discursive Captain Martin I had met in the owner's office little more than a month before. With the discard of his tall hat and broadcloth shore-clothes had gone his pleasant manners and he had undergone a startling sea change. It was my misfortune that the duties of a second mate brought me closely under his inflamed and jaundiced scrutiny in the waist of the ship. He left nothing unsaid in criticism of my activities. He had no name for me; I was not even Mister-ed. I became a 'you there' in the many quick commands and often harsh reprimand or reproof he roared out from his post on the poop as we made all sail. Exerting myself to the uttermost, I envied the lesser hands, racing aloft to loose canvas, in their ability so quickly to make distance from his harangues.

But the excitements of making and trimming sail, of observing the increasing lean of the ship, and the heightening of the spur of foam alongside as, to a shout, the great yards were mastheaded, brought its own relief from the torrent of abuse. Perhaps the Old Man was only working off the vapours of a sailing day? The depressing mood of the outward bound on the day of departure was well known to me. Already, with the hills of home fading out in the mist astern and in prospect of devious happenings of the long voyage before sighting them again, I was myself in no good spirit of charity. *Hutt!* I found myself repeating the snarl in the Old Man's voice as dutifully I passed on his many orders.

Chapter IX

BULLY MARTIN

WE had taken our departure from Ailsa Craig in a freshening wind from S.S.W., and I had expected we would make a fair wind of it and steer for sea room in the north Atlantic; but I was to learn quickly that the Loch Line wool-clippers were built to go to windward, and even in his old age Bully Martin was not the man to be driven from his track by contrary winds. His voyage was to Adelaide and Melbourne, and these lay to the southward, so, instead of sailing free in the north channel as a lesser seaman might prefer, he tacked ship at frequent intervals, possibly gaining some advantage by skilful use of the tides, but certainly imposing hard work on a none-too-willing crew, for all hands were kept on deck throughout the night and day, standing by to jump quickly to stations at the call 'About ship!'

In that long beat down Channel, the Old Man did not spare himself. He held the deck almost continuously, and his loud commands to ''bout ship' were relieved only by frequent admonitions to the steersman—'Keep her close t' th' wind, you there!'

On the second day out the wind abated and there were often patches of calm in Cardigan Bay, where we had sailed far inshore in the effort to gain a weatherly berth from which to make a long board to the neighbourhood of the Tuskar; so far to the eastward had we sailed, indeed, that the quartered fields and hedgerows and villages, even the horse-drawn traffic on the coastal roads, were all plainly visible. It had turned out a fine summer's day, although the head wind against which we had tacked down-channel from the Craig had fallen light, and progress was slow. The crew, still mustered at 'all hands on deck', wearied perhaps by the long hauling of the yards in working ship and unrefreshed by fitful snatches of sleep—but, as it seemed, newly invigorated by the sight and savour of the smiling landscape so nearly under their eyes—were clustered

60

at the bulwarks forward to enjoy the fair prospect. To their number was added a small group of emigrant passengers come from their quarters in the nearby deckhouse, and as eager as they to remark the features of the coastline. It was an occasion of high spirit and good, if noisy, humour. An animated gathering of adventurers setting to sea. There was confused talk, often rising to cheerful oath and banter among them, the sailor hands loud of voice in recalling the fleshpots of the land they were leaving and promising themselves a fuller measure of its fruits in some ports abroad; the emigrants, less noisily perhaps, talking apace, but mostly gazing long across the calm waters to register the impressions of a last farewell.

It was a pleasant and heartening scene, that forepart of a splendid well-manned ship with its gathering of friendly fellows in the adventure. Looking on, I had the thought that it could not do other than promote good feeling among us all, passengers and crew alike. Near me there stood the Mate, alert to carry out the Captain's orders; we grinned together at some quip that sounded out in the windless air. But my thoughts of amity in the ship were rudely dispelled. In some break of the seamen's rhapsody, a sudden and vicious outcry from the poop brought silence—

'Damn you, Mister Mate! Have you nothing else to do but hearken to the rowdy ongoings forward there? Send the hands to stations! Put these chattering apes out o' th' way for going about!' The Old Man indicated the bewildered passengers by a contemptuous wave of his big hand. 'Stand by t' go about, Mister!'

Mr Nicholson reddened somewhat under his tan, but said no more than 'Aye, aye, sir,' as he moved away smartly, beckoning to the emigrants to stand clear and ordering all hands to their stations.

Putting the ship about was now a difficult manœuvre. The wind had died away and broad belts of glassy calm set mirrors in the Bay. The ship was still moving, however, but the little breaths of wind gave us no more than an almost imperceptible steerage way. Soon we were becalmed, with all sail drooping and ineffective to turn her one way or the other. Then followed a lengthy period of working ship, carried out under constant objurgation from the frustrated old seaman who commanded us. No sooner had we hauled yards to meet a phantom breath of air than—its existence palpably denied— we were hounded to stand and haul to some new trimming of the great iron yards, a state of sail in which the canvas hung down as

61

windless as before. The glassy calm that held us motionless
stretched far within the Bay, but out to seaward in the west a ribbon
of darkened line on the horizon showed where a breath of wind was
blowing. It was to that point of the compass that the Captain's
anxious gaze was ever returning.

When, as occasionally happened, a catspaw of wandering air
ruffled the sea's surface, there was immediate 'let go and haul' to
capture it; as though entreating the casual draught to fill his sails, the
Old Man would stamp impatiently on the poop, his lips pursed
to give vent to a hopeful *Ssss-sh! Sss*—his invitation to the
wind!

In the late afternoon weariness overcame him and he was con-
strained to go below. As he paused at the companion-way for a
look round before descending, one of the cabin passengers—Mr
Walker, as I remember, a wool buyer on his way out to Melbourne
—made some friendly remark to him, something about the weather
being fine. The Old Man did not reply: his look was baleful.

It fell to the Mate to trim the yards to a light breeze that sprang
up just before sundown. We had thought it the wandering zephyr
that so often before had called us out to futile labours. But no, this
time it was no vagrant zephyr to arouse our hopes, then earn a
fleeting deep-sea curse as it died away, but a real messenger of the
winds sent out by the coolth of the evening temperature. It came
from northward, faintly rustling the reef-points of the sails before
strengthening to bring them flat aback. Quickly heartened, we
hauled the yards and manœuvred to bring the ship a-trim on the
starboard tack, then watched the gladdening eddies form up astern
as steerage was gained and we sailed westward.

Roused by our hauling cries and the *thrrr-ap* of running coils
thrown from pin-rail to the deck above his head, the Old Man was
soon on the poop again to scan the northern sky and search the set of
sail. The feel of the wind on his cheek seemed to have banished all
his former bitterness and rancour. Almost instantly he was friends
again, promoting us all to good fellowship, even the strolling
passengers being greeted in kindly terms. In high good humour, he
came near to patting the steersman on the back as he set course for
the Tuskar and the freedom of a wider sea. I, too, came in for my
share of his relief and satisfaction. I was no longer 'you there' or
'Hey!' to him, but was hailed 'My lad' when, the breeze holding

finely and every stitch of sail drawing well, he set me to the heaving of the log.

We were all his able men again in this atmosphere of content engendered by the boon of a fair wind down-channel.

At night-time in the fine weather of the trades the relief of the other watch was often attended by an exchange of confidences; as the voyage progressed, I came to relish these all-too-brief conversations I had with Mr Nicholson. With the ship's course repeated, the state of sail and the incidents of the last watch discussed—perhaps a last injunction of the Master duly conveyed—one could revert to the incidents of the day or recall some odd experience in seafaring. Curiously, one's former background when on shore or the detail of home life there was rarely mentioned. We were far at sea, and almost all our topics were of sailing matters.

Nicholson—I cannot remember, or indeed I may never have known his christian name—was only about four years older than me, but he seemed immeasurably my senior by reason of a grave bearing and an enviable ability in every duty he undertook. He had sailed with Captain Martin on previous voyages and had hopes of obtaining a command in the Loch Line ships before long, for many of the serving Captains were up in years, and steamships were claiming the younger men in increasing numbers. His continued service in the *Loch Ness* was a surprise to me, for in his vile tempers old Bully spared no one, and his abuse was often most bitterly directed to those nearest in office to him. I had quickly determined that one voyage with the tyrannical old man would be enough for me and, in the confidences of the night watch, I had spoken of 'looking around' when we arrived out in the Colonies. My wiser shipmate counselled patience. Of course, the Old Man's frequent outbursts were hard to be borne, he agreed, but he had come to look upon them much as a sailor would look upon sudden squalls out of thin air: as something one just had to put up with, something to be endured and weathered.

'After all,' he would continue, 'look at what you can win from him! Every trick of seamanship the Old Man has is a masterpiece, and we're both here to pick it up. What does it matter to us if he dislikes the passengers?'

When we had docked at Melbourne, I thought there was now no

need to 'look around'. Donning his longshore clothes, Captain Martin had reassumed his genial longshore manner, not only towards the Mate and me, but also in converse with the passengers whom he had ignored or flouted on the voyage. As we passed up-river under tow of the paddle-tug *Racer*, he was at pains to enlarge on the growth of the port and harbour as he had remarked it on long acquaintance. He was in high spirits. Gone was the embittered old tyrant with the goad in his sailor tongue; gone the testy and taciturn autocrat of the cabin table, the quick contestant in argument on even the most casual topic. In his stead, an amiable and courteous Commander, at one with his friends in hailing the successful outcome of a pleasant voyage. At the dock-gates where the ship was held for a small rise of tide, his many Melbourne friends boarded us to welcome him in and bear him away to a lodging at seaside St Kilda on the outskirts of the city. There he lodged during our stay in the port, and save for an occasional brief visit to the ship we saw little of him while the unloading of the cargo was in progress.

No, there was no need for me to 'look around' in Melbourne. But it was not wholly the Old Man's novel countenance when harboured and well in a famous city that brought me to change my mind about that. I had vivid memories of his often urgent deeds in the storm and stress of the latter part of the voyage when we were far south of the 'roaring forties' and steering easterly. By his consummate skill in seeking wind, wind, wind, that well he knew he could harness, he had captured my imagination. I would win from him something of value, as Mr Nicholson had said I would. Rebuffs, sneers, savage objurgations, were only small coin in suffering to expend for the uncommon knowledge of my trade I was picking up under his often cruel command. There was no need for me to look outboard the bulwarks of my ship for a better example: I could always discard its tempers . . . or so, in my youth, I thought.

A few days after our arrival at Melbourne, most of the crew were paid off. How different this was from the practice I had known in the *City of Florence*, when arrived in a Californian port, where the boarding master and his brawny runners decided all issues in the manning of ships. Here, the matters were straightforward. It was understood that there was no need for a large body of seamen to be employed while their ships were immobilized in dock. Men of sailor

The *City of Florence* in San Francisco Bay, 1892

Captain 'Bully' Martin, about 1880

type were the most desirable of emigrants; why deny them a chance to 'look around'? It would be time enough for them to think of the sea again when the wool-clip of the season was ready for shipment overseas. Although the men had signed for the round voyage —out and home—there seemed no objection to discharge 'by mutual consent' at the office of the Port Authority.

When the outward cargo had been discharged, we shifted ship to a less congested berth in the dock and lay there awaiting a charter to load for home. Other ships joined us in that quiet corner in expectation of engagement and gradually we formed a small community of idle windjammers. For many years the seasonal wool trade had been the only competitive event within the range of a sailing-ship's employment. The lordly China trade had been lost to us by the advance of steam, and now only on the long, stormy route by way of Cape Horn was there a shred of profit to be earned in sail. . . . Near us at the berth, a large grey-hulled ship, the *Avenger* of Liverpool, lay as idle as we, awaiting the turn of the freight market. She had arrived from Valparaiso some weeks before us with her Captain seriously ill. The port doctor had diagnosed some internal malady and the patient had been removed to hospital on shore. Just at about the time his ship was chartered to load for home, he died. For some reason the Mate of the *Avenger* was ineligible to succeed him, and her agents (who were also ours) appointed Mr Nicholson to go in command of her. Doubtless Captain Martin would have had a word in the agent's ear when the appointment was under consideration. When Captain Nicholson transferred to his new command, no one was immediately appointed to take his place. Like the Mate of the *Avenger*, I felt myself ineligible for promotion—having only a second-mate's certificate—but with other ships of the Loch Line arriving in port, I thought it strange that the vacancy was not filled from that source. In the *Loch Ness* we had come on the berth to load for Glasgow, and again the positioning of the deadweight was the important matter that occupied my earnest attention. It was high time that whoever was to avert the Old Man's wrath when events proved difficult on the homeward voyage should now be busily engaged in figuring out the loading plans. We thought it strange that no appointment was made until we were almost full loaded and ready for sea on a late date in December, when Mr Cunningham from the *Loch Tay* came to sail with us. From him I learned that there was no competition for service under our redoubtable commander.

I did my best to attend to affairs, and was not quite alone. I could well understand that Captain Nicholson's new duties and greater responsibility in the *Avenger* would demand so much of him that he would quickly have to dismiss any interest in his old ship—and in his former shipmate—but he was not the man to leave any reef-points untied, and I was grateful for his frequent visits and much helpful advice in carrying on with the loading plan he had previously employed.

The main body of the crew having been paid off on arrival, and with only the apprentices and a small group of selected hands to be supervised, the work of the ship did not call for urgent direction. In the main, it was devoted to the maintenance of a goodly appearance, for we were now in the splendid company of some of the world's finest sailing-ships. Almost daily there were new arrivals at Williamstown and in the dock, brought in from far abroad to share in the transport of the season's wool. I own to a catch of the heart in recalling the names of the lovely ships that lay with us at Melbourne on what may have been almost a last assignment—the sunset of brave endeavour. . . . The *Loch Garry* (Captain James Horne), *Peleus* and *Melpomene*, the *Mermerus* (Captain Cole), *Sierra Moreno* and the old *Dharwar*, the *Blackadder*, and the barque *Braemar*. Not least of the splendid ships were the many sisters of the Loch Line fleet—the *Loch Tay*, the *Loch Ryan*, the *Loch Katrine*, and the famed *Loch Torridon*.

In such distinguished company we had need to exert ourselves in upkeep and embellishment, and not all the working hours we spent on the garnishment of our ship came within our bounden duty. I remember the long job I undertook in my spare time—the renovation of the carved and gilded escutcheon displayed across the shapely counter of the ship to proclaim her name and port of registry. At Barclay, Curle's shipyard on the Clyde where she was built in the sixties, there must have been a master craftsman employed to fashion it, so finely carved was the hardwood exhibiting a bold design of ropework that enclosed the lettering and the picturesque medallions. It is improbable that the sections, so firmly bolted to the plating of the stern, had ever been regilded and restored since the day of her launching, and only the lettering had from time to time been repainted in some yellowish colouring. Regilding it was out of the question, for I had neither the money to purchase gold leaf nor the skill to apply it, but something could be done with buff-colour paint and a shading of burnt sienna. As I quickly found out, it was an ambitious project that occupied long evenings after the regular day's work was done. It was no easy pastime. Swinging in a bos'un's chair under the counter was almost an acrobatic feat when I employed it to reach the remote curlicues of the design. The work was completed at length, despite the often derisive remarks and rum advices of my sailor friends from the other ships, whose evening recreation seemed to be a saunter along the quayside to see how Bone was getting along with his advertisement. But some were complimentary. The Mate of the *Dharwar* said it was 'a bloody work of art, nothing less' when I had finished and the bos'un's chair was finally hauled aboard.

I was proud of it. As the loading proceeded towards the stowage of a full cargo, I was often at the quayside to study the draught marks, in the hope that my calculations would produce the exact trim the Old Man demanded. It was at the least encouraging to see above the numerals another extra job successfully completed. . . . Often I wonder if the little landscape I repainted on the central medallion of the escutcheon—a representation of a highland lochan, with its blues exaggerated by the flaming purples of its surrounding bens and glens—survived the old ship's later days, when she drowsed in harbour at Port Adelaide, coal-hulking for the grimy steamers that had driven her from the open seas.

Chapter X

THE JAIL TO THE RESCUE

THE new Mate, who had appeared diffident and not quite sure of himself when he came to us from the *Loch Tay* ten days before, was better pleased with his appointment by the time we were loaded and ready for sea. The work of the ship was reasonably forward when he took over his duties and he had found Captain Martin as amiable as I had done on early acquaintance. All seemed to go well as we hurried with preparations to complete loading and sail with the first of the new season's wool-clip. Only the task of finding seamen to replace the hands we had paid off on outward arrival had given Mr Cunningham cause for concern. Few seamen were available for engagement and even men of indifferent experience of the sea were quickly signed on at first appearance on the gangway. Owing to drought, the season—with its demand for casual labour up-country—had continued for a longer period than was usual, and sailormen who had sought employment there had not yet drifted back to the seaports in any number. While we had not done badly in keen competition with our companions of the wool fleet who were in similar plight, we were still some hands short of a full complement when we towed down from the dock and had to anchor off Williamstown to complete our manning.

We had company at the anchorage. Other loaded ships that had been our berth-mates in the Victoria Dock had brought up off the little port for the same purpose, while some, having been more fortunate in their enlistments, lay there awaiting the help of busy harbour tugs to tow out beyond the Heads. Offshore, only two vessels of the 'first-to-load' series, being fully manned, had succeeded in putting to sea and were already under sail, leaning away to the eastward towards Bass Strait. These were the old *Dharwar* and the *Loch Ryan*, the latter a sister ship of the *Loch Ness*. There was said to be a considerable rivalry between old Bully and Captain

68

William Weir, of the *Loch Ryan*, a younger man, and it was not without interest I noted our Old Man's rising choler as he recognized the leaders of the fleet. The light sou'westerly wind that prevailed was at the moment fair for the passage of the Straits, but there was no promise of its continuance in the cloudless sky above. ... Quickly, there was storm in the Old Man's narrowed frown, in his stamping footsteps, in his protesting hands as he conned the situation. Then—the sudden vicious outburst! ... To me it was small wonder that his fury was aroused by having to anchor under a fair wind; but to the Mate, striving to put his best foot forward, the sudden blast seemed to be directed especially and publicly at him—a quick, malevolent snarl from a source he had thought considerate and friendly. Highland bred, and as quick to anger as the old tyrant, he resented the Captain's hasty charges that he had been neglectful of his duty. Could he make men? he countered. Could he make men the way one made a hank of spun-yarn?

Out-shouting the Mate's remonstrance, the Old Man heightened his flaming invective as he hailed the tugboat that had brought us down-river and ordered her to come alongside and embark him for the shore. Yes, he would make men, he roared. He would get able hands, even if all his officers had failed him! ... 'Damn you for a worthless fellow,' he exploded at the astounded newcomer just as the *Eagle* hauled alongside. 'Have you no eyes? Look at the *Loch Ryan* there!' He waved an arm in the direction of the open sea. 'Look at her! Under way from the dockside and at sea already. ... How th' hell can she find her men? ... Eh! Tell me that? But her Mate has energy and persistence in harrying th' waterfront for the men he knew were there. God, Mister! Have I to do your work for ye as early as this on the voyage?'

Fuming and storming, the Old Man stepped outboard on to the sponsons of the tugboat and signalled the skipper to steam ahead and make for the shore. His last satirical outburst had faintly coherent reference to a graveyard where sailors lay: he would find men there, he spat out—better men than the goddam impostors he had now to suffer. Including me in his baleful glance at the receding gangway of his ship, he stepped down from the sponson as though loathing the sight of her.

For long after the tug had cast off and sped on her way to Williamstown jetty, Mr Cunningham followed her progress with resentful eyes, then turned to me for support. Only too well could I read his thoughts. At the Melbourne quayside, I had heard a lot about the even-tempered old Jerseyman who commanded his former ship, the *Loch Tay*, and I could realise Mr Cunningham's dismay at the changed prospect confronting him. Was this the promotion he had signed for in the transfer? I remembered how, in the night watches, Mr Nicholson had counselled me to exercise patience in some similarly bitter reaction on my part to old Bully's harsh sarcasms. I tried to convey to my new shipmate something of that good advice, saying the Old Man's angry manners when sailing his ship at sea had to do with some urgency he could never restrain. Maybe, I said, he hadn't seriously intended to be so brutally frank and had let his words run away with him. Mr Cunningham said nothing in reply and there was still resentment in his eyes as he turned away. Perhaps he thought me case-hardened to the Old Man's rancours or even that I was cowed by the master's bitter tongue.

We spent a busy afternoon on last-minute preparations for getting under way, and this occupation brought the Mate some relief from his exasperations. We agreed that whether he succeeded in finding sailormen or returned without any, the Captain's first order would be to 'up anchor' as soon as he came on board and that it would be well to be prepared for it.

Before sunset there was a stir at the jetty and, through the long glass, we saw the Customs launch put off in our direction. We recognized Captain Martin in the cockpit. But who were these up-standing men in tunics buttoned to the chin and wearing old-fashioned cheese-cutter caps? Beside them in the roomy afterpart of the launch, we could make out a small group of men—recognizable as seamen by the bundles and sailor bags piled up near them. As we were soon to learn, the Captain had no need to visit the grave-yard in quest of able hands. In some way known to him from his long familiarity with the resources of the port he had set about quickly to seek them in a penal lodging. His offer to relieve the Colony of the expense of maintaining five errant sailormen in the local penitentiary was accepted, provided that—paying the wages of the port to the delinquents—he embarked them for the long voyage to the United Kingdom.

It was as well we had set the gear in readiness and coiled down clear for running, for a tug was not employed to tow us out when we hoisted topsails and got under way, steering out towards Port Philip Heads in failing winds but favoured by the ebbing tide. Darkness had fallen and there was moonlight at the anchorage when we raised anchor and quietly took to the wind. Beyond giving orders in an even voice, the Old Man—apparently recovered from the morning's tantrums and gratified by his success in signing hands —left all sailing matters to the local pilot who had come off with him in the Customs launch. That handy harbour craft was retained alongside until we had skirted the shoals and passed the Heads. There the pilot disembarked. With him in the launch there went back to less tonic duty the prison warders, well content with the parting glass and the Old Man's signature for the persons of our 'volunteers'.

During the night the sou'west wind strengthened and when the dawn came in we held a good sailing breeze. As the light grew, two ships were sighted broad off on the port bow. One of the strangers was thought to be the *Avenger* which had sailed from the anchorage about four hours before we did. At first sight she was 'hull down' and the revealing features of her deck structures could not be made out. But when, bringing the strength of the wind with us, we drew nearer to her, I was astonished to recognize the *Loch Ryan*—the Captain's rival—for, knowing her as a speedy ship, we had little hope of sighting her again. In our ignorance, the Mate and I thought Captain Martin would bear off to close her and mark his satisfaction at coming up so soon with the leaders of the sailing group by exchange of friendly signals, but instead he hauled closer to the wind and before long we had lost sight of the ships on the northern horizon.

The Mate and I were at a loss to account for such a deliberate avoidance, but the establishment of the ship's position by the sun at noon brought enlightenment. Well knowing how nearly alike in sailing qualities the sister ships were, it was apparent that the Old Man had no wish to keep company with the *Loch Ryan* and engage in day-by-day manœuvres on the regular sea routes. By the course he laid off on the chart, it could be seen that he had now decided to steer for Banks Strait on the northern coast of Tasmania as preliminary to adventuring the often difficult passage between the North and South Islands of New Zealand. To that end we made good progress, but were unrewarded in the outcome. The winds fell light and baffling in the Tasman Sea: calms were frequent, and when a good sailing breeze did spring up in the north-east, the best we could make of it was to sail south of the Islands altogether and steer on the Great Circle that curves on the icy fringes of the Antarctic. Whatever advantage the Old Man sought on that inclement southerly track to the Horn—the cruising area of the lumbering old whalers—he did not say when setting the course at noon each day.

As the variable winds steadied in the westward and the long days became colder, it became clear to the Mate and me that—unlike the ships whose company we had avoided—the *Loch Ness* was to have no rallying period in less Antarctic latitudes, when we could tighten up our sea tackle and exercise our men against the rigours of Cape Horn. The Mate could make no sense of this 'Arctic bloody exploration', as he called it when, day after day, the state of the weather debarred him from 'shipwork as requisite' to earn for him a good word from the owners on arrival at Glasgow. Though I too was ill content with the reeling ship and the almost constant thrash of water on the maindeck, I had some inkling of the Old Man's purpose. On one occasion when reporting my feeble navigations to him and finding him in good mood, I remarked the doubtful character of my observations, quickly taken in a rift of the morning sky. There had been some days of rain and overcast weather and it had not been possible to establish position by sights of the sun or stars. In the middle watch, I had been lucky to take an observation of a star before dawn. I thought it of little worth, a snapshot for longitude. Later, on working it out, I found its position considerably to eastward of the dead reckoning. I was not at all confident that the Old Man would even look at it, but he did and seemed uncritical. Apologetically, I mumbled something about a favourable current.

'A favourable current,' he repeated gruffly. 'What on earth do you think we're doing down here, Mister?' Then, in less derisive accent, 'Ever stir your tea, young fellow?' Surprised, I said I had, but what——

Curiously smiling, as he so rarely did at sea, he rolled his fingers in the action of one using a teaspoon and likened it to some revolving force of the great west winds stirring the vast area of the southern seas around the Pole to urge us on. There was certainly an east-going current, he affirmed, calling it his dividend on risking hardship in high latitudes. From this reflection, inevitably his talk rolled on to criticism of the seamen of the day. It was my watch below. I had a need for sleep, but this unusual confidence bestowed on me was awakening, for I had never known him as discursive as this. He said firmly that it was the deterioration of seamanship amongst crews that led the modern shipmaster to seek the 'gentler' sea route wherever possible; that, and the economies of owners now confronted by steamship competition. In his younger days, only the ships sailing from Sydney took the northern route from that port to Cape Horn, all the others following the harder route on which the whalers cruised for sperm. I was a good and interested listener, but had the presumption to mention the *Loch Ryan* up north and wonder how she fared. That was my great mistake, his genial mood came suddenly to an end. I was no longer 'young fellow' or 'my lad' and he surveyed me coldly once again.

Chapter XI

SAIL TO STEAM

ON my former arrivals in the United Kingdom from far
abroad it had always been to distant outports that the *City
of Florence* had been directed, often to the west coast of
Ireland, there to unload the cargo she had brought in. Instruction as
to the final port of discharge was rarely given when she sailed, for it
might well be that the ship's cargo was sold, resold, and sold again
on the long voyage home. It was generally as the outcome of a call
at Falmouth or Queenstown 'for orders' that we put out to sea
again on a short coastwise passage to a port of discharge. Upon
arrival there, and the ship securely moored, the voyage was at an
end and the men of the crew were paid off to go their several ways.
But there was still shipwork for the brassbounders who drew no
pay. It was usual for the Mate and the apprentices to be retained
aboard for some time after arrival, before leave to journey to their
homes was approved.

There was much to be done in a sailing-ship just in from sea
to safeguard her sailing gear and cordage against misuse by the
longshore labourer—a makeshifter if ever was, who saw no
sailor's lifeline among the ropes that lay so nearly to his hand.
Certainly, riggers could daily be engaged at any seaport—old
hands, able to unbend sail for harbour storage and to stopper all
the ropes in the rigging out of reach of the cargo-workers—but
they too required an overlooker who was someone familiar
with the ship's sail-lockers and her routines. Always there was
work and enough when the hatches were uncovered and strangers
swarmed up the gangway to roust the lading from the holds
below.

But even if our little group retained on board could not as yet
'return in safety to enjoy the blessings of the land, with the fruits of
our labours', there was always a postal pillar-box not far from the

74

dock-gates and news of the wanderer's return—so often the theme of the poet and the dramatist—could speedily be conveyed and his early appearance at home be expected.

In the *Loch Ness* there was no doubt about our destination and neither need nor opportunity to correspond. It was thus a wondrous and newly welcome experience for me to enter my own home waters under sail, as I had left them nine months before. With no need to seek the Channel for orders, we had steered from a position off the Azores to make a landfall on the north-west coast of Ireland. Sailing large through the North Channel in the night, we watched the matchless beauty of the western Scottish coast unveil as the growing daylight spread abroad on its hills and lowlands. What happiness I gained from that bright morning vision in the clear April weather, what joy aroused by the prospect that—did the wind but hold—we might win to port before darkness came again!

As we trimmed sail, standing to the north-east under the high rugged hills of the Cantire peninsula, the fine wind that had favoured us beyond the Mull lessened, then died away, leaving us mirrored in calm off the south end of Arran. For an hour or more of precious daylight we lay making no progress, our hopes of reaching port abashed. Drifting seaward on the ebb and with the day's outgoing of steamer traffic to mock us by their swift and easy passage, I found it vexing to accept the limitations of sail. But, having the splendid view of Arran from my post at the compass, I could enjoy the sight of snow-clad Goatfell in the north and the nearer outline of the range of the Sleeping Warrior. . . . Curiously, the Old Man did not fly to anger at this maddening check to his design, nor was it in wrath that he stepped his paces on the gangway near me on the poop. Rather, his was a patiently expectant tread as he walked fore and aft. He would know (as I did not) that observant eyes ashore had for long been fixed on us. Our need was known, and when the *Flying Dutchman*, a powerful Clyde Shipping tug, roared out of Ardrossan heading towards us, he seemed in no way surprised by her opportune appearance.

But there was much to arouse my surprise when the tugboat rounded under our stern within hail. I had expected a tiresome 'bicker' of haggling over towage charges between the Old Man and the tugmaster, and all the while the glorious daylight fading; but there was none of that. Hailing the Old Man by name and in the tone of an acquaintance, the skipper—would it be Captain Mac-farlane who had the *Dutchman* then?—held out a bulky envelope as he brought his tug alongside. His orders were to take us in tow right away, he said. 'They' were in a hurry for us up-bye. . . . How grateful to the ear were the modulations of the Highland tongue as the skipper passed the word to us!

Furling all our drooping canvas, we came under tow to the Tail of the Bank at Greenock, an alert and towardly arrival—even though our passage of eighty-three days from Port Philip Heads was not to be considered any special achievement. Nor did this for-tunately even performance end there—as some of us had feared—among the anchored ships that lay awaiting the grant of a berth up-river to unload cargo; for, as we were to learn, industry was boom-ing on Clydeside and there was dearth of quay space in the Glasgow docks. With a second tug brought off from Greenock to assist in the windings of the river, we lay-to for a while at the entrance of the dredged channel, awaiting a sufficient rise of tide to bear us up-stream. When the news was spread in the ship that we were to proceed on the tide to Glasgow, it was scarcely believable that our old clipper should be given such quick despatch, while the urgent and self-propelled steamers were held idly at anchor. Surely, we thought, the new season's wool-clip we had loaded and hurried round the Horn must be in frantic demand in the world's markets for this uncommon preferment. Or, could it be that—as late as 1897 —owners of square-rigged shipping had at last realized that the challenge of steam could not ever be met by any traditional suffer-ance of delay in port? Hitherto, dependence on winds and the weather had been accepted as a good plea for 'lie-by days' before the sailing-ship was berthed at her final port and bulk was broken there. For too long it had been tacitly agreed that preparation of the ship's papers, the checking and amending of her cargo manifests and the recognition of later-date consignees whose interest had been acquired whilst the ship was on passage, could not always be done in advance of the ship's arrival in the port. For many ships of that date the ocean sailing tracks were far off-shore and no sig-nals could be made to coastal stations. Wireless was unknown, and even the telegraph and the overseas mails were not entirely predictable. Perhaps a brief line of print in the columns of a shipping journal (its date long past) might tell of one sailing-ship spoken all well by another on the high seas and be the sum of information an owner had of his ship since she had cleared from a port abroad. It was only with the steamship on inshore and regularly scheduled voyages that pre-arrangements could be planned.

Whatever the reason for the quick despatch we were given at the Tail of the Bank when we towed slowly through the press of anchored steamers, its continuance on the passage up-river heightened the glad spirit that thrilled us all on that remembered day. The Captain had put on his shore clothes (and the genial manner that went so well with them) and was no longer distant with the Mate and me. We were promoted to an unusual fellowship with him as the ship towed quietly between the river-banks. Already he had agreed to continue Mr Cunningham in his post as Mate on the next voyage and had said he would recommend me to the owners for appointment as Mate in the Loch Line when I had obtained my next certificate.

Conversing with the Mate about the prospects of the coming voyage, he spoke of a matter that had troubled him. Among the letters that the tug had brought off from the shore, the owners had written to him a project for altering the rig of the *Loch Ness* and others of the company's ships. It was proposed as a matter of economy to reduce the sail area and cut down the numbers of able seamen correspondingly. The ship was to go out barque-rigged on her next voyage if it was thought that a worth-while saving in crew's wages could be effected. . . . Economy? The Old Man stepped a pace or two, growling in his beard. Then, as though prompted by the word he contemned, passed an order that enforced it. It had been a sunny, if coldish day, and the sails were dry. We were to save a pound or two on the 'Harbour Bill' by unbending courses and topsails before docking, and thus eliminate the expense of employing a riggers' gang when the ship had come to port. It was no specially skilled task, but it would have to be done quickly if the great square-sails were to be unrigged from the yards and sent down on deck to be rolled up—each in its own special way—and consigned to the sail-locker before we reached the dock. Eyeing the beacon on Donald's Quay at Bowling, which we were passing at the moment, the Old Man thought there was just time enough.

Grimacing wryly (doubtless in thought of the pitiful retrenchment involved), he strode off to his restless pacings again, stepping
heavy-footed and cursing the tenour of the day in shipping
matters.

'Economy! Economy!' He growled contemptuously as his gaze
fell on the mizen-mast, so soon to be bereft of its square-sail.
'Where the hell is it all to end?'

It is not usually the part of a sailing crew to unbend sail in the
river when on point of entering the dock, but this was our special
day for quick despatch and we swarmed aloft to carry out the order.
While the Mate remained on deck, my duty on the main topsail yard
was to hasten the completion of the job. But I had no need to chide
or exhort the men aloft there. All hands worked well and quickly
—even the Melbourne 'volunteers' displaying a turn of sailor-work
that had not been noticeable on the voyage. When the last of the
greater sails had been lowered away, I lingered in the main-top to
survey the scene below. It was then about four of the afternoon and
work was at its height in the shipyards that lined the banks of the
river. As the *Loch Ness* towed steadily past the gaunt and red-rusty
frames of ships to be, the thunderous din of the riveting hammers
seemed curiously lessened, as though the labouring men had paused
in their work to look at our old ship, the product of another
generation; then, *ram-stam*, the thundering of the hammers resumed
its working pitch.

In that significant hush there was food for thought. Was the
sailing-ship already such a monument of the old days that the
modern shipbuilder would pause in his labours to watch her pass?
Again, I could not see one fine-lined hull among the many upstanding structures on the ways designed to carry sail. All were great
cargo-carriers, flat-bottomed steel ships, broad of beam and of
heavy ungracious line. I thought I had no heart for them. I had
much to learn.

With the familiar scenes of my boyhood days now coming in
sight as I came down from my task aloft, I pondered my own situation when paid off from the *Loch Ness* and looking for another post
at sea—a mood of self-questioning that had occupied my thoughts
the more as we drew near to the land. I had still three months of
qualifying service to put in before I could sit the examination for a
First Mate's certificate. I was twenty-four now and could no longer

play around, seeing the world. Another voyage in sail would take me too far from the examination room perhaps, and I might become, as so many I had known, a confirmed roamer 'out abroad' with no firm ties with home and family. . . . No, it would have to be in steam now I would sail the seas.

Chapter XII

PIER-HEAD JUMP

WHEN I sought sea employment after leaving the *Loch Ness*, I made every effort to find a post in a steamer trading on short voyages, preferably of about three months. The managing clerk in a shipowner's office at Glasgow assured me that their S.S. *Strathmore*, in which a second mate was required, was on a firm 'time charter' to Sloman's of Hamburg and sailing on Atlantic voyages of short duration. But sub-charters are not unknown in the shipping world, and when I had sailed in her and arrived out in Brooklyn, I learned that she was to load a general cargo for Chinese coastal ports. I had to carry on in her for nearly six months beyond my needs. But the experience of ship-life in the China trade was well worth my overstay in the *Strathmore*, and I returned home resolved to seek my fortune in a ship out there when I had acquired the necessary certificates.

I had good reason for mending my roving ways, for I had fallen in love, and service at sea (which I had thought a sufficient mainstay) needed family support and land-based upholding. In that voyage out east, I had become a good correspondent and my letters reflected the resolution. I felt that I had to seek good service in a ship 'on the coast' and settle down in the comfortable circumstances I had remarked among the pilots and other seafaring friends I had made in the Treaty Ports.

On return from that voyage I lost no time in obtaining a Mate's certificate, but found it not so easy to secure employment in the service I preferred. I made the rounds of the shipping offices, but seldom succeeded in gaining the ear of anyone of higher standing than the clerk at the outer desk. But there were other informations, and I learned from a chance acquaintance that a Japanese firm, the Nippon Yusen Kaisha, was building a number of modern steamships, mostly on the Clyde. Captain Brown, a Scottish shipmaster who

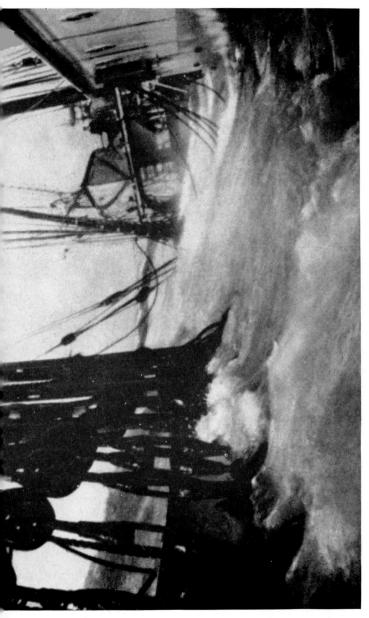

'Running the easting down'

The *Loch Ness*

The Anchor Line flagship in 1899, S.S. *City of Rome*

was acting for the owners while the vessels were under construction, had all to do with the appointment of masters and officers in the ships and was said to be partial to sail-trained men. Although he had an office in the city, he was not often there and it was on the deck of one of the ships I saw him about a job. (This ship, the *Kanegawa Maru*, had just returned from an unsuccessful trial trip. It was the second time such an incident had occurred and the wags in the shipwrights' squad at Meadowside had aptly renamed her the *Canna-gang-awa' Mary*!) Despite the mishap, Captain Brown was affable. When he turned over the few papers I had to recommend me, he paused long at old Bully's large handwriting, in which it was stated that I was a good seaman, able and alert. I saw Captain Brown's lips form a soundless '*M-mmm!*' and, as I thought, there was a renewed interest in his second glance at me. He said he knew Captain Martin. He would be glad to have my application, but it was a pity I did not have a higher grade certificate. He would bear me in mind, he said.

I came away quite pleased with the interview. I had already learned something of the trade in which the new Japanese ships were to be manned. Carrying both passengers and cargo between Japan and London, they were built to a very high classification at Lloyds. They were manned by their own native seamen, but all the commanding branch of the officers was European. Of course, one would be sailing under the flag of the Rising Sun, but it was shining amicably upon us in 1898. The wages were good too. I had great hopes.

But others were as eager as I to serve in foreign ships at such attractive terms and my hope of a speedy appointment was dimmed as the days wore on. Captain Brown was well enough inclined to take me on, but what could he do with so many experienced men with senior certificates crowding him to the issues. The best he could offer me was a post as fourth officer, which I did not accept.

My lane had its curious turning. Meeting my father in Union Street in Glasgow when on these unproductive rounds of the shipping offices, I began to tell him about my latest disappointment. As we talked, a well-built and smiling man came down the steps from the Anchor Line office, and gave my father a hearty good-day then stopped to chat.

I had not met Captain McFee before, but knew of him as an

important figure in Clydeside shipping circles. He was the Marine Superintendent of the Anchor Line, the very man I had long sought to meet. I had tried to gain his ear on many occasions without success, for there was always a self-assured young clerk at the outer desk who told me how busy his principal was and adding—as he regarded me—that there were no vacancies for a deck officer at the moment, but he would take my name.

It was not of the sea and ships that the talk ran. I was briefly indicated as 'M'son, David' and their common interest in literature was quickly resumed. It came out that Captain McFee was the author of a narrative poem that had just been published in Glasgow. My father spoke well of it. He thought *Norman : A Poem in Five Duans* a very special effort for an Ayrshire seaman to compose. How strange it was that I should then consider an indulgence in imaginative verse unfitting in a hardy follower of the sea!

The Captain was surprised to learn that his old acquaintance should have bred a sailor son, and particularly one at a loss for employment. To his inquiry as to why I had not come to see him about a job, I could only explain that I had just come from his office, where a clerk had told me there were no vacancies, but that he would take my name. The Captain did not seem in the least nettled by his clerk's method of fending off casual applicants, but he did say something about counter-jumpers, then asked me what my qualifications were. It then appeared that the junior's information was incorrect. A third mate was needed in a hurry for the S.S. *Australia*, which was due to sail from Glasgow that very afternoon. It was then about twelve noon and the tide served at three. Could I be ready in time to get aboard? I could, and I did. It was thus as a 'pier-head jump' I joined the Anchor Line, in whose service I remained for nearly fifty years.

The *Australia*, a screw steamship of 3,600 gross tonnage, was perhaps the ugly duckling among the graceful sisters of the company's large fleet. Built as a speculation in an East coast shipyard, she had been purchased for service in some emergency calling for large cargo-carrying capacity rather than the speed and fine lines demanded on the Company's passenger routes. At the time I joined her it was said that she was up for sale as being no longer suited to the business of the Line, but—in the late summer of 1899—it was as well that no purchaser had come forward, for great events were in

the making and in such troublous times the value of a sound keel
had become tremendously enhanced. The United States was at war
with Spain and the menace of our own war in South Africa loomed
near.

We sailed out to Bombay on my first voyage in the *Australia*. I
remember her as the luckiest ship I ever sailed in. In that, I mean
lucky in her engagements—a remarkable breadwinner in her good
charters. The mere report of her arrival in a harbour was a tonic in
the freight market: and even if the market rates held stubbornly to
low figures, some incident on the passage was sure to recoup her for
any losses on the round voyage. Loading at Bombay for Marseilles,
Liverpool, and Glasgow, there was often a considerable portion of
the cargo consigned to the French port. When that cargo had been
discharged there, it was not often replaced by exports from the continent, and the ship would have much vacant space in her on the
passage from Marseilles to Liverpool. That was the sailing trim of
the *Australia* on my first voyage in her, when, high and light, she
crawled crabwise down the Costa Brava at nine knots, homeward
bound.

It had not been intended to call at Gibraltar, for there was little
profit in the uplift of the Garrison's empty beer barrels, but when
off the Rock at daylight we were signalled in to the harbour by an
urgent hoist of flags on Lloyd's staff. It appeared later that a substantial addition to the earnings of the lucky old ship was in prospect. A Newcastle steamer loaded with a full cargo of fruit—mostly
oranges in boxes—had gone ashore during fog in the Straits.
Salvage tugs had wrenched her from the Pearl Rock and towed her
to safety at Gibraltar. Her hull plating was seriously damaged, for
the Pearl is fringed by razor edgings, and she was only kept afloat
by the pumps her salvors had quickly set going. Repairs could be
effected in the port, but the cargo, much of it as yet undamaged,
would have to be unloaded before entering dry-dock. There was no
storage available for perishable fruit in the dock area and the cargo
had been put at auction. There was no ship available to load it
either, and no bids were made. That was the situation when the
Australia rounded Europa Point and steered to an anchorage off the
neutral ground. Shrewd negotiation by our agency secured the
damaged ship's entire cargo at the cost of removing it from her, a
stipulation being that all of it—good, bad, or indifferent—was to be

taken out of the ship. She was a smallish vessel—as most fruit-carrying freighters are—and her cargo was transferred to us by bonus workers in record time. In forty hours we resumed our passage, the holds stowed tightly enough but our weltered decks piled on high with damaged boxes which harbour regulations obliged us to carry out to sea before dumping overside. Our ocean route to the United Kingdom was conspicuously marked by a trail of bobbing orange boxes, and a week later the 'fruits of our labours' were selling in the streets of Liverpool at four a penny. What the Anchor Line gained in the transaction I never learned, but it must have been considerable.

Chapter XIII

BOER WAR TRANSPORT

THE Boer War had broken out while we were on that same homeward voyage, and again the *Australia* was in urgent demand for service. Unloaded in haste at Liverpool as we had been, she was quickly available for fitting out as a horse transport and as such we sailed for Cape Town early in November 1899. Heading south in cold but settled weather, we were fortunate on most stages of the long voyage, for the ship, insufficiently ballasted on the instructions of the hastily organized Naval Transport Service, was in very light trim and became almost unmanageable in anything like a stout breeze. How she rolled and wallowed in the Atlantic swell! How the cavalry chargers drooped their lovely heads on the forebars of the stalls and only made complaint in wearied eyes!

In my schoolboy days at Garnethill, a younger boy named Cox became a special friend. His father was, I think, the R.S.M. of the Glasgow Yeomanry at their headquarters in Blythswood Square. As a playmate of his mischievous young son, I was often included in some of the equestrian outings of the Squadron. Sometimes I was even allowed to 'camp follow' the Glasgow contingent to the annual muster on Lanark race-course and had become attached to the splendid animals that Hendersons, the jobmasters, provided for the occasion. Little wonder that on the voyage out to South Africa I had sympathy with the patient animals we had listed for cargo and, in my leisure time, was a frequent visitor to the lines.

My interest in the horses was noticed by the military officer in charge, Major Sir Anstruther Anstruther, and although he had junior officers and an efficient farrier staff, he was never very far from the lines himself. From him I learned much about the care of animals in a ship, an odd branch of sea trade that later was to help me when in charge of race-horses and polo ponies—wild animals too—on shipboard.

Belatedly, we staggered into Cape Town to find that the tide of
war had rolled onwards and that the *Australia* was now required to
proceed to East London to disembark the horses and military
details. We lay anchored for some days, watering and taking on
more ballast, for the ship was now high and light. Our orders were
brought off to us where we lay out in the Bay, and I remember that I
thought it a strange duty for a young naval officer in uniform to
deliver a letter at the gangway and make a protest that the ship's
master was not there in person to receive him. It was a new experience for us to come under the orders of the Navy in this way, and
our early relations with its Transport Department were not as harmonious as they have since become. But the young sub-lieutenant
soon unbent when, Captain Tait the master being ashore on duty,
we sought the news of the day. Of war news he had little to add to
the sea-pilot's story when he boarded us off the port, but was out-
spoken in his news of the water-front. It may have been that our
manning of lascar seamen impressed him favourably as he watched a
bucket-party passing water to the horses. That led to a comparison
with the white crews in the great assembly of merchant shipping that
lay anchored in the Bay under war orders. It was no wonder that
his disorderly ways did not recommend the merchantmen to cordial
acceptance by the Naval authorities, now making our acquaintance
for the first time since the days of the Crimean War. Our visitor
told us that one ship in particular had given Captain Chichester, the
senior naval transport officer in the port, no end of trouble by the
uproar and indiscipline of her people, mostly firemen, when on
shore. Many of the delinquents had been put in jail, and the ship
herself had been shifted to the outer limit of the anchorage, whence
contact with the shore could not easily be made. The speaker raised
his arm to point out the errant merchant ship among the press of
anchored ships.

Looking in that direction, I saw the most beautiful steamship I
had ever sighted. Her long black hull sat gracefully in the still water,
dwarfing all the shipping near her. She was four-masted with yards
crossed on the fore and main, and the rake of her three symmetrical
funnels corresponded with the step of the masts; the bows of a
clipper ship and the stern of a yacht completed the handsome picture of a 'greyhound of the Atlantic'. I learned that, having disembarked the large body of troops brought out from Liverpool, she

was awaiting the tardy arrival of a collier to supply the large quantity of fuel needed for the homeward voyage. Her stokehold crew, the officer said, was completely out of hand. The townsfolk of Cape Town would be glad to see the last of her, he was sure, and certainly the Navy would be relieved by her departure. Fearing the loss of his esteem, I did not tell him that—let the Clydeside rowdies prove ever so troublesome—I was somewhat proud of the Anchor Line's fine flagship, the *City of Rome*!

Sailing from Table Bay to our new destination at East London was no great distance, but the passage occupied four days; so slow was our progress against the strength of the Aghulas current and so much greater the rolling and labouring of the ship as coal and fresh water were consumed. As there was no sheltered harbour for unloading at East London we anchored offshore at the mouth of the Buffalo River, where the ship was exposed to the prevailing groundswell. In this hazardous position we did our best to hoist out the horses and lower them to flat-bottomed barges, in which they could be taken to landing-places on the river-banks, but the incredibly violent rolling of the ship during operations caused many accidents and injured animals had often to be humanely destroyed. A halt was called on the second day of such a lamentable proceeding and a meeting held to consider the situation. It was a wizened old native bushman, one of the labourers brought off from the shore, who told us what to do. 'Put horse in water make 'um swim,' was his suggestion, but we soon found that a horse in wide water always needs to be steered, and the river bushmen reaped a substantial harvest in the employment of their frail canoes to guide the frightened chargers to a landing on the beach. After that, the cattle-pistol was little used, and soon we were north-bound on our way to Gibraltar to load mules for service in the war. We remained in that employment until peace came in 1901.

I recall my further service in the *Australia* as a period of happy sailing in a comfortable old steamer that had never any special urgencies to bedevil her occasions in the 'flying-fish' weather of the Indian trade. There was a good atmosphere of contentment in her and changes were infrequent among the small band of officers in the ship. Only, promotion was slow—and for a curious reason. Three main services were operated by the Anchor Line, the most important being the transatlantic trade between Glasgow and New York;

the Indian service to Bombay and Calcutta was lucrative and held promise of expansion, and the emigrant traffic between Italy and the United States was still actively engaged in, although now restricted by national control in some degree. At that date, it seemed to be the policy of the company to keep the services separate as far as the appointment of Masters and officers was concerned, and it was only rarely that an interchange was made.

If advancement seemed tardy, there was all the more time for study in preparation for it and, as well, for exercise of one's abilities in other ways. It was at this period of my sailoring I revived an interest in writing—a pursuit I had not followed since my schoolboy days. I was now more ambitious and found my subject-matter in the scenes of ports and passages and the waterside characters I met on my voyages. Local colour was a feature of these early efforts—a lure well spread to gain acceptance in seaport publications. The *Glasgow Evening News* encouraged me to write about the dockside and its characters and, later, a full-scale reminiscence of my brass-bounder days in sail. A new adventure 'touched' by the *Australia* gave my writing a place on the back page of the *Manchester Guardian*, to which I was proud to contribute for many years.

The Manchester Ship Canal had not long been opened when the old *Australia*, striking topmasts, pushed the muddy little flood before her and gained a berth in Salford Docks. The super-efficients had not then made night journeys possible in the Canal and it was the practice for ships, caught by the incidence of the tides at Eastham, to tie up for the hours of darkness at some convenient lie-by. On these occasions there was opportunity for an inquisitive young sailor to climb ashore to investigate life on the littoral, be it marked by the strains of an orchestrion at the wakes of Old Quay, or stimulated by the sight of the pipe-stem funnels of the ancient paddle-tug, the *Merry Andrew*, that had so often strained on the stern ropes to keep us in the fairway of the Canal when fog was our portion, lying junked at last on the foreshore of the upper Mersey. . . . These were simple sketches of casual observation, and I found happiness in writing them.

Chapter XIV

ANCHOR LINE TAILORING

IT was with some regret that I came on shore from the old *Australia* for the last time at Glasgow early in 1902. I had been happy in her for many voyages in over two years of interesting service. I had come to like the Eastern run, with its long seasons of predictable weather and the ease of management with a docile native crew. I was loth to sign off and part from the many good shipmates with whom I had sailed. But there was small hope of advancement in sea service without a master's certificate. With marriage in view, I had come to plan seriously for the years that lay ahead, and I saw my first task to be assiduous study for the final examination.

My father's house in Glasgow, with its friendly rounds and the company of my many brothers (clever lads, who had shot ahead of me in matters of the mind), did not have quite the right atmosphere for study, as I thought, so I sought out a less distracting lodging in Leith, where I attended James Bolam's Nautical School at the docks there. Finding me assiduous, the Principal encouraged me to prepare for the higher and voluntary examination. Largley due to his personal interest and lucid teaching, I passed for Master in May 1902, and a week later was successful in the honours examination for Extra Master in sail.

Mr Bolam, the Principal, was a remarkable man, still remembered with admiration by many old shipmasters as one who strove always to promote a high standard in education for all young sailors. Not himself a seaman, he possessed every sterling attribute a navigator should have, and these he laboured to pass on to his scholars in the dockside nautical school he conducted for so many years. At this time the Scottish education authorities heard about boys going to sea at an early age, expectant of making progress in the life they had chosen but unable to earn it because of insufficient elementary schooling. Belatedly, the Board decided that something must be done for them. James Bolam had been agitating for such an action—although he well knew it would mean the closing of his and other private schools—and the plans for teaching in what is now the navigation department of the Royal Leith Technical College were then in his hands for consideration and report. . . . For a short term after my marriage in June 1902, to Ella Cameron, a Glasgow lady whom I had long known, I tried a post as an assistant teacher in his old school, but quickly realized that I was not the patient missioner to serve that worthy tide in a place on shore. It was always the sea I wanted. There, as I thought, I might help James Bolam's good cause by promoting study among the youngsters who sailed with me.

Thinking again of sea service, my inclination was to stay on with the Anchor Line, whose management had invited me to reapply when I had secured the senior certificate. But I hesitated to visit Captain McFee too soon—so strong, doubtless, being my conceit of myself after success in the examination room. I was eager to make up for the time I had lost so pleasantly, if unprofitably, in the junior ranks, and was disheartened—now that I was married and needed an income—to think over the slow promotion I had noted in the Indian ships. I would be grown old, I thought, before attaining a command. There could be no harm in looking around. If nothing better offered, I could ask Captain McFee for a transfer. I had heard that promotion was more rapid in the company's Atlantic service. I might do better there.

'Looking around' in the shipowners' offices at Leith and Glasgow in my quest for betterment, I learned quickly that owners and their superintendents had no particular regard for the Extra Certificate I had been at such effort to gain. While they would know of it as valuable to a candidate for a shore post with the Board of Trade or to a teacher of navigation or seamanship in one of the new Technical Schools, it is likely that they thought of it as something of a nimiety for a workaday mate to possess. Ships officers were of no great account at this time, for they were many and the ships too few. A measure of our standing then is contained in the plaint of a ship's carpenter when sent to make an alteration in the cabin of the second mate of the *Ethiopia*. The new occupant, a six-footer, had protested that his bunk sleeping space was too short for him. 'Chips', disgruntled at being put on the job, muttered, 'Why th' hell could they no' get a shorter second mate?'

With reserves being heavily drawn upon, and having no success in my quest for speedy advancement, I soon decided to set out again on the road that at least I knew.

Captain McFee was glad to see me back, but he did not favour my request for a transfer to the Atlantic service. He had sailed in that trade himself; one had to be a 'hard case' in ships like the *Furnessia* and the *Devonia*, he said. Stretching himself to his full height of about six feet two, he told me the Western Ocean passage required big strong men, good fighters, to handle the tough crews that signed out of Greenock and Glasgow. He thought I could do better where I had already been, in the calmer conditions of the Indian trade. Often since then I have wondered just what it was in my lesser stature that led him to think me a man of gentle character—if that was what was in his mind. But the Marine Superintendent would have to consider many matters in his selections, and perhaps I should not have mentioned as one of my qualifications that I had learned to speak *Lascari bat*—a useful accomplishment when sailing with native crews. In any case, it was to a 'curry-and-rice' ship I was sent, sailing as a relief to the second mate of the steamship *Dalmatia* on a voyage to Calcutta. I was promised a better appointment on return.

A new practice that came into usage in these days was the wearing of uniform by the officers of merchant ships. In sailing days, few mates wore monkey jackets, buttoned and adorned; only the apprentices upon first joining a ship sported brassbound uniform and mounted a badged cap set jauntily at the back of the head. ('*Die junge? It is for de brass botton dey goes to de sea out' Nein;* I was once informed.) We had a sort of pride in appearing nondescript. Bowler hats were often worn at sea, but the establishment of the great steamship lines brought about a ruling in our duty dress on shipboard. Most companies had a clause inserted in the articles of agreement that obliged both officer and man to 'wear the Company's uniform when required', and that livery, which was not provided by the owners, was often an expensive addition to the officer's salt-stained wardrobe, one that he could ill afford without long credit from an outfitter at his home port.

Among these worthy tradesmen supplying our needs on the waterfront of the Clyde, James Boyd was outstanding for the liberal credit he extended to the seafaring customers of his tailoring establishment, particularly to those in the junior ranks of the Anchor Line. Always on friendly and confidential terms with the departmental superintendents at Stobcross Quay, where the Company's ships were then berthed, he had his sources of information. Be that as it may, he took his risks. It was said that, whatever his record of competency or conduct in the Company's ships, no officer was ever sacked by the Anchor Line while 'Jeemy Byde's' account remained unpaid.

It was doubtless his genial spirit together with merit as a fine singer that commended the stout little tailor to the shore officials of the Company. On occasion, when the state of the tide at Glasgow was unsuited to the embarkation of passengers, the transatlantic liners were sent down the Clyde on the night before to anchor off Greenock in order to take on passengers and mails there before sailing for New York. It was not uncommon for the Company's shore staff concerned with the despatch of the vessel to take passage down-river in her. Often the night's proceedings were enlivened by song and story. Mr Boyd, a stirring baritone, was frequently invited to join the party. The breezy little tailor was a star performer —his rendering of 'Scotland the Brave' eliciting such applause as to afford plain evidence of his standing with the important shore officials of the Line, a circumstance of which he did not fail to profit in pursuit of custom around the departing ship. Often he would combine the part of an astute salesman with that of a friend in need. Hearing, as so often he did, of an impending vacancy in the ships for a junior officer, he would pass the news of it to a likely prospect, adding his word of encouragement—

'Ye'll get the job, all right. I'll speak to the Captain for ye. I ken him fine. But, come awa' up to the shop and I'll measure ye for a "swinger". Ye'll need that!'

A 'swinger' was an important garment, to be worn on sailing days at the gangway to impress the embarking passengers. It was a fairly well-cut uniform frock coat, naval pattern but mounting no less than twenty-eight brass buttons. An expensive and not often used item in the salt-stained wardrobe of a poorly-paid young sailor. But 'Jeemy' was patient and understanding and could afford to wait for a first promotion before hinting at a payment on account.

The S.S. *Massilia*, to which I was appointed on return to Glasgow, was a new ship, built by Stephens of Linthouse for the Eastern routes of the Anchor Line. Of over 5,000 tons gross, she was one of a new class designed to replace the mixed group of veterans that had hitherto provided a monthly sailing to Bombay and Calcutta. The character of merchandise exported to the East had altered and the fine old barque-rigged steamers were unsuited to modern cargoes. Mills, factories, mines, great industrial schemes were springing up throughout the length of Hindustan at the start of the century, and the heavy lifts, boilers, and machinery for these enterprises could not easily be stowed in the restricted hold spaces of the old-timers. The opening up to navigation of the Manchester Ship Canal too, whence so much of this profitable freight was drawn, demanded ships having special features to take advantage of it. The new ships were fitted with removable funnel sections. (Entering the Canal at Eastham, one could always tell what ships were on the berth in Salford Docks by the patterns of the steamships' tall hats checked in near the big crane, there to await their owners' return from Manchester.) With new tubular masts duly telescoped, we were able to steer safely under the many bridges that span the waterway, and once docked in the big city could open up our hatches and load all the cargo its industry could offer.

To this convenience the shipbuilders had added passenger accommodation for about sixty. The older ships had embarked greater numbers, but these were berthed in lesser space—a hardship that could not now be tolerated. The Indian route was no longer a reserve for high fares in ocean transport, and there was a demand for a cheapening of fares. Let the nabobs still enjoy the swift and splendid service of the mailboats, there remained a need for less luxurious travel. Accommodation in the new ship was restricted to 'one class' passengers and was provided in quarters that were not luxurious, but sported all comforts a reasonable traveller could demand. Speed was improved, but regularity in sailings and arrivals was rather the Company's aim and that essential seemed to find favour with a sufficiency of eastern voyagers.

I sailed in the *Massilia* for nearly ten years, successively as Second and First Officer and latterly in command. In these long years, dating from her maiden voyage, I marked the gradual development of personality in the ship herself and saw it fostered by the people who sailed in her, crew and passengers alike. . . . How its pleasantry differed from old Bully Martin's repressive manners in the *Loch Ness*!

I had not served in a passenger steamer since my short experience in the *City of Agra*, where, as a duty-bound sailor, my only contact with the passengers had been to chalk out the patterns for the games they exercised when the morning sun had dried the smooth planking of the upper decks. But now, in the new ship, I was a messmate of theirs, sitting at one end of a long table in the dining saloon and, in the twenty-day passages out and home, making many enduring friendships with those who sat with me there.

In some of the Company's ships—notably in the North Atlantic service—such friendly relations between passengers and the vessel's officers were frowned upon: not by the owners but by the older captains, who saw in it a situation that might lead to a lessening of the rigid discipline that had been imposed on them in earlier days. That illiberal belief did not obtain in the *Massilia*, where Captain John Thomson, a generous host, encouraged all his officers to join with him in maintaining a friendly atmosphere in his fine new ship.

At the first I was badly out of training for such an unusual atmosphere. I had not been brought up to it, as were the young cadets signed with us, who, knowing nothing harsher, could accept longshore manners without question or amaze. On deck I found it not difficult to reply politely to the greetings of amiable passengers, but at table I was tongue-tied by a curious embarrassment. For the most part, the partaking of meals aboard ship had been, for me, an animal affair, no more entertaining than the satisfaction of an appetite. Conversation on such occasions had largely been confined to gruff interrogations and surly comment between us—the few officers who sat with the Master—all the talk having reference to the fortunes of the voyage and being punctuated by the Old Man's significant glances at the tell-tale compass overhead, to warn us that the ship was possibly off her course and it was high time we dished up and went up on deck again. Only in the *Australia* did I find a difference. We were more cheerful there. Although the old world-crusted tramp carried no passengers on her Indian voyages, the routine of the Company's good catering was observed and, with Indian stewards and cooks, the smoother manners of the East prevailed in her. Native Goanese were employed to attend to our domestic needs and some attention was devoted to the civilities—

even to the provision of a menu card at meals on which Fernando de Noronha, the dusky butler, coloured his English sometimes by spelling out such odd dishes as 'An shovey poshteg' and 'Rose-bastard'! There was genial companionship in the old *Australia*: no one was embarrassed for want of a word there at table.

But this was different. I was ill at ease on my first setting out in the *Massilia*, sitting mumchance while pleasantries were readily exchanged across the board. But I soon discovered that passengers were not averse from talk concerning their own affairs, and—with that the topic to be encouraged—I quickly found my tongue. From these friendly causeries I learned much of interest bearing upon the everyday life of Europeans in India. Much of this information I found of use in the occasional short articles I submitted to various journals. These included the *Times of India*, often the *Weekly* issue. In its pages I admired greatly the contributions of E. H. A., whose essays dealing with domestic life in the country revealed to me a humane and generous observer. Later, Mr E. H. Aitken sailed home in the *Massilia* and sat beside me. I had read his book *Behind the Bungalow*, a classic of domestic life in the mofussil, with avid interest. I had much kindly advice from him on the passage. I was at the time revising a series of articles about sailor life in a sailing-ship which I had contributed to the *Glasgow Evening News*, and had the hope of putting them into book form. I had good advice from E. H. A. about that.

The Brassbounder, my first book, was published later in 1910. Edward Garnett, who was then literary adviser to Duckworth's, thought well of it and sent a copy to his friend Conrad when the book came out. In some way Conrad had gained the impression that I had the intention of giving up the sea and devoting myself to literary pursuits. He wrote me a charming letter strongly advising me against such a course. 'If I may be allowed to put in a word,' he wrote, 'let me entreat you not "to leave the ship". Never "leave the ship"—least of all for literature. . . . I left because I was no longer fit for the life—otherwise I can assure you that I would have never published a line.' . . . Sound advice, but no one could consider such a kindly letter as expressive of more than anxiety that the recipient should not enter upon a new employment without grave thought. I did not cease to write, but took his advice and continued at sea, to my profit and great happiness in it.

Friendships develop quickly on shipboard and are easily maintained in the sequence of the long voyage to the East. Passengers who book in the smaller 'one-class' liners are not usually bedevilled by the mischief of ostentation, and the 'hotel' atmosphere, which in luxurious mail steamships so often promotes envy and ill-feeling among the dowagers, was not encouraged. We were a small community sufficiently interested in one another's ways to remain companionable, and our passenger list included few titles or great names of the day. Army officers of junior rank, minor civil servants, railway executives, merchants, and the heads of business houses, missionaries—these were the people for whom we catered. Wives and children formed a goodly part of our complement, and it was perhaps specially to them the ship offered the greatest conveniences; as I remember it, the *Massilia* was the first ship on the India run to afford a nursery for small children. I knew that playroom well, remembering it chiefly as the place where I gained confidence enough to compose a doggerel in praise of it. This exercise in the vernacular was aimed to please the often wan little British children who had not yet learned English, but spoke only the Hindustani of their devoted ayahs. My spoony rhyme (obviously based upon 'I saw a ship a-sailing') was indifferently painted up on one blank wall of the space; English phonetics of a kind were used. The jingle began boldly, '*Hum chota jehaẓ banaiaa!*' (I'll build a little ship), and went on to describe the items to be loaded into her. It ceased somewhat abruptly when a homely convenience was suggested by one of my young prompters: '*poti*' is not a good rhyming word in any context. . . . I think my ill-painted holograph of that early poetic effort was still legible in the nursery of the old ship when last I saw her in 1930. Sold to be broken up after long and faithful service, she was—at full speed—rammed on shore at Bowness in the Firth of Forth.

Chapter XV

WORLD WAR ONE

WHEN war broke out in August 1914, I was on holiday with my wife and children at Port Erin in the Isle of Man. That long-promised holiday was something I had looked forward to for many years. But for an occasional break due to a survey or a casualty of some sort, I had not been absent from my ship for more than a few days. I hardly knew my children: Freda, aged ten and David, a baby of two. My long watch on deck may fairly be reckoned by the reply of my little daughter to the kindly inquiry of a neighbour at my home in Helensburgh.

'Oh, Daddy!' she repeated. 'He's staying with us just now, but he's going home again on Saturday.'

But the war altered that. I was at once recalled to Glasgow and posted as Chief Officer in the *Cameronia*, the flagship of the Anchor Line, which was then feverishly refitting in preparation to sail for New York. Alterations were being made in her to accommodate the vast numbers of distracted citizens of the United States fleeing from the storm that, so suddenly, had overwhelmed all Europe. Upon leaving the *Massilia* a week before I had been expecting a command in one of the Company's smaller ships due soon to arrive in a home port. It was a disappointment for me to take up a subordinate position again, but 'number one' in the *Cameronia* was looked upon as a plum in the service and one rarely allotted to a 'curry-and-rice' man. There was emergency in it, too, and I felt assured that I would not suffer by striving to do my best in the new job.

The passenger season in the Atlantic had been a busy one in the spring and early summer of 1914. Certainly, there were the rumblings of distant drums on the Continent, but a great war between civilized nations seemed unbelievable to the throng of American tourists that had crowded the eastbound liners to enjoy their vacations abroad. Now, startled and dismayed, they had swarmed back to British seaports seeking immediate transport in any west-bound ship that could rig up a berth for them. But passage in any direction overseas was difficult to find. The sudden violent outbreak of war had disrupted all sailing schedules. Many of the great transatlantic liners had been requisitioned for naval service; others had been taken from their routes to serve as detention ships for enemy internees. Added to the rush of travellers with return passages previously arranged, there came crowding to the offices of the shipping lines and agencies in every town the many stranded Americans—these mostly of Teutonic stock—who had booked return passages by the German liners. But no fine German liners were venturing to sea. As we were so bitterly to learn in a few eventful months, the freedom of the seas to an unarmed merchant ship was not a gospel the Reichsmarineamt would entertain. German passenger-ships were all held in port at Bremen and Hamburg, or if at sea were ordered to seek harbour in some neutral port abroad.

With all these anxious travellers converging on the city, Glasgow's resources to accommodate such an influx—never adequate at the best of times—were overstrained. Every hotel, boarding- or lodging-house was booked to the roof; even private householders were urged to extend hospitality to the troubled voyagers. The offices of the shipping lines and those of the cable and telegraph companies, the banks, consulates, and passport offices were thronged all day by anxious suppliants—while we, in the one ship available on the Clyde, were dredging rust and grime and coal-dust from the empty bunkers to clear spaces on which to erect passable ship quarters for the numbers so constantly being multiplied.

The *Cameronia*, built at Meadowside in 1911, was a strong and splendid passenger-ship of 11,000 tons gross. On a normal voyage she could embark about 1,500 passengers: her crew numbered 328. She had a fine appearance as she lay alongside the quay at Yorkhill on the day I joined her, her lines enhanced by the long vista of empty quay space where she was moored. Tier upon tier, her superstructures, newly freshened in a coat of white paint, gleamed brightly under the sun. In outboard appearance she showed no sign of the confusion and activities within, but I was not left long in ignorance of these complexities and the part I had to play in hastening her completion. I was proud of my new appointment, though perhaps not altogether confident of my fitness for it: there would be new and unfamiliar duties awaiting me, doubtless many tasks for which my long service on the Indian run had not prepared me. I was soon to learn that much more was expected from the second in command of an Atlantic liner than from the most hard-working of First Officers on the Eastern service. Once aboard and established in my post, I found myself become a central consultant on almost all the business of the ship. The Head Steward protested that the steam on the deck winches was insufficient to hoist his barons of beef from the quay-side; the Senior Wireless Officer needed hands to rig his aerial for an exercise; the stores department vanman was alongside clamouring for someone to accept delivery of fish-knives or fire-bricks or per-colators. At the door of my cabin there was ever a host of irritators rushing to shed their responsibility for this or that on my threshold. But I was put on my mettle, and had already decided that Captain Francis Wadsworth who commanded the ship was not one to be denied.

There was one source of serious disquiet to me—the unruly con-duct of the ship's seamen, on whom so much depended in clearing the under-deck spaces, now urgently required for the operations of the shipyard workmen erecting accommodation for extra passengers. 'Absence without leave' was frequently reported during the hours of work, for at Yorkhill Quay a ship lies over-handy for the distrac-tions so enthusiastically acclaimed in the stoker's jingle as he rattles his shovel on the footplates to call for more coal—

> Here's rub-ee-dubs for the bonnie wee pubs
>   That stands in the Kelvinhaugh.
> Stands in the Kelvinhaugh, four o' them a' in a raw!
> Then here's rub-ee-dubs for the bonnie wee pubs
>   That stands in the Kelvinhaugh!

We sailed on a Saturday afternoon—the 15th August, as I remem-ber. All was then well below decks. The paint that had been applied to the new construction in such haste was barely dry and the pungent smell of it, fortified by an excess of patent 'dryers', assaulted the throat and nostrils on every visit. By some omission (probably mine), sufficient space had not been set aside for the storage of the vastly increased amount of baggage that had been brought along-side. The only space by now available was in the lower hold and, as the baggage was hurriedly lowered there, 'wanted on the voyage' labels had to be callously ignored. But the ship was manifestly bound out to sea at last, the Blue Peter fluttering significantly at the fore. After many days of hopes deferred, the stranded passengers were at length embarked and much could be tolerated on such a sailing day.

Only one protesting voice was raised. The leader of a group of Lithuanian emigrants on the fore-deck was sure that he and his people had been embarked in the wrong ship. Holding out his passage ticket, on which there was displayed an illustration of the three-funnelled *Columbia* (a much smaller vessel, long since towed away to the shipbreaker's yard), he called upon all and sundry to witness a deception. The *Cameronia* had only two!

Until late in 1916 merchant ships on commercial voyages did not come under naval control on their voyages abroad, but were advised to avoid meeting the enemy at sea by deserting the regular ocean routes. Long accustomed to the fog and mist—the ice, too—of the northern Great Circle between Innistrahull and Cape Race in New-foundland, Captain Wadsworth sought a lonely passage for his ship by steering yet farther to the northward in search of low visibility to veil her progress. Certainly it was a wise decision, for not even the sound of another vessel's foghorn was heard as we pushed on at our best speed, but it was bitterly cold to such a 'flying-fish sailor' as I!

In the vastly different manner of seafaring almost on the fringe of the Arctic I had quickly to adapt myself not only to weather changes and alterations of routine but even to certain variation in the standards of navigation. With the sun or the stars so rarely visible in these misty latitudes, it was largely by 'dead reckoning'—an estimation of the course and speed—that we measured our progress. To me, 'coddled' for long years in the Indian trade—the sun a daily visitor and the nights full of stars—dependence upon such fallible conclusions appeared unwise. I said as much on one occasion when, for the fourth day running, we had had no observations and were approaching the eastern edge of the Grand Banks of New-foundland. Smiling at my naïve distrust of the only course possible in the continued thick weather, the Captain reminded me that we could at least rely on the lead. Pointing to the chart that lay out-spread before us, he bade me remark the shape of the Bank—a great triangle of comparatively shallow yet not shoal water, its apex pointing to the south. 'Old Father Neptune was very good to bewildered navigators when he shaped his bed like that,' the Old Man said. His reference was to the establishment of a sure position by an approximation of the distance run between the east and western edges of the bank. Manifestly, the greater that distance the further northward the ship would be. I was to have the Kelvin sounder in readiness for a cast of the lead at 4 p.m., he ordered. 'A cast every fifteen minutes', he repeated, 'until we find the hundred fathom line.' . . . I learned much from my master in the *Cameronia*.

Command at last! In August 1915, I was promoted to command in her. A vacancy had occurred in the marine department on shore which Captain Wadsworth thought more suited to his advancing years. What brought about my selection I shall never know. I suppose the need for an immediate appointment ruled out the senior candidates who were in service far abroad, but I was indeed fortunate in my promotion. I had already served a trial period as Master of the *Massilia* on a voyage to Bombay during Captain Thomson's leave on shore, and that successful probation may have commended me to attention when Captain Wadsworth decided to 'swallow the anchor'. . . . But I was not heedless of my inexperience when I sailed out on my first voyage in confirmed command. There was some difference between the long-familiar pattern of routine I had followed in my brief command of the *Massilia* in peace-time and fair weather and that in the thrice-larger *Cameronia* lurking far north in fog and among the ice during the early days of the war. A great support in that time of trial was that, on each returning voyage, I could relate my problems and discuss my handling of them with my late Commander, now seated in the chair of the longshore mighty at Yorkhill Quay.

Since about 1912 the Anchor Line—one of the oldest shipping companies in North Atlantic trade—had linked with the Cunard Line in matters of joint interest in shipping. For a time we, in the lesser Indian services of the Glasgow firm, knew little or nothing of the matters involved. It was not until the outbreak of war in 1914 when the news of it came to us from 'Jeemy Byde'. He said that an alteration was to be made in the company's uniform. Instead of the twisted gold braid that had been a shoulder-mark on our 'swingers', we were to conform with Cunard uniform, mounting a half-inch band or two of gold lace on the cuffs—but without the Admiralty curl—to denote our office in the ships. Whatever the relations between the two great companies may have become in later years, they proved useful in 1914. Practically all Cunard's strong and speedy ships were commandeered by the Admiralty on the outbreak of war, and the passenger sailings of the Cunard–Anchor Lines were largely maintained by the *Cameronia* and the *Orduna*—the latter a fine ship chartered from the Pacific Steam Navigation Company.

In my early days of command in the *Cameronia* we were not over-looked in the demands for troop transport, but the carriage of mails, specie, and passengers could not of course be entirely abandoned. We were hard run on our voyages. When, sailing out from the Clyde, we had put in to Liverpool to embark passengers and had then made our northern passage to New York, it was not to linger there for some days, loading at leisure. Hurrying to land our passengers and cargo—the latter often including millions in gold and specie—we backed out into the Hudson to make haste up north again and embark Canadian troops at Halifax or Quebec for the United Kingdom. Homeward on such occasions, it was generally in company with other ships we made the eastbound passage to Devonport. That was my first experience of sailing in a form of convoy, and although our early efforts to keep station were often ludicrous, I saw in this old and tried adventure a counter-action to the now alarming menace of the ocean-going enemy submarine.

For some time in these early eastbound voyages from Canadian ports we were not armed with artillery, but it was usual to mount small armed boat-guards in the outswung lifeboats when in the 'danger zone' of the Atlantic. We did not expect to sink submarines with our 'pea-shooters', but, with so many sharp eyes directed outboard, a helpful look-out was always maintained. The riflemen were instructed to open fire on any seeming flotsam that was sighted. Needless to say, there were many false alerts, but I know of one instance when, off Malin Head, the rattle of small arms and the up-throw of spray from bullets in the sea gave me warning in time to turn away, the torpedo racing close astern as we swung to starboard.

Later, the ship's stern frames were strengthened to carry a heavy weapon and a six-inch naval gun was mounted there. Its 'papers', which I had to hold, showed the piece to have been mounted first in

H.M.S. *Terrible* in 1901. I wonder if it was a replacement of the artillery so quickly landed and adapted for land operations by the *Terrible* in the Boer War. . . . Another oddity was the light-weight casing built round the emplacement to conceal the sizeable weapon. Constructed largely of hinged plywood and painted to resemble a deckhouse at the stern, it was designed to fall apart, all sternward ranges cleared, at the pull of a lever. Rarely, it did—but we had to weight it by attaching firebars to get a sudden drop and keep the whole simulated structure from flapping in the wind. If the concealment gave us cause for misgiving, that was as nothing to the uproar it brought about when, relying on our status as a merchant ship armed only for defence, we arrived at New York and docked at the Chelsea Piers. . . . Neutral America had read all about our 'Q' ships in the Sunday papers, and we were thought a pirate ship of some new type! Captain Guy Gaunt, the British naval attaché, was summoned from Washington to support our submissions to the port authorities in what had become almost an international situation. How matters were resolved I cannot clearly remember, but we were advised to discard the offending and unsightly theatrical contraption that had provoked so much argument. When this had been done, I liked better the new and purposeful appearance of our naked weapon. It looked now as though we were in earnest.

We had need to be in earnest as the closing months of 1916 drew on. Ship losses from enemy action were alarming. Concentrating almost all his naval energy upon one specific form of sea offensive, the enemy had developed the submarine arm to a high degree of efficiency. To all intents, the U-boat had become a surface destroyer of lengthy sea-range and with the added advantage of being able to disappear at will. Our merchant shipping—that included troop transports—was being sunk at a rate that boded ill for our campaigns oversea. In the Mediterranean, where atmospheric conditions gave long sight in the periscope, a vast tonnage was quickly destroyed—many of the ships being large troop carriers, heavily embarked with reinforcements for our armies in the Near and Middle East.

For some time past we had wondered at the long retention of the *Cameronia* in the Atlantic trade when ships of our type were so urgently needed elsewhere. One after another of our sister ships had been taken from the route and we had learned of their loss by enemy action in distant waters. We had not long to await a change of duty. On return from New York and Halifax in November, the ship was requisitioned by the Admiralty and refitted as a troopship at Glasgow. Six weeks later we sailed for Salonika packed to the guards with reinforcements for the Doiran front.

Chapter XVI

TORPEDOED

WE did not return to the United Kingdom when we had disembarked the troops in Salonika. The Germans had resorted to attacks on hospital ships, and these specially illuminated vessels—clearly marked with the Red Cross—were for a time sparingly employed in the Ægean Seas, and it was probably as an effort to lighten the burden in removal of the sick and wounded from the Eastern Front that the *Cameronia* was detailed to carry many of the less serious cases to Marseilles as a stage on their homeward journey. From that port they were transported overland in hospital trains. Malaria was rife on the Doiran front and we were often over-berthed in the emergency of the moment.

In this duty the ship was busily engaged, sailing out from Marseilles or Salonika on an almost weekly routine. Two destroyers were allotted to us as escorts and a frequent variation of the route was made. The most dangerous area was thought to be in the inter-island channels of the Cyclades, where the enemy may have had his sources of information, but the same channel was rarely used on successive voyages. Only once did we sight an enemy submarine, and that too distant to be of interest to us or to the destroyers. On these comparatively short passages—Marseilles to Malta, to Suda Bay and on to the Macedonian coast—we discovered a new and most welcome merit in the ship: a performance the economics of frugal ship management in peace-time had hitherto held in check. For over-long I had listened to the complaint of the ship's disgruntled firemen that 'thae rocks an' stanes o' Bannockburn wull jist no' burn' when the speed was lamentably low. (The reference was to the coal supplied by a colliery near Stirling whose ownership was not unconnected with the board of the Anchor Line. It was said that all the slag and stones of its refuse bing were reserved—to promote foaming blasphemy in the stokeholds of the Company's ships.) Freed now by an ample supply of first-grade Admiralty fuel, the speed of the ship was miraculously improved. I had known that she was built for an Atlantic crossing at seventeen knots, but we could now do at least nineteen on a turn away when one or the other of our escorts gave warning of a suspect note in his hydrophones. Each passage seemed to confirm our confidence that by keen look-out and our best speed—together with the eccentrics of a zig-zag course in clear weather—we might elude the fearsome shifts of the U-boat.

The confidence I had in these protective measures was rudely shocked on a bright Sunday afternoon, the 15th April, 1917. A change had come about in the direction of our trooping voyages, and at Marseilles the ship had been heavily embarked for a different battle front, still farther to the East. We had sailed from our base port two days before, and now, bound out to the Shat-el-Arab in the Persian Gulf and steering on a zig-zag course for Port Said and the Suez Canal, the voyage had gone well. The day was fair and the sea smooth: on each bow the escorting destroyers—*Rifleman* and *Nemesis*—swung out from time to time in conformation with the angles of our rambling course pattern. It was clear right to the horizon, and nothing else was in sight.

I had heartening reflections, up there on the wing of the bridge, as I surveyed the length of the ship, with her decks enlivened by the activities of our people. One could wish they had not been so many embarked in one ship in perilous seas, but needs must in time of war, and there was encouragement in the swift progress we had made and the promise of its continuation shown by the foaming waters at the stem. In a few days, I thought, we would pass through the Suez Canal and put the big shield of Africa between us and all the new and deadly inventions of the enemy. For myself, I might find rest from the fatigue of almost constant alert in the quiet and— as yet—pacific Eastern ports I had known in other days. There could be——

An alarmed outcry from the look-out aloft wrenched me back to reality. The man was pointing out towards the port beam. I saw nothing there but, on the good sailor principle of canting towards a danger, called out for '*Hard a port!*' The steersman had no time to act, for a rending explosion almost underfoot threw us all into confusion. The upthrow came on the moment of the torpedo's impact. Broken hatch-covers, coal, shattered debris, a huge column of sea water, soared skyward in a hurtling mass to fall in torrents on the bridge and bear us down. . . . Then, silence for a stunned half minute—only the thrust of the still turning engines marking the heart beats of the stricken ship. Then they too died.

At this long date since my first command was lost at sea in wartime, I find it difficult to preserve a sequence in the narrative, for everything seemed to happen at one time. It was quickly apparent that all our careful plans and drills for the emergency might be set at nought by the vast numbers we carried, now crowding together on every plank of narrow deck-space the ship afforded. I recollect my terror of an immediate panic when—instinctively, perhaps—the young untried recruits, of whom our numbers were largely composed, swarmed towards the outswung lifeboats on the upper decks and started to fumble with gripes and lifting gear. Then—my relief when, ever so slowly in the press of struggling men, I saw some of the ship's and troops' officers pushing through. It seemed long before the turmoil was arrested. A similar situation on the fore-deck, where a surge of troops from the mess decks below had jammed all gangways, was suddenly disentangled by a small ship's boy—William McKinnon, a bridge-deck messenger—who used my megaphone to marked if unauthorized effect, 'Steady up, you men doon there,' he piped in youthful treble. 'Steady up. Ye'll no' do any good for yersel's crowdin' up the ledders!'

On the bridge, I had no touch with the ship's people below. Telephone and speaking tube had been destroyed and no messenger could get through. All I could guess was that No. 3 Hold was open to the sea and that the ship was likely to go down by the head unless, by pumping, some buoyancy could be preserved. The ship was now stopped and bowing to the lop of a slight easterly swell. Craning overside from the wing of the bridge, I could see a strong outflow of water from the bilge discharge and knew that at least an attempt was being made to carry out previous plans. It was heartening to know that the engine-room appeared intact. A little later, the Chief Officer pushed through to tell me that the wounded had been taken up from the troop decks forward. Some men had been killed there. He did not know how many. With him, I shared my fear that the ship would not remain afloat. Had the *Cameronia*'s bulkheads been carried to the height of the weather decks, a more hopeful view might have been taken, but Mr McBurnie and I were agreed that all energies must first be concentrated on getting our people off the ship. About twelve minutes had passed since the blow was struck. The sands were running out. Already the bows were lower in the water, and sinister rumblings sounded from the damaged hold below: the troops massed on the fore-deck were restive, despite all the efforts of their officers. We decided that she would not stay for long. I hurried below to bring up the weighted bag in which to jettison the secret papers. On return to the bridge, I found the Chief Engineer there. He had no hope of improvement below and had ordered his hands on deck. I told McBurnie to let the Officer Commanding Troops know that we had decided to abandon ship.

It cannot be pretended that the last despairing effort went well. There was accident and disaster—again the loss of life as tackles parted under overstrain and at least two lifeboats crashed in the sea alongside. Some men preferred to trust to their cork lifebelts, and the sea around us was quickly strewn with bobbing figures amidst the wash of shattered planking and the swirl of debris. But the work went on as quickly as diminishing strength could further it.

About twenty-five minutes had gone—I could hear the loud *ping* of the zig-zag clock in the wheelhouse—and still the numbers on our decks did not seem to be reduced as swiftly as the emergency required. For a time I had had no communication with the escorting destroyers. Beyond signalling my fear that the ship was vitally holed and in immediate danger of sinking, there was little positive information to be imparted. Both destroyers had remained in company astern, engaged in a pattern of their own and dropping depth-charges to withhold the enemy from further action. . . . Now, with nearly all our boats away and still a frighteningly large body of men grouped on deck and awaiting action, I signalled *Rifleman* for help. It was quickly given. Leaving *Nemesis* to continue the watch astern, the commanding officer of the *Rifleman* skilfully brought his ship alongside us at the very lip of our foundering bows. The *thrr-ump* of landing feet that quickly followed as our men leapt to the safety of the destroyer's deck was a glad sound to me as I noted the rapid dwindling of our numbers. How many of our men the *Rifleman* took off in this way could not then be counted, but hundreds must have gained her decks before Commander Fletcher signalled he could take no more and drew slowly away, his gallant little ship listing awkwardly under the weight of our men on her weather deck. Later, the *Nemesis* came alongside to duplicate her sister's performance. Seeing the fore-deck cleared by her action, I was thankful for the amazing feat I had witnessed. My hope grew. The Germans could have the ship, but they would not have all our men.

When all our serviceable boats had been manned and lowered, and our upper decks looked cleared, I was heartened by the thought of our purpose achieved. But this cheering reflection was quickly and apprehensively chilled, for in a sudden reaction, I realized that an end to the adventure could not be far away—for me and the remaining few on the deck of the ship.

We were not many now. Of the military, the O.C. Troops with a few of his juniors and a group of other ranks; the senior officers of the ship with a small muster of seamen and firemen: the Second Engineer and a leading stoker—a small group, perhaps twenty-five in all. Gathered near the bridge, we expected no further help from outboard the ship. Our last resort was a damaged ship's boat, the only one remaining, that we were unable to heave out and lower because its working tackles had parted under strain and caused the boat to be bilged on the chocks. Striving and wrenching to manhandle it, we succeeded in pointing the craft outboard and awaited a deepening of the ship before launching her on a last throw. We had only this hazard, or the chances of a grip on floating wreckage, to count upon for survival.

The ship was sinking by the head. The sea was curling and lapping over the bows and gradually extending along the fore-deck to make it shine wetly under the sun. A strong ship, the *Cameronia* had endured her vital wounds nobly, but the strains were now too great. Her stern was high upraised above the line of the horizon, and foothold on the sloping bridge-deck had become increasingly hazardous; one had to seek hand-grip at every step, for we were standing-by. . . . Standing-by for something to happen! How often had I not done that, loitering in unease and expectation to await a trend of great winds lessening or hauling to advantage, or peering into fog or mist—all ears a-cock—for the distant whisper of another ship? There was silence between us all, up there on the boat-deck or on the bridge, as we awaited the end. She could not possibly remain for long. A sudden rupture of the leaning bulkheads below would quickly flood out the buoyancy that remained and send her down.

It seemed like a nightmare to be in peril on such a brave and shining day—the sky a cloudless blue, the sea calm and sparkling in the radiance of a westing sun. Standing off, beyond the scattered groups of our overloaded lifeboats and the ragged area of bobbing flotsam and wreckage, the two destroyers of our escort were still maintaining watch, but they were no longer swifting and circling on a search, but lying-to—weighted as both ships were by the burden of the men they had rescued from our foundering fore-deck.

In a sudden startling movement, sheering deliberately towards us, *Rifleman* took a grave but calculated risk. Unheeding the warning shouts we gave, as further rumblings from below told us that the sands had almost run, she bore down perilously near our submerged bows, then backed astern to close with our dying ship. Steel met steel with a grinding, jarring note that was almost a tortured scream.

There was no need for the hails and cheers, the admonitions and appeals for haste that rang out. Commander Fletcher's intention to take us off was plain and its urgency understood. By casual lifeline and swaying boat ladder, our small company scrambled overside and gained foothold on the destroyer's deck below. . . . What possessed me to remain on the wing of the bridge when my sterling shipmates had left her, I cannot conceive. I must have held odd views about ships and the sea in those far-off days. I was young then. The *Cameronia* was my first command. I thought her mine, whereas I belonged to her in that last hour. . . . Shouts from overside rang out. Commander Fletcher was beckoning from his bridge.

But it was the *Rifleman* herself that urged me to take a last chance. Some movement of hers caused a widening off from our side and I thought her under way, but again she leaned towards my stricken ship—her mast with its wireless span and signal yard, listed by some movement among the crowds on her deck below, almost touching the wing of the bridge where I stood. I had not to reach far out to seize the half-inch wire of some span or guy or brace. It held. Hand under hand, as my old sailing rules had taught me, I climbed down to reach the destroyer's deck in time to gaze at my first command for the last time as she went down.

Chapter XVII

A VISIT TO ADMIRALTY

SENT home from Malta to report on the loss of the *Cameronia*, I had opportunity on the journey to ponder the circumstances of the disaster. In port there, some days had passed before our total numbers had been confirmed and casualties were known. Of the 2700 troops embarked in the ship at Marseilles, one military officer and 128 other ranks had been lost; two officers and 14 men of the crew did not survive. That was bad enough, but for some troubled nights I had been haunted by the vision of countless soldiers on the upper and lower decks, all facing towards me on the bridge, and I was soberly relieved to learn from the official figures that losses had not been greater. Among the dead was Mr McBurnie, who was lost at the very last moment in trying to aid a man who had fallen overboard from the side of the *Rifleman* as she surged away from the sinking ship. Mr Black, the ship's Troop-Deck Officer, was missing; we could not learn in what manner he had met the end. I had not known of the loss of these good shipmates until, late on the day following the sinking, I arrived at Valetta. As soon as I reached the deck of the *Rifleman*, I begged her Commander to put me in one of the *Cameronia*'s lifeboats lying-to nearby. This he did, and also approved my plan to exchange some of the troops that crowded her for a few of my own seamen who had come from the sinking ship. Rowing quickly back towards the scene of the disaster, we succeeded in taking many men from the water. When, at about three on the following morning, we were picked up by a searching sloop, H.M.S. *Hydrangea*, we counted over ninety in a boat designed to carry sixty-four.

I thought long about the sinking of my ship when composure returned. I was puzzled by the U-boat's ability to come within the screen of the two destroyers and make an attack without detection, and had wondered if a station on the quarter instead of four points on the bow for the escorting vessels might not deter a submarine commander from using his periscope ahead of a rapidly advancing patrol boat. What I thought might have happened was that the enemy, having sighted us in the clear of the weather at a great distance, had established our true course and approximate speed without difficulty. Submerged later, and on hearing the sound of the destroyer's propellers rounding overhead, he had pushed up his periscope for a sight of us from the broken water in her wake, then fired his torpedo from a position on our bow. I did not, myself, see the torpedo or its track, but others had, and there was ample evidence that it had been fired at comparatively close range.

I had been given the hospitality of the Union Club in Malta (I was known there as the only man ever to have boarded one of His Majesty's ships 'by wireless'), and it was not without considerable misgiving that I expressed my opinions in the expert naval company I met there. While most of the officers thought that the usual escorting position on the bows, being largely dictated by the need to conform with a zig-zag course, was preferable—a few, and they mainly submarine officers, concurred with my theory. In the summing up, all were agreed that naval occasions could not for much longer be served by the provision of two destroyers to escort any troopship, however fast, crowded, or important she might be. We did not have enough escorting ships for that, they said. I gathered that a serious situation existed in the anti-submarine struggle. We were being hard hit at sea in the spring of 1917.

Upon arrival in London I was welcomed by my brother James and his wife and lodged with them at their flat high up in the Temple. James was the London editor of the *Manchester Guardian*, whose office in Fleet Street was conveniently near. . . . Was there ever a better port of call for a D.B.S. working his passage home from a harrowing experience in far waters? I had been continuously engaged at sea since the outbreak of war, with only short infrequent visits to my home at Helensburgh on the Clyde, and I found it a consoling experience to enjoy again the comfort of longshore dwelling—and in the heart of London, of all places, in this time of war.

It was late on a Sunday evening when I came up from Folkestone, tired out after a long journey overland, and it was later still before my story had been told. But I had the happy prospect of an undisturbed 'all night in', so different from the broken snatches and wambling cat-naps that had been the sum of my rest periods when out at sea. (We turned in 'all standing' there, fully clothed for the emergency we felt was always near.) I recall the grateful quiet of the little room facing out over King's Bench Walk towards the tower of the Inner Temple Hall and, throughout the night, how kindly to the ear were the chimes that sounded from it. And in the morning, when it was time to rustle the curtains back and lift the window-sash, how refreshing to gaze out over the green trees, lawns and gardens of the Temple and gain reassurance from sight of the brave old buildings that flanked them. There was the spell of ancientry about, and even the whistle signals of shipping on the Thames near-by recalled no anxiety. I found it hard to realize that a state of war existed—but London had wakened with the day's work to be done and the sound of many footsteps from the slope of the Walk below and the increasing din of traffic on the Embankment rose to the opened window. . . . It was a strange and memorable experience for me to sit there at that time of the morning reading and revising the text of my report on a cruel disaster at sea. Ill scrawled on my knee in continental trains and written in pencil on nondescript sheets, it was no clean copy for any official eye. I would have to get it typewritten somewhere, and that quickly.

To whom I was to make report to Admiralty on my arrival in London Vice-Admiral Ballard had not said when instructing me to proceed from Malta, and I was unfamiliar with naval methods of approach in such bureaucratic affairs. But many doors are open to the Press, and my dilemma was cleared for me by a fortunate intro-duction to Mr C. P. Scott, the famous editor of the *Manchester Guardian*. I had just collected the typewritten copies and was dis-cussing the report with my brother in his office when Mr Scott called. He, too, was interested in the narrative of the loss of my ship, of which only a bare statement had appeared in the newspapers. It may have been my submission concerning the positioning of escorts that seemed important to him, for he questioned me about it. When he had read the typescript, he asked me to whom the report was to be submitted. I replied that I did not know—'The Admiralty' was all the direction I had had. I had already tried to find out. In the afternoon, while my paper was in the typist's hands, I had gone to the inquiry desk in the hall of the old Admiralty building. The Chief

Petty Officer whom I found there was helpful—even if it was with distaste that he eyed the Maltese tailor's slop-built suit I was wearing —when I told him of the matters, but all he could do was to advise me to return there when I had got my report. . . . Mr Scott re-read it, then kindly offered to accompany me to the Admiralty and see that it was placed in the right hands.

As a result of this fortunate meeting he took me straight to the First Lord's room, and there presented me to Sir Edward Carson without the delays and interrogations I had thought likely. The First Lord was friendly and said many warm things about the war work of the Merchant Service. Accepting my report, he scanned it hastily, as though only too well he knew the full and alarming tale of our shipping losses. I had thought my duty done, and awaited some sign that it was time to go when, quite suddenly, Sir Edward asked me if I had ever sailed in convoy before?

Recalling my experiences when, in the *Cameronia*, we had carried Canadian troops on eastbound voyages in the early days of the war, I replied that I had sailed in scheduled company with other ships but had not joined convoy, if by that was meant a large group of ships keeping station abreast and in a number of columns. I spoke of the eastbound crossings and said we were only four ships or five, sailing in line ahead, which I thought not difficult after a little practice. But I had been apprehensive at first, particularly in fog and misty weather, so often met with in the North. I said that all our previous training at sea had been to keep well clear of other vessels.

Sir Edward, pondering my reply, left the room for a few minutes, then returned with a senior naval officer in uniform who may have been Rear-Admiral Duff, then head of the Trade Division at Admiralty. The newcomer greeted me pleasantly and we talked of the loss of my ship. He spoke in handsome terms of the comparatively moderate loss of life in the sinking, which already he knew, but did not question me on other particulars. I saw that he held my report in his hand. He did not refer to it, and I am still in doubt as to the best position for an anti-submarine escort. In this manner was my well-loved *Cameronia* effaced from the Registry.

But that the protection of merchant shipping lay deeply in the Admiral's thoughts became clear when he, too, asked me what knowledge I had of convoy practice, then hurried to question me on many matters concerning its operation by merchant ships. It was at once apparent that he had an intimate acquaintance with our way of life. . . . While my recollection of that interview is vivid enough, even at this long date, I can recall only the gist of what was said, for I have no memorandum or diary now to guide me. In the later stages of the war we merchant seamen were forbidden to keep personal records of service in it, but an understanding Providence often grants the sailor good sight and long memory, and the trends of the conversation remain with me. His questions were mostly concerned with the routine of duty within the ship. The enforcement of black-out, methods to reduce excessive smoke from the funnel, the disposal of refuse—it was about such lesser details that the Admiral was inquisitive, but I thought it odd that he should ask:

'How do you get on with the engineers in your ships?' Noting my surprise, he added: 'What's the reaction of the officer in the engine-room when he takes an order from the bridge?'

I took my time to answer that one. I had not thought that the occasional frictions that occur between shipmates in any ship could have attracted such distinguished attention. Certainly I had known dissension, but never considered it of importance. On the whole, we were good shipmates, and if we did have different points of view —well, that was the spice of argument. My own experience had been that orders from the bridge had always been carried out with reasonable despatch. Recalling minor difficulties in adjusting speed on the few occasions I had sailed in 'line ahead', I mentioned them. Questioned shrewdly on the points, I replied that the difficulties might have been due to communications between bridge and engine-room being unsuited to convoy practice. Long accustomed to the bridge telegraph being used with casual margin, the count of revolutions at every alteration was something the engineer had not been asked to make. He might be sore at that. Then again, not many of our ships were fitted with telephones. Most ships had a speaking tube—an indifferent pipe affair. Hearing was made difficult by engine noises below there.

The Admiral smiled indulgently at my long-winded explanation of tiffs on shipboard, then inquired quizzically what were the faults of the bridge party. I admitted that we were not blameless. We were not trained in the pitch of voice to be used by telephone or speaking tube, and our 'tops'l halyard' shouts only made matters worse. Nor were we patient enough in adjustments of speed; we made too many alterations, and these often too large. We had a lot to learn. He agreed, and said that one of the first lessons was that there must be good understanding between the deck and the engine-room if we were to succeed in convoy.

Coming away from that historic old building, I wondered if I had not said too much. As a last question the Admiral had asked me if I thought we merchant shipmasters and our people could adapt ourselves to sailing in convoy. I had said, 'Yes'.

Chapter XVIII

MERCHANT CONVOY

THREE months later I stood on the navigation bridge of the *Elysia* anchored offshore in the approaches to New York. We were waiting for daylight to sail eastwards on a return voyage to the United Kingdom. After a welcome interval of rest at home I was again at sea, assigned to relieving duties in the Company's ships, taking command for a voyage to give a respite to their tired and sea-worn masters. Some of my former officers, returned home after the loss of the *Cameronia*, sailed with me in relief of their opposite numbers on deck and in the engine-room. War casualties had seriously reduced the tonnage of the Anchor Line fleet and not one of the Company's transatlantic liners had survived. To keep the important route to New York in operation, ships from the Indian service had been brought in. The *Elysia* was one of them, a fine intermediate vessel of 6,757 tons and twelve knots speed. She had large cargo capacity and, on her normal route, accommodated about a hundred passengers, although none was carried on the Atlantic voyage, for the cabins had been tightly stowed with mails and special packages of war material.

Standing by for daylight is often a prudent measure in a ship when an intricate sea channel has to be traversed, but it is one rarely taken by a full-powered vessel in open waters. Near where we lay anchored the Ambrose Lightship, that marks the sea-gate to the Port of New York, flashed its welcoming beacon at timely intervals, but we sighted no incoming vessels bearing in for the channels nor did any out-bound ships steer past us on their way to sea. This was greatly in contrast with the busy traffic of the early morning I had so often remarked on previous voyages. Right from the outbreak of the war it had been the practice for belligerent shipping to take advantage of darkness when in neutral waters. But now the circumstance was different at the outer buoy of the Ambrose Channel.

The United States was no longer neutral, and we lay anchored there in the half-light of early morning in readiness to sail together at the coming of the day. Allied with us, America was in the war. We were the first merchant convoy to sail eastbound from New York.

Around us in that open anchorage, and dimly to be made out in the dusk (for we showed no lights), was a group of fifteen deeply laden ships listed to sail in company across the Atlantic. On the day before, a conference of masters and senior officers had been held at the Chelsea Piers and there we had been instructed in the new duties of concerted action out at sea. We were to proceed at nine knots in a formation of five columns and the distance between ships in columns was to be two cables. On a large blackboard our respective positions were chalked in with an exactitude that none of us felt competent to copy in action. But we could try, and it was in that spirit we left the waiting-room and returned to our ships.

As daylight grew on us at the anchorage, we made a grotesque and gaudily bedizened assembly, for merchant-ship camouflage had newly come into use and we were streaked in bewildering patterns. None of the ships was of large displacement: we were mostly of the tramp class, or cargo liners of moderate size and speed. The *Elysia* had been chosen as the 'Guide' to lead the group of merchant vessels and, beside me on the bridge, the naval Commodore of the convoy looked out over the darkling waters at the ships he was to conduct in company overseas for the first time in the war. He was Commodore Herbert J. Haddock, R.D., R.N.R. I had known him earlier in transatlantic service when he was Master of the *Olympic* of the White Star Line and, like every understanding seaman, had been thrilled by his skilful and gallant action in her when attempting to tow to safety the sinking battleship *Audacious*, mined off the northern coast of Ireland. . . . The tedium of our waiting moments was relieved by the Commodore's amusing reference to some incident of his last employment, as Flag Officer in charge of the British 'dummy' Battle Fleet, anchored specially for the enemy's persistent aerial observation in far Loch Ewe or Loch Eriboll. . . . And now we were to be shipmates on the slow and perilous passage across the Atlantic. I looked forward with eagerness to learning something from him of the operation of a merchant convoy. I remembered the Admiral's question at the conclusion of our interview in London.

Would the difficulties prove me overbold in my declaration that we merchantmen could succeed in it?

The coming among us of an American warship put an end to these reflections. Daylight was now abroad, and it was time to weigh anchor and proceed astern of the cruiser. She was the U.S.S. *Albany*, detailed to escort the convoy overseas until arrival at a rendezvous in 15° W., where it would be met by a group of British destroyers. Under way at last, we steered out in a ragged and disorderly procession, crowding up on one another in slight resemblance to the positional 'line ahead' the Commodore had ordered. Strangely, he seemed little perturbed. 'Come and go' was apparently to be expected from us at the beginning of a first convoy passage, and the ships made crazy patterns in avoidance of their neighbours. It was clear that there was a wide range of error in the estimation of one another's speed. In the *Elysia*—as guide of the convoy—our duty was to maintain steady progress while steering a straight course, but often I found it hard to curb my instinct to forge ahead when our next astern came perilously close. In this manner we straggled on to a position south of Fire Island, where, with the wide Atlantic before us, Commodore Haddock decided to take up ocean-sailing formation in five columns. A hair-raising experience, through which the *Elysia* plodded on steadily as a standard for troubled mariners! But some lesson had been learned during our erratic progress from the anchorage: as the ships fanned out to take up the new positions, there was not the crowding and overtaking that had marked our earlier efforts. We were now inclined to hang back. The manœuvre took long to complete, but in time we formed up some appearance of steaming order. We had met the first requirements without casualty.

From then on I recall my first ocean convoy as a period of constant alert. It was not that the enemy pressed us, for of him we saw nothing on the route, but rather that our own errors required unremitting correction. There were many lapses from the text of our convoy instructions. We made too much smoke; unthinking, we jettisoned our garbage in daylight hours; we showed lights during the night and our black-out was not efficient. As the centre for convoy direction, the *Elysia*'s signal yard was rarely free of flag-hoists indicating admonition and reproof. But, as the long days of the voyage wore on and practical experience supplanted the dry conference instructions, the Commodore's naval signalmen gained a respite from that disagreeable duty and the Commodore himself relaxed in confidence that something had been done. Sailing for so long in company we came to know one another's reaction to a common circumstance—how 'A.3' would fall back at nightfall and spur up at daybreak, or 'B.1', our next in column, slip ahead when he had cleaned his fires. In fog or misty weather lay our most searching trials, and I recall few more anxious moments at sea than those dismal days when, holding speed, we heard the trumpets but had no sight of our charging fellows. Was ever a sailor's relief like ours when the fog miraculously lifted and a count revealed the ships all present, if ill assembled?

Taking a southern route, intended for the George's Channel, it was a long passage at much less than the nine knots we had so gloomily accepted at conference in New York. There had been much additional mileage to be traversed, due to frequent detours ordered by the *Albany* when some unfamiliar *pin-ggg* was heard on her hydrophones. But we had no sight of the enemy, and daybreak of the twelfth day out found us somewhere west of the Blaskets, explaining ourselves to the Senior Officer of a formidable destroyer escort. Merchant convoy had proved itself.

Chapter XIX

MY ARTIST BROTHER

FOR long it had been my ambition to write a book about the Merchant Service in the war, but the regulation which prohibited the keeping of any private diary or memorandum while serving in a ship at sea withheld me from writing down day-to-day accounts of events as they occurred. The Admiralty ruling (which demanded also the surrender of every merchant ship's log book immediately upon arrival in a home port) came into effect after the Battle of Jutland in 1916. It appeared that a chest of drawers from one of our warships was found later floating with other debris in the battle area. It contained an officer's complete diary of current naval operations, which might easily have fallen into the hands of the enemy. Although naval secrets were not generally known to the merchant shipmaster, there could be disclosure of shipping routes and rendezvous, or war channels and protected harbours, in the careless jettison of scrap papers when out at sea.

Nevertheless, in the intervals of leisure at my home in Scotland, in the carefree days that came between relief assignments in the Company's ships, I had busied myself in writing a rough memorandum of personal experiences since the outbreak of the war.

My brother Muirhead had seen these jottings and knew of my plan to use them later in writing a book. Indeed, his interest in the project led him to suggest a collaboration in which his war drawings of seaports and merchant shipping would supplement my story of merchantmen-at-arms throughout hostilities. Muirhead was the first of a group of artists officially commissioned by the War Office in 1916 to record in pictures drawn on the spot the life and actions of our armies on the Western Front. Few drawings so well represent the weary stages of static warfare and the desolation of the field as his: his dramatic and awe-inspiring lithograph of the first military tank in action is known to have produced an atmosphere of dismay when a copy fell into the hands of the enemy's Intelligence. In the same capacity of official war artist, he saw service with the Grand Fleet and in naval establishments, docks, and shipyards. All his work at this time came under close inspection by the naval and military authorities before being released for reproduction and subsequent exhibition. These drawings became the property of the nation and are mostly held in the Imperial War Museum.

When I arrived at Liverpool from New York in the *Massilia* and handed her over to her well-rested former Captain, I had the surprising news from the Anchor Line that my services had been asked for by the Admiralty, not—as I might have hoped—to sail ships, but to write a book about them. I thought it odd that the request should have come from the Naval Censor's Department, a branch of the Admiralty that I had always associated with reticence and reserve—and sharp reproof at times. I was speedily corrected in my opinion when, with my brother, I was interviewed by Captain (later Rear-Admiral) Sir Douglas Brownrigg, the Chief Naval Censor, in London. In his reminiscences of that exacting post, *The Indiscretions of the Naval Censor*, Sir Douglas recalls its 'productive' side—its enterprises in art and literature. He expresses his disappointment that in 1918 the story of the Mercantile Marine which he had in mind had not then been written, despite his approaches to a number of competent authors. It was to repair that omission he had thought of me when Muirhead, a frequent visitor to his office in Whitehall, had mentioned that I was likely soon to be on leave. As a result of that interview, and the Anchor Line being willing to extend my leave, an arrangement was made for my brother and me to travel together all round the coast; he to make drawings and I to gather material for a book on the war doings of the Merchant Service.

I recall that roving commission as a handsome reward for long sea-keeping and happily remember the bright companionship of my brother throughout our uncommon journeys to tide-water. We made many friends at the ports we visited. Well documented for our coastal rounds, we had no difficulty in gaining acceptance from the naval and port authorities at the larger bases; but in the smaller seaports it was thought suspicious to have a military officer in uniform drawing pictures of ships in the port and plainly interested in some untoward doings behind the breakwater. I recall particularly the agitation of an elderly harbour-master at Padstow. Muirhead had innocently inquired about the purpose of a foreign-looking coastal barge—the *Drei Geschwister*—which lay at the quayside, her two long guns barely concealed, just under the windows of the Harbour Office. The old Captain's perturbation was only allayed by the immediate production of our credentials and the subsequent dis-covery that long, long ago, in the days of square sail, our respective windjammers were in port together in San Francisco and we two—then brassbounders—must sometime have met at the Sailors' Institute on Market Street!

The fine days of the summer of 1918 lined out as we travelled from port to port. While my brother worked away steadily at his drawings, striving always to perfect an impression or capture the very essence of some fleeting activity of shipping in the docks or on the river, I was the onlooker who stood idly by or cast about in quest of information that might help me to write a masterly text to accompany his amazing drawings. Not often did we find the work on which we were engaged clearly understood. It was assumed that I, the writer, could only be interested in statistics and the technics of ships and oversea transport, or perhaps the wartime efforts of the port workers to speed the operations of the merchant ships as they came in from sea. I thought this concept an unusual compliment—that sailors and their ships should be considered as unremarkable and as faithful as the tides; but when, at the end of the day, I dis-burdened my brief-case of much official material, it was over my own rough notes of personal contacts with my fellows on the water-front I pondered. There lay my story.

Frequently I found the copy I sought in almost any assembly of shipmasters and seamen, pilots or port workers where, once con-fidence had been established and one was known to be of the fraternity, much could be learned of the war-time happenings at the port or in its nearby waters. A favoured rendezvous was the duty room of the Pilot Station at Deal or Plymouth, Gravesend or Gourock on the Clyde. We found it best to intrude there at the 'x' period of the tide—an hour or so before high water, when pilots 'on turn' for duty gather to await their assignments. The institution of convoy had crowded these gatherings, for mass arrivals of ship-ping called for every available pilot to report for duty—at some ports even retired pilots were recalled to serve again in the emergency.

One would have thought that in such a busy and often noisy assembly there would be small opportunity for an artist to concentrate on his drawings. But my brother found just such stirring scenes greatly to his liking. How quickly he would have his pencil and paper out and the board a-tilt on his knee, and how easily in the airy pilot-house find a sheltered corner with the lighting for his purpose! He was not easily distracted from his task, and the stir and clatter of the duty room seemed in no way to disturb his drawing. Nor was he averse to joining in the conversation from time to time. I recall with amusement his discussion with an elderly pilot on the recognition given to art by seamen in their ships. That was in the Pilot House on Gravesend Pier on a bright day in August. A large convoy was due inward at almost any moment, and the old man (probably one of those recalled from retirement) punctuated his remarks by frequent use of a large telescope fitted in a window-frame, through which he scanned the seaward reaches for first sign of the incomers. He held an enthusiastic brief for the Chinese artists of Hong Kong, who, as he said, excelled in their paintings of the sailing-ships of the old days. At his home nearby he had a splendid picture of the *Norman Court*, in which he had served, beating against the monsoon in the China Sea. We were invited to inspect the masterpiece. . . . But the curl of smoke that he had watched growing up over the Essex shore could now be identified as shipping under way in the distant reach, and the invitation was not further extended in the rush to collect handbags and oilskins—not forgetting the bundles of old newspapers that would ensure the pilots being given an especial welcome on boarding the ships in the river.

In the autumn, our journeyings together suspended for a term, I settled down to my writing at home in Helensburgh, while Muirhead took up an assignment that sent him to the Grand Fleet at Scapa Flow. That was in late September, and up to that date no definite arrangement had been made for publication of the projected book. But before we parted in London, my brother and I were asked to call on Arnold Bennett at the Ministry of Information, where he was then assisting Lord Beaverbrook. Bennett, a keen admirer of Muirhead's drawings, was really interested in the plan for our joint effort to produce a book about the Merchant Service in the

War, and gave us every possible encouragement. The title I had in mind, *Merchantmen-at-Arms*, seemed to appeal to him. Nothing was suggested regarding official sponsorship of the book, but it was through Bennett I came to know Frank Swinnerton, who was then literary adviser to Chatto and Windus. From Mr Swinnerton I gained valuable advice in planning the text, which, it was tacitly understood, was in time to be submitted to 'Chatto's'.

Busied with my task, I had not given much thought to the amazing rush of military events that, in early November, brought the war to an end, and it was a surprise to receive a message from my brother to join him again in London. This arrived on the 8th November, and together we observed the scenes in London streets on Armistice Day. Memories of that great day when the load was lifted are strangely dim in my thought of it now. Crowds, crowds, and yet more crowds swarming in the City streets; traffic hopelessly congested by merry-makers intent upon communal excitement. But when darkness fell, it seemed that the moment had come for a proclamation of freedom once again established. Amazingly, the lights came on! I remember standing in the shelter of the portico of St Martin-in-the-Fields, joining the great crowds that had assembled there at nightfall. I did not know of any official relaxation of the civic black-out, and the sudden illumination of Trafalgar Square and the high buildings fronting it came as a happy surprise. . . . A big bonfire, conjured swiftly by a group of resourceful soldiers from a nearby hoarding, had been set alight on a southern angle of the paving; seen from where we stood, the brave gleams lit up the fluting of Nelson's Column and cast a glow on the upturned faces of the milling and wildly cheering crowds. As always, Muirhead lost no time. Although the light was dim beneath the portico, it seemed visible enough for him to complete a dramatic sketch of the relief and rejoicing.

A week later I was at sea again; not sailing, but as an accredited member of a Press group boarded in H.M.S. *Melampus* to see the surrender of the German submarines off Harwich. My impressions of that day of victory, made gloriously manifest, form the concluding chapter of *Merchantmen-at-Arms*, which was published in 1919. I had hoped that my brother would accompany me on that last assignment, but Admiral Brownrigg had a more spectacular occasion to offer him and had sent him off to H.M.S. *Queen*

Elizabeth in Scottish waters, where from her foretop he made his mighty drawing of the surrender of the German Battle Fleet out at sea off the Firth of Forth.

My brother Muirhead died at his home at Oxford on the 21st October, 1953. He was seventy-seven. Sailor-like, I accepted his passing as though a well-loved shipmate had sailed in another ship after long companionship and happy days of voyaging together. When he died, his lifework as one of the greatest British graphic artists was the text of many tributes.

Rear-Admiral Brownrigg, to whose book *The Indiscretions of the Naval Censor* I have referred, and who died in 1939, said this of him while both were still active in the First World War—

'This artist has a passion for work surpassed by few people I have met. When he was staying at Admiralty House, Rosyth, with the late Admiral Sir Frederick Hamilton, he would disappear out of the house immediately after breakfast, and not infrequently before that meal, and reappear when the light failed him. That was during the summer. But those who remember the magnificent black-and-white drawing of H.M.S. *Lion*—"Surveying Cables"—in dry dock at Rosyth can imagine what the artist endured, standing for hours in the bottom of a dry dock (which really had about six inches of water on its floor) in the depth of winter and in almost incessant snowstorms. His fingers at times were so numbed that he could not feel them. The material with which he worked frequently froze, so that he had to get near a stove to thaw himself and them.

'He returned from each of these trips to the fleet, having made hosts of friends and bringing back with him literally scores of drawings. He has a heart big enough for ten men, and when he wished to give an officer or man, to whom he considered he was specially indebted for some little act of kindness, a sketch as a memento, he would work on Sundays, "in his own time". For he was so scrupulously honest that he would not part with any work he had brought down, since all that was the property of the British Museum.

'Eventually, and as might be expected of such a worker, he

broke down and was off work for some nine months, fretting away all the time at doing nothing, and thus retarding his complete recovery. However, we got him back presently, and I think his first work was a very large black-and-white drawing of the *Vindictive* on her return from Zeebrugge. That drawing —in my judgment one of the finest of its sort that he has ever executed—was sent over to the United States and toured the country in company with other war pictures. I am glad to say that this picture is also the property of the Navy.

'He followed up this job by the tour he made with his brother, Captain David Bone, for the preparation of the book on the Mercantile Marine, of which I have written in a previous chapter. I pumped good advice into him, and especially did I charge his brother to see to it that he didn't allow him to overwork again, else the whole scheme would be wrecked. I am glad to say that he returned "all correct" and with an enormous mass of sketches, from which the two brothers must have had trouble in selecting what was necessary for their book.

'Bone was one of the artists who went up to the Grand Fleet to see the surrender of the German Fleet, and he was accommodated on board the Fleet flagship *Queen Elizabeth*. Once more he got lost. At breakfast time inquiries were put about as to whether anybody had seen Bone? Nobody could find him. He turned up about 7 p.m., having been in the foretop since 7 a.m. without a scrap of food. What an enthusiast, and what an artist!'

Chapter XX

RECONSTRUCTION

WHEN peace came in 1918, the return to normal commerce at sea was not speedily effected. While the ocean transport of the world's goods might loosely be served by tramp-ships the war had spared and by the hasty new construction of 'standard' ships, the grievous losses of troop transports and other large passenger liners could not quickly be made good. As always after crises in Europe, a high flood of emigration crowded every westbound ship, but these were few in number. Pending completion of new vessels, shift was made by recalling to service many older ships that in normal circumstances would have been sold to the shipbreakers. A few large and speedy vessels which, at the outbreak of war, had been commandeered by the Navy to serve as auxiliary cruisers were handed back to their former owners and hurriedly refitted to enter the sailing lists.

The Anchor Line had suffered gravely in the loss of all its larger transatlantic ships in the war. Two intermediate vessels were taken from the Indian service to make Atlantic crossings in the summer of 1919, and in June of that year I was sent to take over a standard ship —the *Vindelia*—which the Cunard Line had been operating in freight service for a short term. At that date much interest had been aroused in long-distance air flights, and there were those who predicted a future in the air for both passengers and cargo transport over the 3,000 grey miles of the Atlantic route. A transatlantic flight had already been made, but with a stop for re-fuelling in the Azores. In May, Harry Hawker and a companion took off from Newfoundland with the intention of flying direct to the United Kingdom, but were forced down at sea many miles from the nearest point of land. It was known that the plane had come down, and the aviators were given up for lost, but a week later they were safely landed at an English port, having been miraculously picked up at

The *Cameronia*, the Author's first command in 1915, torpedoed and sunk
in the Mediterranean in 1917

The *Columbia*, ex H.M.S. *Columbella* in first World War

The *Tuscania*

The *Tuscania* passing an Atlantic iceberg, 1924

sea by the Danish steamer *Mary*—a small vessel that had no wireless.

When about to sail in the *Vindelia* from the Clyde on the 12th June, 1919, I was told that two British officers of the R.F.C. were in Newfoundland about to launch out above the Atlantic in a Vickers–Vimy converted bomber. I was asked to keep a specially good look-out for them, as the Great Circle course we would be steering on the passage to Cape Race would be the reverse of that used by the aviators. Two days out we had information by wireless that Alcock and Brown had set out from St John's, Newfoundland. But the weather being dense fog, we saw nothing of them, though they must have passed not far from our position during the night. I recall something of my own feelings during that stretch of thick weather as I paced the *Vindelia*'s bridge thinking of these gallant men aloft flying blind, for little confidence could be placed in the aerial compass of the day. It was still foggy far into the afternoon of the 15th June when we learned that they had landed safely in Galway— the first direct flight from North America to Great Britain. . . . A month later, while I was still commanding the *Vindelia* but at the time visiting my Uncle George at New Haven in Connecticut, I saw the British Airship *R. 34* sail majestically overhead bound southerly to an aerial anchorage in New Jersey—the first direct flight from Britain to the United States. . . . I, who had handled square sail in my youth, had much to ponder on the arts of the new aviform of navigation when I returned to my home port at Glasgow.

A new *Cameronia* was being built in Beardmore's shipyard at Dalmuir, and when I had been relieved in my temporary post in the *Vindelia*, I was detailed to represent the Company's interest in the new ship's construction. Beyond having satisfied the examiners to the modest degree set out in my pass for extra master, I had made no special study of shipbuilding and felt singularly ignorant of the duties I might have to undertake. But I was well received at the great shipyard where so many of our finest ships had been built. Quite probably the shipyard officials and the working foremen were inwardly amused by my artless inquiries, but I was tolerated and in time acquired sufficient cunning to conceal my inexperience. With the new *Cameronia* launched and fitting out in the basin and Captain James Blaikie—recovered from his sufferings as a prisoner of war in Germany—standing ready to command her, I was sent to take over a fine old ship—the *Columbia*—which, with notable distinction, had served throughout the war in the Tenth Cruiser Squadron as H.M.S. *Columbella*—a somewhat oddly musical translation of her given name, deemed necessary by the Navy having another *Columbia* already in commission. De-requisitioned, ungunned, and returned to us in the spring of 1920, a temporary conversion was hurriedly carried through and we sailed westwards in April, fully embarked with 1,400 passengers. They were largely emigrants seeking to better their fortunes far from war-torn Europe. A feature of the embarkation was the amazing assortment of household equipment the emigrants had saved from the wreckage of their homes. I had not known that bedding could be thought so precious in the States.

For myself, I had much to learn on my return to peaceful transatlantic service. Upon arrival at New York I found a remarkable stiffening of the rules of immigration. Extremes of narrow nationalism had been bred and nourished in the war years and kindly Uncle Sam had come to feel that he could no longer welcome all and sundry to his shores. A new Immigration Act had become law in which a monthly quota, based on former numbers, had been established, and only incomers previously approved by American consulates abroad were at once admitted. Gone and almost forgotten were the free-and-easy days when Patrick *avick* (himself only a week arrived in the land of promise) could shout out cheerfully, 'Putt on y'er bonnet an' y'er shawl, Bridgid. It's a grand day for an outin'. I *guess* we'll go down t' Castle Garden t' see th' greenharns land!'

But the new regulations in the ports could not be enforced without conflicting with other authoritative matters of port administration. So great had become the press of entrants at eastern ports that the Immigration Department at New York or Boston and Philadelphia could no longer cope with the arrivals. The monthly quota, too, had brought about a state of the utmost congestion towards the end of the month, and a curious form of ship racing developed among the old crocks engaged in the emigrant trade. No blue ribands were conferred; only disturbed harbour conditions grew out of it, and there was often a dangerous crowding among the vessels awaiting clearance at quarantine. It was realized that some other plan was called for.

Although the *Columbia* on that first post-war voyage was officially cleared for New York when signature was made in the Custom House at Glasgow, I was told before sailing that some other port of destination on the eastern seaboard—where the harbour management might have more berthage—might be signalled to me on the voyage. We made good time on the way, but when south of Sable Island I received an instruction from New York to alter course and proceed to Portland, Maine—a pleasant pine-enshrouded harbour where, as I think, almost the town's entire population came down to the waterfront 'to see the greenhorns land'.

Another, and a more disquieting difference from the old days of plain sailing was the often precarious trim of the ship when, with coal fuel, fresh water, and stores in part consumed and the passengers baggage brought up on deck for quick unloading, we staggered into port at the end of a westbound voyage. The old *Columbia* had always been regarded as a strong and upstanding ship in any circumstance. Had she not, in 1905, reached port safely after a heavy collision with an iceberg in mid-Atlantic? I was worried to find her listing badly as we steered in shallow waters towards Portland.

Built at Meadowside in 1902, she was, like other merchant ships of her day, constructed to burn coal, which was carried in her bunker spaces. This she drew upon on the voyage out, and with every mile of progress her stability was to some degree impaired. Fresh water and other stores consumed added to the insufficiency of stable deadweight. In pre-war days this inclination to lean over when in shallow water at the end of a voyage could be disregarded, for there was always a compensating factor in the deadweight of the cargo to hold her upright under most conditions of the weather. The Glasgow-to-New-York trade was good in these palmy days. A keen demand for Scottish products existed in the United States, and only rarely was the ship not loaded to her marks on outward sailings. But in 1920 we were 'high and light' when setting out from the Clyde. The war had slowed production of goods for export, and the great new experiment of Prohibition in the United States had put a stop to shipments of Scotch whisky in cask and case that for so long had made our ships 'sea kindly' in the most testing of Atlantic seas. Other weighty consignments had also vanished from our cargo manifests, for in the war years our fishermen had enlisted to net submarines instead of Loch Fyne herring, and the export of salted fish had fallen away. . . . At the end of a westbound passage the ship could only stagger into port, listing lubberly to one side or the other as emigrants on the crowded upper decks mustered to see the sights of New York harbour.

I recall an occasion when the ship was stopped to embark the New York pilot off Sandy Hook in fine, calm weather. It was at the end of a protracted passage, and the rush of passengers to the port side of the ship to observe the incident of his boarding caused the 8,000-ton liner to list so badly that the suspended boat ladder swung violently outboard, giving the pilot a perilous climb before he gained a foothold on the deck. Well might elderly Mr Stoffrieden speak of the old wanderer being 'half seas over' when, breathless from his exertions, he reached the upper bridge. Half seas over! But it was no excess but rather the insufficiency of strong waters packed tightly in our lower holds that had caused the *Columbia* to behave so badly to an old familiar.

Some months later, in winter time, when the press of emigration had lessened somewhat, advantage was taken of a long-delayed survey and general overhaul to deal with this unsteady behaviour at the end of a week's oversea voyaging. Ballasting—the loading of an unprofitable quantity of sand or stones as stable makeweight —was suggested, but, as eastbound cargo was increasing in volume and to make space for it the ballast would have to be discharged on every arrival at New York, that proposal was ruled out. Then, again, it was not now thought that the *Columbia*'s employment would be only a temporary measure to keep a sailing list in currency until the four new ships were completed and in sea service. The construction programme was badly in arrear. Labour troubles in the shipyards had slowed building operations and the dates of probable delivery were now far off. It was decided to recondition the old ship for extended service. Her hull and twin-screw engines being in surprisingly good state, she was converted to become an oil-burner, the fuel being carried in the double-bottom tanks. A 'separator' was installed to deal with the known antipathies of oil and water. When these and some state and public-room conversions had been made, the fine 'old timer' was herself again and speedily recovered her old prestige in the service. Under almost any condition of sparse loading, salt water could be run in and tightened up in the tanks to maintain her steady and upright on the Atlantic voyage.

When the restored *Columbia* was brought back into service, a running mate had to be sought for her to conform with fortnightly sailings from the Clyde. None of the Company's Indian service ships had speed enough, but suitable German 'reparations tonnage' was available and the *Yperanga* was acquired. She was a good-looking steamship of 8,000 tons, built for the Woermann Line at Kiel in 1908. She carried about 400 passengers but, as the trade in which she had formerly been engaged was favoured by tropical weather, she proved a somewhat chilly vessel for the North Atlantic seasons. In the war, the German Admiralty had fitted her up as a heavily armed commerce raider. As such, we did not know of any action at sea in which she had a part, but it is possible that her wolfish intention towards the Allies' shipping fold was remembered when the question of renaming her to conform with the Company's naming system came under review. She became the *Assyria*, and was sold back to the Germans in 1929.

Although I had often sailed into the port of New York in the war years, I had not come to know the city well, and up-town beyond Twenty-third Street was a hinterland I had never explored. An occasional train journey to New Haven to visit my American relatives, long settled there, was about the extent of my shore-going outside the area of ship's business at the seaward tip of Manhattan. I had few acquaintances then in the city or its nearer suburbs, and the war-time business of loading special and unusual items of cargo often held me to the ship for long hours. . . . But it was now peace-time again, and there was no need for me to be on daily and nightly attendance in the ship when she was safely tied up at the Anchor Line pier in the North River. I had opportunity to adventure up-town and discover what lay inshore of the towering cliffs on the waterfront. This new routine of scheduled voyaging, with its regularity of comings and goings, recalled to me the amenities of the Indian trade, where, with a round of at least ten days in port at Bombay—discharging one weighty cargo and loading another—I could find time and occasion to take part in longshore social life. At thought of that, I could feel again the glow of happy anticipation I had often known when the domes and towers of that regal city arose at break of morning in the calm sea-line ahead, and I could plan once more the pleasant interludes of sailor life that I recalled so vividly—

'Would the H.L.I. still be established at Colaba Barracks, and could I expect an invitation to a Mess Night there? Had Hargreaves returned from his business tour in the Deccan, or was Meldrum back from home leave in Australia? Anyway, I could be sure of finding someone I knew at the Gymkhana to bear with me on a round of patmore golf on the Maidan!' . . . Quite suddenly I remembered. The men I knew in the Highland Light Infantry did not long survive the retreat from Mons. Meldrum had met his end in Mespot, and Hargreaves—where? There were not many left of that group of longshore friends out abroad. It was time I took to shore-going again and sought new companionship on the beach.

Chapter XXI

THREE HOURS FOR LUNCH

PROMINENT among the tenders and harbour craft that swarm alongside an incoming liner when she has arrived and lies anchored at quarantine in New York harbour to await clearance, there will surely be a U.S. Coastguard cutter, fully embarked with a crowd of visitors to the ship, for often there are celebrities on our passenger list, and America is eager to know something about them. The reception party is accompanied by representatives of the Press detailed to report the occasion, ship-news reporters and photographers, often a glee club or a song-and-dance team if we have a stage star aboard. In such events there is useful publicity for the ship, and naturally we put ourselves on the best of terms with the journalists who provide it. With many of the 'regulars' the ship's people establish a long and stable friendship, fortified on the one side by talk of sea experiences on the Atlantic, on the other by authentic word upon current events and the latest news of the waterfront. Rarely do these friendly callers arrive to board us down the Bay without a bundle of the latest newspapers, or even a lately published book.

It was thus in the newly furbished *Columbia* when she arrived and anchored handily in the Narrows on a bright summer morning in 1920. We had made a good voyage, and had no special incident to report. Nor were complications to be feared with the Immigration or Customs authorities. There was good prospect that we would quickly be cleared and sent on our way to dock at Pier 64, North River, on the run of the tide.

As the Coastguard cutter rumbled alongside, I peered over the bridge rail to see who was attending to the business thus early in the morning, hoping that one particular friend would be among the newsmen. I wanted to let him know that the novel he had left with me on the previous voyage was fully up to his enthusiastic

135

recommendation. Mr Williams (known as 'Skipper' Williams among his colleagues) was a staff writer on the *New York Times*. He had sailed at sea in his younger days, and combined a taste for good reporting with sane views about ships and seafaring. What he had to say about the book he had given me—*Casuals of the Sea*—could be listened to with respect, and I had thoroughly enjoyed my reading of it. I had not known any work by William McFee and was eager to learn more. I had heard that he was an engineer officer in British merchant ships. *Casuals* revealed him as an uncommonly good writer, a forthright and sincere if somewhat caustic commentator on the moods and manners of shipboard. At first impression I thought his style of writing 'sea lawyerly' and was mildly roused by what I then considered an overly critical attitude to the sea life I had known. Who was this fellow, I mused—a shop-trained steamboatman—to cavil at points of real seamanship? I was to learn later that he was born in his father's lofty ship at sea; that at six he was voyaging under square sail!

Another glance overside satisfied me that Williams was not among the newsmen in the cutter. But John Regan of *The World* was there, and came up to my quarters. It was a Saturday, and he thought 'Skipper' was attending the sailing of a new Italian liner due out from her pier at noon. But Regan relieved my curiosity about the author of the book. He, too, commended *Casuals* and mentioned a second book that had lately appeared, called *Aliens*, which he thought even better. I made a note of that and spoke of my interest in McFee's work. I wondered if he was still actively employed at sea. Did he ever come to New York, I asked?

'Why, yes,' Regan said. 'McFee is still sailing. He's in the United Fruit steamers; docks in the East River at times. If you want to find out when he's in port, have a look at Morley's column in the *Post*. Chris often mentions his kinsprits in *The Bowling Green* . . .,' Kinsprit? Some interruption occurred, and I was not then enlightened about kindred spirits and their ways of doing.

A month later, when I had become an admirer of Christopher Morley's bright column in the *New York Evening Post*, my reading was rewarded by an item that confirmed John Regan's surmise. It appeared that *The Bowling Green*'s compiler had adventured on the deep of the East River and had something to report of its perils and casualties. Visiting a friend in a vessel at the pier there, he had been careless enough to tap out the ashes from his favourite briar against the rim of the port-scuttle in his friend's cabin. The pipe-stem broke and the long-polished bowl was lost overside in the mud of tidewater.

I thought that incident a somewhat trifling preamble to a column largely devoted to literary topics, but I had found it 'wisdom to perpend' when reading Morley's text. Sure enough, a further paragraph reported a stimulating exchange with his seafaring friend who, as I thought, could be no other than William McFee. Conrad's latest novel—*The Arrow of Gold*—came under discussion and someone remarked that Conrad, for all his command of English, had his entanglements in the use of 'shall' and 'will'. Having myself heard Conrad speak of troubled understanding when serving as third mate of the Scottish ship *Loch Etive*, I ventured to write to *The Bowling Green* suggesting that any difficulty the greater writer had in choice of the fitting verb may have been influenced by the authentic voice of Glasgow he had to live with on his long round voyage to the Colonies. It was not unknown for *shall* and *will* to become conversationally synonymous north of the Border. As an instance of this variant, I quoted the laconic reply of a Fleet Street editor to the appeal of a Scottish reporter, teetering hesitantly at his half-opened door. 'Will I come in?', the man inquired, flourishing his note-book as an intimation of a point to be discussed. 'God knows,' muttered his busy senior, not even looking up from his desk.

My letter provoked attention when quoted in *The Bowling Green* and, as subsequently I learned, brought to Morley's overloaded desk in Vesey Street many comments—learned and facetious—on the use and misuse of common forms of speech. Controversy grew out of it; 'shall' and 'will' got out of date and 'who' and 'whom' took place for a while. I did not enter into further correspondence, but a kind letter from the editor of the column invited me to call on him at his office down-town, and in that way there began the long and deeply cherished friendship that remains between us to this day.

Chris Morley, a Rhodes Scholar with an affectionate regard for the old country his father came from, was then nearing thirty—a big upstanding man of hearty smiling manner. Although I was considerably his elder, there was never hint of that in our association. Indeed, in his company I felt myself grow young again, and enjoyed to the full his companionship; it was enough that I could cater to his abiding interest in ships and sailors, while he could at least humour me and my opinions of the printed page. He had already written a number of books and had long been recognized as a brilliant commentator and essayist. Gifted with a prodigious memory for the written word in extensive reading, his column in the *New York Evening Post* had become a jousting (often a jesting) court for high-spirited discussion of literary oddities. The almost fabulous Sir Kenelm Digby was often mentioned in *The Bowling Green*, and had become to many readers a stately figure-head for what was always a bright and never unkindly feature column.

As a thinly anonymous Kenelm Digby, Morley also wrote for *The Literary Review*, a weekly adjunct of the *New York Evening Post* devoted to book reviews and literary criticism, based largely in form and character on the London *Times Literary Supplement*. Later, when the *New York Evening Post* was acquired by a Philadelphian interest, *The Literary Review* was separately published by its former editor Henry Seidel Canby, assisted by Morley, William Rose Benét, and Amy Loveman, all of whom had worked so enthusiastically to found it a few years earlier. In its independency there came from it the idea of 'The Book of the Month Club' that has been so sedulously copied by many book-circulation agencies.

In the United States, and particularly in the ports of the eastern seaboard, the links of friendship are swiftly forged. Morley lost no time in counting me among his colleagues and kindred spirits. If at first I felt not quite at my ease in such an expert bookish fraternity, I was quickly reassured by a spontaneous and friendly acceptance. It appeared that I had come down-town to Vesey Street at an opportune moment for inclusion in a novel and special fellowship that was then forming in support of a *Bowling Green* contention. For some time the newspapers had been concerned with matters of food and drink—with notable emphasis on the evils of ill-considered alimentation under the rulings of the Eighteenth Amendment. This topic of the day was not unnoticed by 'Kenelm Digby', who, in his column, extolled the healthy pleasures of long hours at the table as opposed to the dyspeptic dangers of the swift stand-in at 'Quick Lunch' counters. Among other points, the *Bowling Green* disapproved of restaurants and other eating-houses where impetuous waiters dismantled the tables too early in the afternoon. The brief essay was titled—'How to Spend Three Hours for Lunch', and the column advised its readers to seek it at railway termini and other communal resorts where a less ruthless tempo prevailed and where opportunity and furniture were provided for the talk and restful discussion necessary to enliven good digestion. In a concluding passage it was hopefully suggested that a 'Three Hours for Lunch Club' should be formed.

With the return to the regular sailing schedules of peace-time, old routines came into force with us again. On the day before departure it was only necessary to conduct a general inspection of the ship to ensure that she was 'in all respects' ready for sea. Senior officials of the Company mustered to make the rounds, and after that considerable circuit had been made, what could be more appropriate than that the surveying party should sit down together to sample the creature comforts that had been freshly embarked for the use of passengers and crew on the voyage? . . . At this official occasion guests were often present—generally at the invitation of the Passenger or Publicity Departments of the Company. In port at New York I saw an opportunity of my own to promote more notice of the fine old veteran I commanded, and thought the gaiety of nations could well be served by adding to our table numbers when General Inspection had been completed. Gradually, and in this manner my fellows in 'Three Hours for Lunch'—so nobly conceived by Morley and the elder Benét in the course of a stroll on Manhattan's sea-front—became water-borne (if only at the dock) when the *Columbia* came in from sea and tied up at the western end of Twenty-third Street.

The novel and happy association thus formed went far to break up a sort of solitary habit the reserves and austerities of war service had stamped on me, as on so many other shipmasters I had known in the years of hostilities at sea. In these strenuous times I had been content when in port to limit my shore-going in neutral New York to the round of duty visits to the Company's down-town offices, the Custom House for entry or clearance, the meteorological eyrie a-top the Woolworth Building to seek guidance on weather prospects. On occasion I might ramble farther afield, to the chart-sellers for a new projection—or was that not merely for another appreciative glance at the effigy of an old-time able seaman supporting the bowl of a steering compass, a feature of Negus's shop window in sailor town that I remembered from my first visit to the Manhattan water-

front in 1897. . . . But now my days in port had become all too short
for the enterprises and engagements new companionships had conferred on me. Under friendly pilotage I steered on questing courses
through the City and came to know it well. In time I was accepted
—if not as a fellow New Yorker then surely as a 'visiting fireman'—
entitled to his part in its activities.

With the circle of acquaintanceship being constantly enlarged, I
came in touch with an American interest in my writing that I had not
thought would persist from 1910. Among the many sterling friends
I made at this time was G. M. Acklom, who was the literary adviser
to E. P. Dutton and Co., publishers in New York. He reminded
me that Dutton had published *The Brassbounder* in the United States
when it first came out. I had not remembered that sheets were sold
to the American firm by Gerald Duckworth of London at the time,
and the news that the book, long since out of print in the United
States, was still remembered there by a literary critic was vastly
encouraging. As a result of our meeting, Dutton offered to re-
publish the book if I would write an Introduction to the new
edition. I did that, and *The Brassbounder* met with some success. A
year later Duttons published *Broken Stowage*. It, too, did fairly
well. In slight degree I became known as a writer—but not very
well known. . . . O. O. Macintyre, whom I never met, described in
his column of the *Journal American*, a meeting with me in the
Algonquin Hotel at that date. He wrote that I was a big brawny
Scot, hirsute and bearded, speaking with a strong Scottish *brogue*!
I wonder who that can have been?

It was not long before the pundits of the Club thought of rules
and a Constitution. Admirable in its simplicity, this was devised
and somewhere around there lies an old Log Book, printed for use
in the vessels of the Anchor Line and having the Company's
'Standing Orders' prominently underlined. In it there is inscribed
in florid script—the whole designed by the best limner of our
membership, Franklin Abbott—the RULES of the THREE HOURS for
LUNCH CLUB. As I recall it, RULE ONE decreed—

'There shall be no rules.'

Chapter XXII

THE SCOTTISH CLANS

WE had met with fog and misty weather on all the voyage across from New York and Boston. Although winds had been light and the sea comparatively smooth, the low visibility and a gloomy, overcast sky had dampened the spirit of exercise on deck, and passengers had confined themselves to the brighter atmosphere of the lounges below. This was unfortunate, for the voyage was a special one and we were bearing back to their native land a large membership of the 'Order of Scottish Clans', a fraternal society of Scottish–Americans who had emigrated long back and had prospered in the United States. But the dismal days of the misty passage were quickly forgotten when we reached the northern Irish coast and saw the sun again, shining brightly on the hills of Donegal as we lay awhile off Moville to land an Irish contingent.

And now the *Columbia* lies anchored at the Tail of the Bank off Greenock awaiting a rise of tide to enter the river and proceed to Glasgow. It is a Sunday morning, a day of brilliant sunshine, and the outlines of the Cowal hills and the southern uplands stand out sharply against the cold azure of an almost cloudless sky. Distant in the north, the mountain peaks of Argyll are still snow-clad, for it is a day in spring and the heights take long to clear. A few ships ride with us in the anchorage, but we are early on the tide and there seems little activity in them: only the guard-boat of the Customs Service, quietly and methodically attending her business, gives sign of Sunday's lessened labours in the port.

But there is animation enough among our passengers, who, early astir on this exciting day of arrival in Scottish waters, have crowded to the upper decks to enjoy the smiling face of the land they have long remembered in the passage of the years; and the old ship is herself a-bustle with preparations for arrival at the dockside in

Glasgow, the point from which many of the sightseers set forth as emigrants to seek fortune abroad. It is perhaps especially for them that there is still reserved a source of nostalgic recollection to be savoured in the last brief stage of the voyage. 'The lone sheiling on a misty island' may be far distant in figment or in fact from the muddied river-bank of industrial Clydeside, but the memories that narrow stream of tide-water had the power to evoke could not easily be lost to our returning Scotsfolk. So, in groups or family parties or leaning solitary at the bulwarks, they indulge the memories of days long gone and await the moment when we shall weigh anchor and complete the voyage.

A rude music to suit the occasion of our passage in the Clyde is brewing up somewhere on the fore-deck among the piles of passengers' baggage taken from below for quick unloading at the quayside. Duncan Mackay, able-bodied seaman and the ship's best piper, is tempering the drones of his bagpipes to the right key and volume for playing the ship past the notable points of interest in our course up-river. But we are not yet under way, and the sighing groans and skirls his pipes emit have little resemblance to the stirring martial airs that later he will rouse up as we steer in mid-channel past the high crown of Dunbarton Rock, and the greening howes at Elderslie, then skirt the shipyards on the northern bank, disturb the Sunday quiet of the Rothesay Dock, and earn a welcome home from waterside occupants of the high tenements near Govan Pier. A short rest for him then, while he gathers his wind for a stirring and final rendering of *Gabhaidh Sinn an Rathad Mor* ('We'll take to the High Road'), as the fine old *Columbia*, after canting in the river, swings in to make fast at Yorkhill Quay and one more of her many faithful voyages is at an end.

That is the fine prospect I conjure up from the bridge—on tiptoe to be on my way—as I look out over the gaily expectant throng. . . . Only, a low smoky haze in the eastward—where lies the river channel up-stream—gives me pause. It is part of sailor lore to watch the weather in its growing. There is no wind. The haze lies broody and sinister as a violet cloud-bank, in the valley of the Clyde.

In slight degree I have been worried by the non-arrival of the river pilot when we anchored off Greenock. Usually Mr Bruce, the Company's special pilot, was prompt to meet us and often had clambered on board before the dust and rust from our anchor cables had settled as we brought up in the Bay. But not on this occasion, nor could I see any movement at the Pilot Station that would indicate an understanding of our early flag signals. Through binoculars, I see the pilot cutter still tied up at Princes Pier and beside her the Anchor Line's *Express*—an aged baggage tender. Adjusting focus, I can make out much coming and going on the quay. Clearly, something has not come up to expectations . . . and the tide is making fast.

When, about an hour later, the Company's tender surges alongside we are prepared for an alteration in the plan for disembarkation. A dense fog lies in the fairway beyond Dalmuir, they tell us, and it has been decided to land the passengers at the anchorage. The G. and S.W. Railway will lay on two special trains from Greenock and already we can see their river steamer *Mercury* casting off from the pier to head towards us. All baggage and the mails are to be transferred to the *Express*. . . . Disappointment at the change of plan is not confined to the passengers who had looked forward to the river journey and to reunion with their friends on Yorkhill Quay, but extends to the crew as well. Had the weather at the anchorage been more in keeping with the lack of visibility in the upper reaches of the river, the check to a happy homecoming might have been more patiently endured, but it is with ill grace that the ship's company set about the transfer of the baggage in the mocking clarity of such a brilliant sunny day. We are all in discontent as the passengers, waving good-byes, stream down the gangways to the decks of the waiting *Mercury*, while we are left to await the clearing of a fog that, as yet, is not apparent. But Able Seaman Duncan Mackay is not to be denied his *piobaireachd*, whatever the weather, after all the trouble he has had in mouthing reeds and tuning his pipes. As the exiles returning flock towards the gangways he cheers them by a spirited fingering of 'The Road to the Isles'.

Among the letters brought off by the tender is an instruction from the Marine Superintendent. I am to be relieved in the *Columbia* on arrival at Glasgow. Captain George B. Kelly, an old friend and former shipmate, will take over from me, and I shall be sent to Fairfield Shipyard to attend to the Company's interests in the fitting out of the new ship, the *Tuscania*, which I am slated to command when she is ready for sea in the autumn.

It was with a compound of regret and elation that I learnt of my promotion to a new ship, for I had been happily at one with the manageable old *Columbia* and had no great desire for a change. The new ship would be about twice her size, but I had never considered mere tonnage a special merit in a ship. Still, there were novel doings to be thought of in this transfer. Ocean cruises had been discussed as a source of profitable employment in the winter season when, normally, passenger traffic in the Atlantic was run at a loss, and the *Tuscania* was to be specially fitted up for such excursions. There was, too, in the comparative leisure of a longshore job while she was fitting out, the opportunity to work on *The Lookoutman*, a book of steamship types on which I had for some time been engaged. . . . Leaving consideration of all these matters to be reasoned in their turn, I go on deck again to scan that bank of cloud in the eastward that has robbed us of a notable homecoming on my last voyage in the *Columbia*.

It has risen no higher and still glooms right across the river channel where our course to Glasgow lies. The tide has turned, and yet no out-bound ships, having crept fearfully through the blanket in the upper reaches, emerge from under it and spur joyfully to open sea again. The shrilling of an engine whistle at Princes Pier gives notice that at least our contract with the 'Scottish Clans' has been faithfully performed and its members duly forwarded on their pilgrimage. But I am in ill content with this check to a voyage I had prosecuted with vigilance and not without professional strain. To exorcise my splenetic thoughts, I go below to my cabin to write these sad reflections—

NOT HERE

High Water again at 11.10 *p.m.*

A radiant moon stands in the eastern sky,
The stars shine purely in the lift o'erhead.
The calm and moonlit anchorage is studded by
Bright riding lights. Not here the dread
Fog wraiths and vapours that would have us bound
To slow and stop, then fearfully to steer
Pass endless obstacles, perhaps aground.
'Oh here,' they said? 'Maybe it's fine an' clear,
But—Goad!—Ye'll find it thick at Govan Pier!'

Christopher Morley

The High Seas Bookshop

Author and H. M. Tomlinson in the
Transylvania

William McFee

The Author, Joseph Conrad, and Muirhead Bone in the *Tuscania*
(*Photo by John H. Bone*)

Four Bone Brothers

Chapter XXIII

THE HIGH SEAS BOOKSHIP

LAID down at Fairfield Shipyard in 1919, the completion of the 17,000-ton *Tuscania*—the second large transatlantic ship of the Company's post-war programme—had been grievously delayed by adverse circumstances. In the war years few large and elaborately-equipped passenger vessels had been built, and it may well have been that the craftsmen needed time to recover the finer touches that, for a while, had been held in abeyance. Much ship material of special sort was hard to come by in the stress of construction the coming of peace had inspired. The workers, too, wearied by long exertion in the shipyards, were in a mood of unrest and labour disputes were frequent. For long periods the fine new ship which I was ultimately to command lay derelict and forsaken on the Govan foreshore, her gaunt uprights, on which birds were nesting, weathering to rusty spearheads as the days wore on. From time to time I had attended at the shipyard, but found little to report; then had been called away to take up some emergent sea duty. In the *Columbia*, I had almost forgotten to cast even a glance at her deserted shell as we passed inward or out on our voyages.

How different was her appearance when, having paid off in the old *Columbia* in 1922, I returned to the shipyard to stand-by until I could sail with a new command to sea. There was then the prospect of a maiden voyage in the autumn and the utmost effort was being made towards it. Instead of a rusted hulk on the launching ways there was now a shapely vessel, buoyantly afloat in the fitting-out basin and resplendent in the standard paintwork of the Anchor Line. Inboard, the gaunt red-leaded cubicles of the passenger accommodations had been transformed by paintwork and panelling to some correspondence with the designs already advertised to impress the voyager, the decks were laid and throughout the ship the greatest activity prevailed.

Upon the upper sections of passenger accommodation, Charles Holden's heterodox plans for decoration and furnishing of the public-rooms were being methodically carried out, and as the un-usual features of his treatment became plain to the craftsmen there employed, comment and discussion arose. Some doubt had been expressed when the designs of that distinguished architect were first submitted. For overlong it had been thought that the ocean traveller could only be induced to book passage by the resemblance of his quarters on shipboard to the quasi-theatrical elegance of a luxurious hotel. To that end, and to foster a belief in the rigid stability of shipping when at sea, maritime structures and furniture were designed to have as little 'ship' appearance as possible. Solid dark mahogany panels were no longer built in place in the lounges and other public-rooms; heavy arm-chairs, unfastened to the decks as a weatherly precaution, had taken the place of snug built-in alcoves and, in general, the sea traveller was expected to be un-aware—from his inboard surroundings—that his ship had put to sea.

Such a 'modernization' could have curious results. 'Oh, look, Mother,' a young lady was reported to have exclaimed in one of the lounges of a Superstoria Hotel at New York: 'If this big room only had a Renaissance fireplace at that end, it would look exactly like the cabin of our ship!'

'Hush, my dear,' the mother might well reply. 'I wish you wouldn't say things like that. I begin to feel queer already!'

No one could suffer such qualms in the public-rooms of the *Tuscania*, for she was ship-like in all her interior appointments. When the shipyard whistle sounded for the mid-day break, it was noticeable that not many of the workers employed on the upper decks rushed home to snatch a hasty meal, but preferred to eat the dinner-pieces they had brought with them in the seemly surround-ings they had fitted up. The most favoured rendezvous was the teak-panelled smoking-room of the first-class accommodation. Teak, the most durable of all woods, was rarely used for decoration in a ship, and this expanse was something novel to the eyes of the assembled craftsmen. The panelling was bare. No polish had been laid on to mar the beauty of the naked wood. Later, and shortly before we sailed, when my brother Muirhead's gift to the ship—a number of outstanding lithographs of Clyde shipbuilding—were hung in place, they added an uncommon interest to the simplicity of the walls. Many of the drawings had been made in Fairfield.

It may perhaps have been the atmosphere of achievement that now pervaded the shipyard which encouraged me to work steadily on my book of steamship types, their characters and capabilities, the sea trades in which they usually engaged. It was to be called *The Lookoutman*, and Jonathan Cape, the publisher, was urging me to complete it before I again put to sea. He had made arrangements for H. Hudson Rodmell to do line and scale drawings for it. A visit from this able young marine artist to Glasgow had settled most of our points of common interest, and nothing remained but that I should hurry to submit my text. Employing my days in a fairly constant survey of the technics of the shipbuilding yard and the leisure of the long summer evenings in writing of ships and their trades, I was up to time in delivery of the manuscript—a feat I have never since repeated. When discussing the date of publication, it occurred to me that the circumstance of a new ship and a new book by her master might prove a worth-while conjunction. The spirit of invention and resource I saw displayed around me in yard and drawing office probably led me to think of a novel feature in the new ship. At the time, much had been done by shipowners and builders to gain publicity for the many fine vessels then approaching completion or already at sea. Out and indoor swimming-baths, both permanent and portable, were coming into use; cocktail bars of garish appeal were the unruly rule in even the most conservative of shipping lines; nursery murals adorned the walls of children's play-rooms, a special deck was provided for exercising the passenger's pet animals. All these and other unusual features were widely advertised in the claims for profitable notice in the Press. I, who had handled square sail in ships whose only luxuries were notified as 'cow and piano carried', thought of a High Seas Bookshop in the new *Tuscania* and spoke of it in controlling quarters.

'A bookshop?' repeated Mr Stamp, Chief Draughtsman of the shipyard. 'We-ell, yes. If your people want it, there's still time to rattle one up.' Rapidly, he drew some lines on the back of an old envelope (we were together in a far corner of the ship) and handed me a rough sketch. It was a bookstall or news-stand he had drawn: a shelf or two and a small space for an attendant to stand—and remain standing.

'Oh, no,' I protested. 'Not at all like that. We shall want a real bookshop. One with cases and shelves. Not a counter like that. A table perhaps, and a chair or two where the customers can sit down to examine the stock and perhaps talk about books with the attendant.'

Mr Stamp eyed me indulgently, but with a shade of mistrust. He was a good associate who had humoured me on many occasions when some minor alteration had called for decision. I had quickly realized that he was the one to be approached in the first instance when changes were afoot. 'To talk books with the attendant, eh? The attendant! One more addition to the crew, another berth to be found somewhere. And a table and chairs? A service indent.' My friend rubbed his ear in puzzlement; this was clearly an odd request. 'Gosh! What kind of an attendant? What does a *booksailor* look like, anyway?'

'Purser staff,' I suggested, but without conviction, for I had not then figured out all the commitments of the matter. 'He would have to be a special person, knowing books in general and able to talk about them. 'Yes. Purser staff,' I repeated. 'He should rank with an assistant purser at the least.'

Smilingly, Mr Stamp returned to the drawing office, whence, in due course, a formidable blue-print appeared. With it there came a reference digest of profit or loss in the allotment of passenger space to serve a purpose that could only be considered an amenity on shipboard. Profit was nil, and the loss anticipated considerable. The project met with heavy opposition from many quarters. (I was said to be lining a cosy nest for my own retirement from the sea.) But the plan—chimerical, as it appeared—was aided from an unexpected source. The Resident Director of the Cunard–Anchor Line (as then we were affiliated) was visiting the home offices at this time. Sir Ashley Sparks, always of liberal ideas, thought my project had its possibilities, and the plan went through. We got our bookshop in the ship and I set about to find a suitable *booksailor* who would put up with the somewhat cramped quarters we were able to provide.

After exhaustive trials, the *Tuscania* sailed on her maiden voyage on 16th September 1922. Under instruction to rumble in the gears that had been newly cut for experiment in double-reduction Curtis-Brown geared turbines, we made a leisurely passage out to New York, which received us with the courtesy and friendliness so customarily bestowed on all new ships entering at the Hook. In the Hudson River, the City's fireboats sprayed us a second baptism and the steam whistles of the moored and anchored ships sounded out a welcome to the new-comer. On the day following there was an unusual note in the text the ship-news reporters put before their readers. While much was published about the vessel's size, potential speed, and superb passenger accommodations, much was made of the new feature—the first of its kind to be established in a ship at sea. The High Seas Bookshop was notably introduced.

A news-stand or bookstall would have passed unnoticed, for these are fugitive fixtures on shipboard as a rule, only set up on sailing days as a convenience for embarking passengers, then vanishing until the next sailing day. But the quiet atmosphere of a well-furnished bookshop was something refreshingly new to the hardened pressmen. Mr W. M. Parker, a scholarly compatriot whom we had signed on as 'Master's Clerk' before sailing from Glasgow, had many questions to answer regarding the special purpose of such an unusual department in the ship. He claimed no special purpose for his charge other than the distribution of good literature, but suggested that there might be an international exchange in the ship's far voyaging. He had the hope of introducing the literature of one country to another. He was on the point of indenting for a selection of works by American authors, he confided, pointing to the publisher's lists stacked on his desk.

It is not often the New York shipping newsmen call over their photographer colleagues to take exposures of a shop-sign on shipboard, but that of the High Seas Bookshop was thought sufficiently unusual to merit inclusion with the wide-angled illustrations in the Sunday supplements. The sign, painted by Tom Gentleman, a Scottish artist, was set up above the deck window of the bookshop. It depicted a rubicund and portly master mariner straddling wide-legged on the slanted deck of a vessel reeling in tempestuous seas, yet sufficiently interested in the book he holds in hand to ignore the perils of the deep. Modesty withholds me from disclosing the title of the volume.

Chapter XXIV

TUSCANIA

THE post-war shipbuilding programme of the Anchor Line envisaged five ships of large tonnage, of which two vessels— the *Tuscania* and *Transylvania*—were intended for service between the United States and Mediterranean ports, a trade the Company had been engaged in for over fifty years. It was confidently expected that when peace came a great flood of emigration would call for larger and better-appointed ships than the intermediate freighters we had previously employed. In these sturdy yet deep-laden and crowded cargo ships the lot of the emigrant was not one to be envied, and in about 1905 the Italian Government took steps to regulate the trade. All ships of whatever nationality engaged in it were brought closely under survey in Italian ports, stores and provisions were officially inspected, and a *Commissario Regio*—generally a medical doctor—was appointed to sail with the ship on emigrant voyages.

On our second voyage the *Tuscania* was routed from New York to Genoa to undergo this necessary survey before embarking Italian emigrants. We were then to sail from Genoa to Naples with a group of local officials on board to conduct a sort of trial trip on that coastwise passage. Among the officials there was a body of Italian naval officers—navigators and engineers—but I cannot remember that they made record of any defects, for apparently they all found a sufficiency of interest in the personable Americans who had booked passage with us for the round voyage. Before arrival at Naples we had established our seaworthiness, and when we hauled alongside and berthed at the Molo Commerciale all seemed fair to embark a large emigrant booking for the land of promise.

But when Mr Payne, the Company's local manager, came aboard to welcome the grand new ship to his field of operations, he did not seem at all confident that he could load her to full capacity. Certainly there was the prospect of a good cargo, and the port was crowded by emigrants seeking passage to the United States, but a sudden adverse situation had arisen and he was gravely concerned. What had idly been thought no more eventful than a flaunt of Latin effervescence had grown swiftly and become a major movement. The 'March on Rome' had brought about many changes in the Italian Government. Already, the Fascisti had gained control of most of the Ministries, and even that of Shipping (with its international ramifications) had been forced to accept the narrow nationalistic creed symbolized by a strapped bundle of punitive rods. At the moment our permit to embark Italian emigrants was withheld; exporters were becoming apprehensive about the shipment of their goods, while impassioned young 'blackshirts' paraded the streets of the waterfront shouting aloud for all emigration to cease and for export cargo to be loaded in Italian ships only. The situation had not yet reached such extreme conclusions, but it was evident to Mr Payne that only the scarcity of Italian shipping prevented the application of an immediate embargo in Italian seaports on foreign transport of Italian goods and emigrant passengers. After some days of indecision, we did sail westward from Naples to New York with a small cargo and a limited booking of passengers not listed as *emigranti*, but the prospects did not seem good for a continuance in the service for which the ship had been designed.

But shipping, like the tide, has its ebb and flow. Shrewd observers at the passage office in New York, looking about for alternative shipping business, noted the trends of a rising and profitable holiday exodus from the United States. After the long war-time restrictions in oversea travel, many Americans showed an eagerness to sail abroad and the possibility of employing the ship on pleasure cruises came under discussion; it was an enterprise in which the Anchor Line had not before engaged but one for which the new ship was admirably equipped. A well-known tourist agency having worldwide connections took an interest with us in a Mediterranean cruise and in June 1923, the *Tuscania* sailed on her first voyage of this description, a venture she was often to repeat. The new departure had the merit of keeping the new ship and her claims for attention within the purview of the Italian Ministry of Shipping, in the hope that saner counsel might someday prevail. To that end, the itinerary for our Mediterranean cruises included Genoa, Leghorn, Naples, and Venice. Frequent calls at these familiar ports gave us at least the opportunity to display at the masthead the Company's 'house flag', which had always been well known in Italian harbours. Perhaps, in that way, something was done to hearten and restore confidence in the shipping agencies of the ports who had served us well throughout half a century. But the most they could do for us now was to attend to the shipment of cargo in smaller ships and occasionally to cater to sightseeing trips within the radius of the ports. The dollar profits of the tourist trade made cruise ships' visits acceptable to the Fascisti.

In this new and, as then we thought it, temporary employment we sailors had much to learn. The stiffly formal routines of the Atlantic crossing differed greatly from the easier social manners of a long-extended cruising voyage. Setting out on a transatlantic passage of a week's duration there was always the urgent aim of a tightly scheduled proceeding—to sail, to progress, to arrive—and friendly contact with the passengers was brief. In any case, frank fellowship was discouraged, for it was long the custom in Atlantic liner services to prohibit all social amenities between crew and passengers: indeed, I can remember at least one passage in the Company's now-forgotten Rule Book: '*Subject to answering questions politely, officers are forbidden to associate unnecessarily with the passengers.*'

The Captain was of course exempted from compliance with such a harsh ruling, but where he was to learn about the social duties expected of him in later years was nowhere laid down. To attain command he would have to serve for long years in junior ranks, and the rigid system that then held him moodily to his quarters when not on duty was hardly a suitable training for a future shipmaster. Fortunately for those of us who had served in the passenger-ships of the Indian service the 'rule' was never seriously enforced there, and pleasant relations with cruise passengers were not difficult to establish when the early courtesies of question and reply were exchanged. It was not long before we found ourselves—all hands of us— strangely placed in the collective position of host aboard the ship, amazingly enfranchised in the relation of crew to passengers. On the part of the cruise voyager much the same spirit prevailed. The influence of the ship herself brought that about—even to the extent of joining in praise of her and pitying the unfortunates who elected to sail in other vessels.

One could find solid commercial reasons for the general practice of bringing a cruise ship into a foreign port at dawn and sailing her again at dusk or in the darkness, but I like to think there is more in such a happy practice than the logistics of a carefully-planned itinerary. Some influence of the *genius loci* may perhaps affect the planner, for how better can the spirit of a place be felt than when dawn rolls up the curtain? I am thinking of Madeira at the moment and of the approach to the open roadstead of Funchal from westward. Landfall is made by the flash of Pargo Light while it is yet dark, then the prudent and sight-loving mariner will slow the engines down to make easy progress along the southern coast aiming to anchor in the port at daybreak. Coming in quietly with the daylight there is time, and the moment to see the glorious wooded island growing to the eye as though it had never been revealed in that way before—

> Then daylight came. The placid ocean stirred,
> Wakened, and ruffled gently. From the north,
> Where lay the harbours of a restless sky,
> The freshening wind drave radiant galleons forth.
> Brave aerial fleets with rose topgallants spread
> Holding their stately courses in the blue
> Towards fair southern ports; save one proud ship,
> Deep freighted with the precious morning dew,
> That stranded on the peak . . . frail barque of faery cloud . . .
> And veiled both mount and valley in its foundering shroud.

Chapter XXV

JOSEPH CONRAD

IN a former chapter I have related an early correspondence with Joseph Conrad to whom, a little fearful of his opinion, I had sent a copy of *The Brassbounder*. He was good enough to reply and an infrequent, and to me precious, exchange of letters followed throughout the years; but it was not until the winter of 1919 that I met him for the first time. The occasion was a gathering in honour of the Merchants' Service (as then we were described) given by the University Club in Liverpool. I had written *Merchantmen-at-Arms*, a narrative of personal experiences in the war of 1914–18, and it was as a representative of the Service I was invited south from Glasgow to be a guest. Conrad was in Liverpool at the time, and he also had been invited. Many Liverpool shipowners were present, and the dignitaries of the University made a friendly show of interest in the master mariners they so hospitably entertained.

Conrad's appearance did not agree at all with my preconception of a robust sailor and a gifted and successful author. Here was a reflectively quiet man, obviously apprehensive of a public dinner occasion. He, too, had been asked to speak. He confided to me that he was nervous, never having spoken at such a gathering before. Nor had I, but it was perhaps my temerity in presenting the merchant sailor's cause in the hearing of so many learned dons and shipowners that encouraged him to speak. As I remember it, he spoke of the resolute character of seamen with whom he had sailed in his sea days under square sail. . . . All I said had best be forgotten, for it was a long dinner with fine wines, but I did get attention when forecasting a strange future at sea in the merchants' ships. I said that in the years to come there would be little need for captains in ships. The whole business of navigation and administration would be done by the shipowner himself using wireless control from the pier-head. I instanced the hypothetical case of such a remote controller seated in his office at Liverpool, scanning the wireless situation and its picture of his ship out at sea, then suddenly reaching for the desk telephone to call up a fellow shipowner in London:

'Oh, hullo! *Hullo!*—Oh, Jones! Your infernal *Procastria* and my *Fadantic* are closing in mid-Atlantic. There's a fellow in yours: cook, I think—see his high white hat—craning his neck through a port-hole. If you don't do something quickly, he'll get his damned block knocked off!'

Since that date I had not seen Conrad, although our signals were still exchanged. I recall an occasion when I incurred a mild rebuke from him. A Russo-American, Karrakis, whose writing I thought good, had adapted Conrad's *Under Western Eyes* as a stage play which I was foolish enough to mention in a letter after Karrakis had sailed across in my ship for the purpose of submitting his adaptation to the author. (Mrs Conrad told me later that the morning my letter arrived, J. C. continued brushing his hair fiercely for at least ten minutes.) He wrote—

'. . . The stage version of the *Western Eyes* has reached me through Pinker. I am very sorry that Mr K. should have taken this trouble. Of all my novels this, especially, is the one I do not want anybody to touch. If there is ever any adaptation it will be done by myself.'

Early in February 1923, Frank N. Doubleday, the American publisher (known as 'Effendi' to his friends), told me at a Three Hours Lunch in the *Tuscania* that he had hopes of a visit from Conrad in the spring. The information was confidential, Effendi said, for J. C. had a horror of publicity and wished to avoid it if he did make the Atlantic passage. Effendi knew that I had often urged Conrad to sail out with me, and thought that I should again stress that invitation. I did, and received a glad reply—

17th February
'I was very glad to receive your friendly letter. I confess that as soon as that project of a visit to the U.S. came up for consideration I formed the intention to stow myself away on board the ship you commanded. In my time the stowaways (to Sydney) were kindly treated.

Seriously, my dear Bone, I am very grateful to you for the

suggestion. The matter however is not quite certain. There is always the possibility of a gout attack knocking me out; and I am sorry to say that there may be the possibility of another operation on my poor wife's knee. I should not like to be away. This is the only reason why I haven't yet rushed to secure my passage in the *Tuscania*. Your brother is a great artist.' (I had told Conrad in my letter that my brother Muirhead was sailing out to New York with me on the 21st April.) 'I don't know his work as well as I ought to do—but enough to have a great regard and admiration for it on something more than a superficial impression.'

A month later, on my return from America, I found all matters confirmed, and Conrad appeared to be in high spirits at the prospect of sailing out, if one may judge from the cheerful tone of his letter I received upon arrival at Glasgow—

'As I imagine you will be home in a day or two I drop you a few lines to tell you that I intend to apply for my ticket (return) on Monday next, as I will be in town that day. I think I will get to Glasgow on the 20th April as I should like to call on James Lithgow whose acquaintance I made in 1917 and who was my eldest boy's Battery-major for some years in France. . . . I look forward immensely to the passage with you and Mr Muirhead Bone. What gave me immense pleasure is that you should have written first to me just as I was preparing to write to you. What delayed me for a day was a doubt as to the name of the ship. . . . Last December Doubleday told me of having met you at Gibraltar in command of the *Berengaria*.

'. . . I intend after getting my dunnage together to sit close at home up to the 17th, working at my novel. On that day, I will attend the National Life Boat Institution Meeting, it being the centenary. After that I will allow myself two more days to say good-bye to various people before starting on my voyage of discovery; for N. America will be as novel a sight to me as it was to Cabot a few centuries ago.'

Conrad duly appeared at Glasgow on the night before sailing, but his purpose to avoid the attentions of the pressmen was not furthered by his journey north. Indeed, much was made of his preference for a passage in an eight-day ship across the Atlantic. We sailed from the Clyde on the 21st April, 1923, and had bright cold weather on the early days of the passage. For this I was thankful, for only in such clear weather could I go below to enjoy the company of my friends. We had a smallish passenger list on that occasion and I could devote myself to my brother and Conrad—with whom he was quickly on the best of terms.

I had thought that J. C. would be interested in the development of shipping and seafarers, since he retired from active service in 1896, but whether the old trade secrets that he knew so well remained with him when we sailed together in the *Tuscania* I could not easily determine. During the forenoon of our first day wide at sea I had taken him to the navigation bridge on a tour of inspection. Quickly, he had understood the use and purpose of the many mechanical devices there installed, but he seemed not at all impressed by their manifest efficiency. It may be that he did not appreciate the need for instancy in curbing the not unknown misconducts of a vessel of such large size and power. He betrayed a faint displeasure that we had come so greatly to rely upon mechanical power to do much that, in his sea days and mine, had to be manhandled by sailor stratagem and strength and resolution. I wondered then if he thought of us in our new estate to have become not hard enough for the rigours of the sea, that we were not quite the men he had known and had portrayed so faithfully. . . . Strangely, for one so understanding and cultured in himself, it was the 'gentility' and apparent confidence of the new ship manners that seemed to disquiet him the most.

I recall an occasion when he was comfortably seated across from me in the day-cabin. It was noon by zonal time and, as we sat, the sweet notes of 'eight bells' sounded out from the bridge above us. Conrad rose with an air of apologetic concern. Had he been keeping me from my duties? Twelve noon, as he remembered it, was the time for the master to set the day in its place and attend to the ship's reckoning. I reassured him. It was a fine clear day and I was at my leisure. In a little while the officer of the watch, having been relieved, would come below to hand in his finding of the position of the ship. Upon hearing of this, Conrad asked me—with charming diffidence—did I not myself take 'sights' by the sextant and work them out as always he remembered doing? I said of course

I did, but largely to keep my hand in. We had at least five excellent navigation officers who could not all make mistakes in their calculations at the same time. In any case, I said, apparent noon at ship (the time for observing the meridian altitude of the sun) would not be until 12.40 p.m. of our current zonal time. If he liked again to use the sextant at sea, he was welcome to the use of mine. We would go on deck together when the time came, I suggested.

He pondered long this explanation. The keeping of zonal time was doubtless something new to him—as almost it was to me in 1923. I surmised that he would maybe be recalling the anxious days of 'running the easting down' in high seas between the Cape and the Leeuwin when he served in square sail. If that were so, I could construct the picture that was in his mind, for often I had seen or taken part in it. The 'Old Man' and his mate, broad-legged to meet the surges of a reeling ship, sheltered behind a scrap of a weather-cloth, with sextants in hand to establish a meridian contact. Time and again they would raise and lower their instruments in the effort to distinguish the sun's visible rim between the shafts of racing storm-cloud. And when at length agreement was reached, the master would say—firmly and with emphasis—'Make eight bells, Mister!' No one but he would give the order, and it would be repeated by the mate in a bull-mouthed shout—challenging the uproar of the westerly winds—to cause the look-out on the fore-end to clang the double strokes on the ship's bell. Thus, the day would be ordered, the watch relieved, and the entry be made in the ship's log.

It was a day of boisterous weather. A moderate southerly gale was causing the ship to 'bite' to windward, and as we passed through the wheelhouse Conrad noticed that the steersman was carrying considerable helm against that tendency. He recalled the time long ago when he would have trimmed or shortened sail to meet such a situation. I remarked that we could neither trim nor shorten the surface we exposed to the wind, for steel could not be furled, and I took him out to the wing of the bridge, whence a good view could be had of the great beam seas running up and crashing on the plating of the hull as the *Tuscania* sped on her course. As one fascinated, he looked down from the height on the maelstrom boiling and curling alongside. We stood at about the height of a clipper's top-masthead, I told him. He agreed that we had to sail on with all our 'kites' set as the builders had planned them. . . . But science and technics had not yet superseded Palinurus, and I think Conrad was heartened to hear that even the largest and most powerful of steamships had to be 'nursed' like any other ship in the great gales and terrific seas of the North Atlantic, and that, though infrequent, it was not unknown for them to be 'hove to' in the height of such a tempest, just as the windjammers were forced to do in the pitch off Cape Horn.

After three days at sea, the weather thickened and the friendly conversations to which I had looked forward were ruled out. But in Muirhead I had a good brotherly remembrancer on all the topics of their constant interchange. I had arranged that the staterooms they occupied should be adjacent—indeed, they formed part of a suite known to the purser's department as a 'super and bath' reserved for wealthy travellers. In these quarters, the twain sat up to all hours of the morning talking happily of art and literature—or even adventuring into the ways of sailoring—a subject upon which my brother was surprisingly well informed. On these occasions Muirhead made many portrait drawings of Conrad, of which at least one was subsequently made a drypoint etching. At the sitting, the artist remarked, 'I wonder if this is the first time you've ever had a picture made of you at sea?' Conrad, somewhat surprised at the thought, admitted it was. Photographs, perhaps, there had been many, he said, and his disapproving grimace as he said that arrested the artist's pencil. But Conrad had yet to hear a commanding news photographer at New York shout out above all lesser clamour—

'Take aff y'er hat, Mister Kahnradh!'

Squeezing modestly into New York between the movements of the *Leviathan* and the *Aquitania*, we discovered that the ship-news reporters had ignored these great ships to hurry to our pier and welcome the great Polish writer to the shores of America. Not only that. Politics were involved in the arrival of a simple truthful interpreter of life that lay within his knowledge.

As we hauled in to the north side of Pier 54, checking on the head-line to bring her stylishly alongside, I could glimpse a flurry of red-and-white skirts on the upper storey of the pier. Dancers in national Polish colours. It was a handsome gesture, I thought. . . . But I thought, too, of another word on that as I watched the reception committee processing to the gangway. I had said to Conrad how extraordinary it was for him, a Polish aristocrat, to elect to tar his hands in a merchant ship, and to become a British subject. He said—

'Bone! I am more British than you are. You are only British because you could not help it.'

Chapter XXVI

THE BOOKSAILOR

UPON arrival at New York in the summer of 1923, the ship
was undermanned to the extent of a 'Master's Clerk', and
the High Seas Bookshop had not been opened for business
on the outward voyage. Before sailing from the Clyde, Mr Parker
had decided that sea life was not for him, and there had been no
time to engage a suitable substitute. From New York the ship was
scheduled to make a lengthy cruise voyage to the Mediterranean,
and I had looked forward to the sales of cruise literature to offset its
already considerable debit. To this end we had laid in a substantial
stock of guide-books, travel literature of general interest, and also
what we thought a profitable 'line' of *My Cruise Abroad* (a travel
diary) in expensive bindings. Something would have to be done.

I spoke of the vacancy when my friends came aboard to greet me
on arrival, hopeful that someone among them would volunteer to
sail with me in the emergency. Nor was I disappointed. But it is
unusual for an elderly and highly senior officer in any service to
take up a position of lesser responsibility than that he had held in a
ship before, and when William McFee told me I need look no further
for an applicant, I was astonished—and highly delighted. I had
known, of course, that he had 'swallowed the anchor' (or whatever
its equivalent in a ship's engine room may be) and had retired to the
beach to ruminate—as his Mr Spenlove does—on the curious
behaviour of his shipmates, but I had not thought of him returning
to sea as a booksailor. But he was in earnest, and we sailed away
together.

His sudden urge to 'go down to the sea again' did not pass unnoticed by the ship-news reporters, and much was written about his
object in signing for service in a cruise ship and that in the capacity
of clerk in charge of a bookshop. Mr S. T. Williamson of the *New
York Times* wrote of it—

'There is something unique about a marine engineer turned author; there is something unique about a sailor turned farmer; but a hitherto dependable thesaurus goes sailing out of the window for failure to raise "unique" to the nth power and give an appropriate term to a farmer-author-marine engineer who has turned bookseller and in a floating bookshop at that.

'It is a question which is more interesting; when Mr McFee brings out a new book, or when he gets a new job? Probably the latter is the more important, for it supplies new inspiration, new scenes and new plots, that later find their way into print. ... So, what is going to result from his latest venture, his leaving his farm at Westport, Conn., to sell books to Cooks tourists? ... Imagination can picture the spectacle of an ocean liner Captain and a former Chief Engineer, both recognized novelists, carrying on a sea-lawyer argument over the selection to be made in wholesale purchases of Tauchnitz and Paris paper reprints.'

No sea-lawyerly disputations obtruded upon the harmony of our respective offices as the voyage progressed. The High Seas Bookshop was still a novel feature on shipboard to me and, until the signing on of a fully-qualified marine engineer to take charge of it, I had not ventured far in its matters of management. The former attendant, whose distaste for the sea had occasioned the vacancy, had done that for me. But now it was thought that 'standing orders' should be composed and enjoined forthwith. Hours of Business was a first matter to come up when, clear of soundings, I sent my compliments to the 'Master's Clerk' in the expectation that he would quickly join me in my cabin on the bridge and help to celebrate the passing of the day—for 'ship' days end at noon, when the sun is well over the fore-yard. But McFee did not appear. Busy, he said he was, and a written order had to be made out that the Bookshop in the ship was to be closed for business at twelve noon and not re-opened until two or three. Then, again, at our first port of call, Madeira, arrangements had to be made for our joint excursion ashore; for it had been agreed that we should not compete with the booksellers of the friendly ports we visited and that our booksailor should turn his key when he heard the anchor 'let go'!

The arrangements worked well for him and me. Only there was

one derangement. Before sailing from Glasgow I had been expecting my book *The Lookoutman* to be published while I was at sea on this cruise voyage, and had made arrangements with the publisher to print a small special edition to be sold only in the Bookshop of the *Tuscania*. A consignment of this edition with its title-page boldly imprinted as 'Published at the High Seas Bookshop' was due to be sent to the ship at Naples. It did not arrive in time before we sailed, and my hope of setting up a novel naval precedent in launching a new publication 'off soundings' did not work out quite as I had planned. But the 'Clerk' I had signed in charge of that department was alert to his responsibilities. Remembering past disappointments in non-receipt of long-awaited replacements needed in his engine-room, the 'clerk' made his protest in a shipshape and seaman-like manner.

> 'Sir, [he wrote to the publisher] I am instructed by the Master to call your attention to the grave inconvenience and annoyance caused by the non-arrival at Naples of the special edition of *The Lookoutman* for the High Seas Bookshop. I need not labour the point that the disappointment of a large number of patrons who had been informed of the advent of the new volume has been correspondingly profound. It is this sort of thing, the Master desires me to state, that gives seamen so unfavourable an impression of conduct and inconsiderate morality ashore, and preserves them from a premature retirement.'

A sentient rebuke that Jonathan Cape thought worthy of wide quotation throughout the trade!

The parcel of books that had been so eagerly awaited followed us on the coast to Alexandria. By that time the Bookshop had no customers, for all our passengers had there disembarked to go on an extended side trip to Cairo and the Nile. When they rejoined later, a wave of economy had set in: there was little business, and McFee had time enough on his hands to settle all accounts of his not unpleasant adventure as a Booksailor.

The manning of the Bookshop by casual labour did not make for profitable operation, however much the notice taken of it might be valued in a factual assessment. My cruising passengers had rarely much tolerance for high seas and adverse weather: the west- and eastbound seasons in the North Atlantic, during which the *Tuscania* had to take her turn between cruise charters, was looked upon by the casual booksailor as *the* season of retirement to the beach and, the Bookshop derelict for a while, I was left at the end of the voyage to face a stern accountant in Glasgow who wanted to know what new scheme I had in mind to entertain my longshore friends at the expense of the Anchor Line.

When Miss Ilah Niehoff signed on at New York and took on duty as a 'Master's Clerk', I had no thought that she would prove any different from the others who had sailed in the ship for a brief period that was largely sight-seeing, but the sea must have been strongly dominant in her ancestry, for she delighted in it and endured its ragings as she enjoyed its calms, like any confirmed seafarer. I had known her uncle, Stephen Pigott, who was a neighbour at Helensburgh, where my home was. He was the representative of the American Curtis–Brown Company in the United Kingdom and later became Managing Director of John Brown's great shipyard at Clydebank, being responsible—among other feats—for the construction of the *Queen Mary* and *Queen Elizabeth*. He was knighted on the outbreak of war in 1939.

His sister, Mrs Elizabeth Niehoff, often voyaged with her two daughters to Scotland, and we had come to know them well. So, when I arrived out in New York before sailing on a cruise in 1924 with the post in the Bookshop vacant, I thought of it as a lucky opportunity for Ilah, whose leaning to literature and to books I knew, to sail abroad. It was particularly a happy chance, for I had my own daughter sailing with us as a favoured passenger on the round voyage back to Glasgow, and the company of a shipmate, whom she already knew so well, added to her anticipations of happiness on the extended voyage. Freda had just completed her term at the School of Art in Glasgow, where she had learnt wood-engraving. A voyage to the United States and on to the Mediterranean and the Middle East was a fitting reward for the years of study and gave every opportunity for exercise of her talent as a book-illustrator.

When Ilah took up her duties in the Bookshop she found it overstocked with much that was unsaleable—for we had too many literary advisers, myself included, eager to laud their own specific tastes, and some of the books on the shelves were rather dead-weight for a pleasure cruise. Still, she had many brighter volumes to offer to the passengers and, being clever and informative, the High Seas Bookshop under her care quickly became a centre of attraction in the ship. The fortunes of the Bookshop—while never of serious account—improved under her skilful management. Not only in the choice of books and the discussion of their merits did this new Master's Clerk consider duty at an end. Getting to know the ship and the ways of shipboard practice, she could be relied upon as a traveller's aid at sea to the less pushful voyager.

Another unusual service this resourceful lady took on was that of the Master's 'remembrancer'. I had for long been bedevilled by lapses of memory where former passengers were concerned, and had had my hot moments of embarrassment when greeting them anew. But that was all quickly attended to when the new booksailor came to sail with us. Scanning the passenger lists at the outset of a voyage, she could always be relied upon to remind me of a former friendship or of a mutual interest a passenger and I had discovered on an earlier ship meeting.

Chapter XXVII

THE CLUB'S FLAGSHIP

AT New York in the summer of 1923 I attended a ceremony that was unusual in the shipping world—the re-dedication of a ship. It was conducted in a spirit of high holiday such as one would look for at a virgin launching of a ship, although the *Sophie* of Sandefjord was already a veteran with forty years of active seafaring to her credit. I had not heard of a similar ceremony in all the years of my service. Certainly, the re-naming of ships is quite a common occurrence, but it has never been a tradition of the sea that such a purely business expedient should rank with the natal baptism and be accorded the same honours, be celebrated with the same rejoicings.

Sailors do not view an interference with the given name of a vessel as praiseworthy: such affairs are usually carried through in an atmosphere charged with dread of unnecessary publicity. Of course, there are the clear and well-understood cases of transfer to another national flag, or the purchase by a shipping line having as a trade asset some distinctive phonetic or classified grouping of vessels' names; but in general the policy of altering a ship's name has the very material aim of confusing or even concealing her identity. For some reason, be it deed or misdeed, a ship may become notorious. Shippers, underwriters, ship-chandlers and storemen, charterers and shipping-brokers view her with mistrust. 'She turns out poor cargoes'—'she is unlucky in her averages'—'she loads late and makes long passages'—in all, she has lost credit in the shipping world and her owners are anxious to discard her as an unprofitable adventure. Her buyers, in an effort to start her out anew, decide to rename her. They insert a brief advertisement in a quiet corner of the maritime press and, no objection being raised, her name is chipped off by a dockside workman and repainted. There is no ceremony about it, no fuss—but sailors recognize her by the ship's bell, which is rarely re -engraved.

In connection with the ceremony I attended there were certainly no just causes or impediments proclaimed. The three-masted full rigged sailing-ship *Sophie* (ex-*Inveruglas*) had no reason to apologize for her past on the day we held holiday and called her the *Tusitala*, in honour of one who loved ships greatly and who also had experienced a change of name, becoming 'Tusitala' (the teller of tales) instead of Robert Louis Stevenson.

It is true that such an incident as a change of name was no novelty to the old ship, for she had been re-named twice before. Contracted for as one of the beautiful 'Sierras'—swift, white-hulled, white-sparred, white-winged—I do not think that she ever took a sailing in that Line: in 1883 steamships had begun to smoke the stately clippers out of the favoured sea trades. As the *Inveruglas* she became a noted flyer in the Australian wool trade. Then, sometime in the great discard of the nineties, when steel came out to sea in the shape of steamer tramps, and only Scandinavians held lingering faith in canvas and square rig, she passed under the Norwegian flag, to be renamed the *Sophie*. (For what had her Norse buyer to do with a remote Highland glen when, doubtless, there was his wife or daughter standing a-tiptoe in plea for a gallant and shapely namesake?)

Certainly, the old ship had no need to blush for her seafaring in all the forty years elapsed since first she put to sea. I can picture her then, about the last of the fine-lined sailing-ships; for the windjammers of a later date were remarkable for swollen lines—a futile effort to compete with steam in which speed was sacrificed to greater carrying capacity. One feels assured that she was loaded with the greatest care on her maiden voyage. Her builders—the famous Steels' of Greenock—jealous for her reputation, would even be prepared to ship a few tons of pig-iron abroad in her, to ensure that her designed sailing trim of four important inches by the stern was not miscalculated in the pressure of events at her first loading.

With what expectations would the Master of the *Inveruglas* survey his new command and watch her behaviour under canvas when the paddle-tug that had towed her to sea cast off and he crowded sail on her? He would judge her by the standards of his last vessel and, as 'last' ships are ever the darlings of the seaman's heart, the new ship would be hard driven in her maiden efforts. The log would spin a frequent and merry reel to measure her rate o' knots in each new trimming of sail and sweating up of halyard or brace. New ropes, new tackle-blocks, new leads in the running gear! New canvas stretching visibly: new mates, new hands! One can imagine the sailormen at the ropes 'chanteying' all the news of it—putting into their hauling songs the protests they dared not utter in prose. On that first day out all hands would be on deck for long-continued duty and weary of the strain of it when, at last, the 'Old Man'—noting the clean run of the passing water under the counter—would shout 'Belay!' to the last dry pull.

Forty years. A long sea life for a hard-driven wool-clipper of her type! Steels' built well; she has long out-lasted the parish-rigged barques that came after her: poor nondescript cross-breeds, squat-masted and over-sparred, beamed to gross proportions so that they could neither stay nor steer; undermanned, and breaking the hearts of countless gallant seamen.

Forty years—a brave sea life. Fair winds and foul, calms and great gales: leaning away to the fine caress of the 'trades' or stagger-ing under low canvas in the heave of the roaring forties. Running her easting down, reeling the miles in the white-lashed fury of long southern seas! . . . Cruel but exhiliarating sea-work aloft with frozen sails and cordage in the winter passage round the Horn. Fog, and ice on the Grand Banks: hove-to on the edge of soundings in the Channel, or labouring in a great gale off Hatteras. Monsoon in Indian seas, a cyclone at the Sand Heads, and a twelve-foot 'bore' in the Hughli River. . . . Lone calls at the island outposts of the world, at Pitcairn, Ascension, St Helena. . . . Brief glimpses of Diego Ramirez or the Ildefonsos; perhaps a misty vision of the Crozets or Paul's Rock standing out sharp on the horizon in illimitable blue.

Forty years! The ports of the world would know her cargoes in all that time. What marketings and ventures and exchanges would be affected by her landfalls and departures! Roving the oceans, she would have many burthens. Flying light with bales of wool screwed into longers in the holds from Melbourne or Geelong (old rails and casks of tallow to give her deadweight); jute and myrabolams from Calcutta to Dundee; palm kernels from the Coast; New York to the Far East with cased oil; Cardiff to load coal for the Argentine; nitrates—to Channel for orders—from Taltal; rolling her spars a-crack with a lading of railway iron for the Bengal Railways or showing an excess of freeboard in the cotton trade from the Gulf.

Forty years! She would put her stamp on countless men of the sea in that long career. Generations of sailormen would be bred in her, bred to a skill in seamanship that is still unsurpassed, bred to independence, to resource, to fortitude. She would prove a hard old-fashioned school with few mechanical adaptations to take the place of brute strength and sailor stratagem. . . . *Sierra Lucena*, *Inveruglas*, *Sophie*. A gallant old seafarer, whatever her alias, the *Tusitala* of New York, as then we named her.

If the ceremony of adult ship-baptism to which we applied ourselves that day was peculiar and unorthodox, the circumstances of the old *Sophie*'s purchase and the identity of the buyers were no less strange. Bought under the auction hammer of a United States marshal, her old debts liquidated, she was saved from the ignoble fate of coal-hulking for her steam-pressed successors—or perhaps a rude despatch under the hands of the ship-breaker—by a group of sea and ship lovers comprised in the membership of The Three Hours for Lunch Club. Mr Seth Low, one of the few surviving friends of R. L. S. spoke at the ceremony, and when he had given her the Tahitian name of *Tusitala*—the 'teller of tales'—he said her purchase by the Club was in acknowledgement of a debt to the literature of the sea. It was not intended that the *Tusitala* should be laid by in some backwater as a relic of other days. Under the Club's house-flag, recently designed by Tait Mackenzie, she was to be stored and equipped for sea again. In the enthusiasms of the day, we were all in optimistic spirit. The old ship would sail again. Some of our fellow-members even thought of a voyage in her to find adventure far abroad, but there were many old sailors among us who could only sail in her in dreams.

It is not easy to define the precise sentiment that inspired a city club, avowedly one of a quasi-literary character, to purchase a sailing ship of 1,700 tons and assume responsibility for her active career. Seventeen hundred tons of old iron! An embarrassing relic of the days of sail. In the matters of employment, the Club's advisers had no profitable future to forecast—however small the figure at which the marshal's hammer fell at her enforced sale. Ocean transport of goods called for speed and regularity that could not be guaranteed by a vessel dependent on the vagaries of the winds. When the *Tusitala* was refitted for sea it became evident that only by special favour could a suitable cargo be obtained, but the Club was fortunate in enlisting the support of a distinguished ship-lover, Mr James A. Farrell, then President of the United States Steel Corporation. Steel products were needed in the Hawaiian Islands and a return cargo of island produce could be obtained there. Towage through the reaches of the Panama Canal was expensive but could be had, and in this special trade the old ship was indulgently engaged. In later years the ship was wholly acquired by Mr Farrell, and, about 1940, became a training vessel.

I sighted her once at sea when, in the *Transylvania*, which I then commanded, we sailed on the same tide from New York. Passing, I steered close to her and could have shouted my regards to Captain Coalfleet, but preferred to hoist my message in flag signals, as always we did in sail. 'Good-bye' and 'I wish you a good voyage' were rustling at the halyards as we steered east for Nantucket and she, her white sails filling, bore away south from Sandy Hook.

Chapter XXVIII

TRANSYLVANIA

WHEN a change of Master in one of the Company's ships took place abroad it did not usually call for long explanation or discussion between the two officers concerned. It could be assumed that all was well in the ship and that the rules and routines of the service, with which both were familiar, were in regular operation. For legal registry a brief entry of the transaction could quickly be made in the ship's Official Log. It was thus when, in the autumn of 1925, Captain William Gemmell was sent out to relieve me in the *Tuscania* at Naples and I was brought home overland to take command of the new *Transylvania*, then completed at Glasgow and about to undergo acceptance trials in the Firth of Clyde. It was perforce a hurried business as the *Tuscania* was on point of sailing. But we had been advised by wireless of the transfer, and there was little for me to do but to sign off and make for the gangway. When that rush was over and from the quayside I watched the ship unmoor and steer out on her voyage without me, I had my moments of nostalgic regret, for I had served long in her and had happy days to muse upon as I saw her go. But here was promotion to a senior ship, and the railway journey through Italy and France found me in high spirits and eager to establish myself in a new command.

Although she was originally planned as a sister ship of the *Tuscania*, much alteration had been carried out in the *Transylvania*, largely as a result of the virtual abandonment by the Anchor Line of the emigrant traffic from Italian ports to the United States, for which trade both ships had been ordered. Now, with the extensive range of steerage accommodation discarded, the demands of cruising services, in which the *Tuscania* had experimented so successfully, were met by extensive re-planning. Passenger accommodation had been re-designed to avoid the seeming segregation of First and

Tourist class bookings. On an early inspection I had difficulty in making out any difference between one stateroom and another, so much alike did they all appear, and I thought that such similarity could be a sensible feature of a cruising liner in which passengers were considered of one class and had 'the run of the ship'.

But the outward appearance of the two ships was not at all sisterly. The *Transylvania* had much finer 'lines' forward, and the fullness of the water-line there, of which both Captain Blaikie in the *Cameronia* and I in the *Tuscania* had complained as causing our respective vessels to pound violently in anything like a heavy head sea, had been fined away during construction. As I stood out on the wharf at Fairfield Basin, with Dr Hillhouse, who had designed the alteration, I could happily agree with him that there was promise there of a better entry than that of my former ship.

I had seen the plans of the new ship while she was under construction and knew that it was intended to equip her with three funnels, but had found it difficult to persuade myself that such a weight of 'top hamper' could ever be thought an asset in an oil-burning steamship which, for her purposes, needed no more than one. . . . Of course, there was the Anchor Line's preference in the matter—as against the new Liverpool austerity of 'needs only must' —and I remembered how that preference stemmed long ago from the profitable managership of the three-funnelled *City of Rome* in 1881. (Built for the Inman Line at Barrow, that lovely vessel did not come up to contract speed and was not accepted after trials. She was operated by the Anchor Line thereafter, and in the capable hands of Clydeside engineers proved swifter than all her rivals of the day.) . . . Three funnels! I would have to review that earlier opinion; certainly, the *Transylvania* looked much larger and more massive than her 17,000 tons, because of them.

While the trials in the Firth of Clyde and on the measured mile were carried out in fair weather and proved satisfactory, the weather was boisterous on that maiden voyage towards New York. The gales and heavy winds we met did not quite amount to the worst the Atlantic could rouse against a newcomer, but the heavy sea and cross swell—doubtless the petering remains of some recurring storm—that shook us on the Grand Banks proved sufficiently testing for the builders' engineers who accompanied us on the voyage. Again, as on my first voyage in the *Tuscania*, no effort was made to work up to contract speed; we preferred to take no chances with the turbine reduction gears and jogged along at fifteen knots to run them in. We arrived off Sandy Hook at daybreak on the eighth day out.

To every sailor there are some special hours of the day to be conjured up in the mind for later recollection, and often the thought of that arrival in the morning watch recurs with me. To come in from the eastward with the sun is a fine and dramatic entry under any circumstance, and it is nowhere more impressive than when Sandy Hook and the nebulous glimmer of the Port of New York appear ahead and the open Atlantic lies astern. The coastline of Long Island to starboard appears almost unreal in its fairy beauty: the bare sandy shore is but faintly visible, and the long chain of sea-side lights not yet sufficiently defined to stand out barren and un-interesting as in the broad of day. Away in the south, Navesink Light, after challenging the darkness hour after hour with its brilliant stabs and flashes, has died down to a valiant but ineffectual diamond point in the darkling mass of the Atlantic Highlands. Anon, the sun comes up and the blue haze that lingers over the Hook and the entrance to the Channel dissolves at the onset of his rays. The yellow hull of the Ambrose Lightship emerges from that misty curtain as we stand on to pick up our pilot for the windings of the Hudson channels. . . . Our maiden passage is thus pleasantly concluded and old Neptune has another shapely vessel to enter in his books.

When the new Cunard and Allied Lines skyscraper at 25 Broad-way in New York was almost completed, Mr Benjamin W. Morris, the architect, showed me the features of his lofty conception and, for a final and wonderful impression, took me up to the roof fifteen storeys or more above the busy streets, whence a stirring maritime review could be seen of the confluence of the East and Hudson Rivers far below—a panorama of shipping and the sea that could not elsewhere be surpassed. A brick structure was being erected almost where we stood to admire the view, and on inquiry I learned that it was to become a 'pent-house' for the convenience of the resident director of the Cunard Line, with which the Anchor Line was then associated. Sir Ashley Sparks was the controller of both Companies in the United States, and when he had moved into his delectable apartment he invited friends—often including the senior officers of the ships as they came in—to share his pleasure in it and enjoy with him the spectacle of the harbour so far below his windows.

To the seaman arriving in his ship and steering in the Hudson River right up the open cleft of Broadway, as we termed that sea-mark for holding the deep water of the approach channel when past the Craven Shoal, the sudden grandeur of the skyline of New York City is there to be admired alike by passengers and crew, but the continuation of that inspiring scene is not often enjoyed by the hastening passenger, eager to disembark and attend to his affairs, and rarely by the sailor. . . . But sometimes the augury was fair for both. I recall my artist brother Muirhead's delight in the striking pictorial interest of that reverse in outlook when, after landing from the *Tuscania* in the bright springtime of 1923, he lunched with Sir Ashley in his remarkable eyrie up there on the very tip of Manhattan.

Lunch was not intended to be a leisurely repast like that of the Three Hours for Lunch Club, for all except my brother and I had business to attend; but it was in fact prolonged and to some of us made memorable by Muirhead's enthusiasm and eagerness to get to work with his paper and pencils. Again and again he excused himself to view once more some feature of the commanding prospect that had claimed his interest. . . . In the upshot, he got our host's permission to make a picture of the magnificent view. The large drawing took many odd days to complete. In that time the mobile objects in the composition of the river's traffic—train-barges and ferry-boats, incoming and outgoing liners, tugs and many-decked excursion steamers—were making a constantly changing pattern, yet there is no confusion of movement among them in his masterly picture. At a private view of it in my ship before we sailed, Mr Kramer—the Pilot Master taking us out—said it might well be called a chart of skilful river navigation for not a ship in it was off her regulation course in the channels!

To the hospitable atmosphere of that apartment on the roof of the Cunard Building, I owe the formation of many enduring friend-ships. For the most part these were with intending passengers who were Sir Ashley's associates in the business life of the great city, for the discerning Director thought that the personality of people in a ship was of some interest to the passenger who sailed in her and could promote a harmony in the voyage before it was even begun. A long list could be made out of introductions thus happily effected

in that sky-high sitting-room. . . . Mr William Woodward was one
I met there. As a relaxation from the concerns of Wall Street (he
was President of the Central Hanover Bank and Trust Company),
this new friend occasionally took a 'watch below' on shipboard, and
a cruise to the West Indies was in prospect at our first meeting.
But his abiding recreational interest was in breeding race-horses at
his Bellair Stud Farm in Maryland.

In general a shipmaster has little to do with race-horses, other
than to lose an occasional trifle on a 'sure thing'; and when the
conversation at that first meeting turned to the subject I had little to
contribute to it. A chance remark was made, however, about the
carriage of horses at sea, for Mr Woodward's white-and-red-dot
silks were well known on both sides of the Atlantic. I recalled an
experience with Captain Leslie Cheape's string of polo ponies sent
home from India in 1914 during the early period of the sou-'west
monsoon. I mentioned my distrust of belly-bands to steady a horse
in his stall when in a rolling ship at sea, and Mr Woodward was
gratified to learn of the care which the crew of a ship took of their
equine passengers on a voyage. . . . What induced him to name one
of his promising colts after me I shall never know, but it was a
happily unusual gesture he made when later we became firm friends,
and one of which I was proud.

I am told that 'David Bone' was very well-bred, being by Camp-
fire out of Medora, and had a colourful pedigree that included
Mediant, who won a Stewards Cup at Goodwood and whose
dam was the winner of a Cambridgeshire. My namesake
won the Wakefield Handicap at Aqueduct, the first race in
which he started, and repeated that success ten days later. Then
ensued a period of ill success, and the colt seemed slow of development.

The Master of a ship in a port abroad can rarely travel far from
the gangway, and horse-racing in the States is a Saturday engagement—Saturday being always our sailing day from the Chelsea
piers. For this reason I never saw my namesake run and only once
did I have an opportunity to visit him in his stall at Bellair. That
was in the days of his doldrums and was perhaps brought about by
a headline in the sporting press expressing the bitterness of casual
backers. The banner headline read—

'DAVID BONE ACTS LIKE A COWARD'

The text that followed related that for three months the colt 'had been working like the wind in the mornings, to come forth in the afternoon and race like a cheap plater. Recently his morning trials have been amazingly good. He has stepped a quarter of a mile in 22 2-5 seconds and five eighths in 59 seconds. But when he is asked to show that speed in the afternoon he failed utterly, and clockers and trainers branded him as a "morning glory".'

But to the sailor, and apparently to the horse, 'doldrums' is a period of ill weather that one must struggle through to gain fair winds again, and that is what my namesake did. Appropriately, his victorious come-back occurred in the Oceanus Handicap, a race for two-year-olds run at the Jamaica track on Long Island which, if not quite within sight of the sea, is at least within its salty atmosphere. Deemed a rank outsider at odds of 15 to 1, 'David' won handsomely, defeating Mrs Payne Whitney's 'odds-on' favourite 'Excalibur' (who started at 3 to 5) by five lengths.

I never learned what happened to the colt in later years, for the turf is almost a closed book to the sailor. But Louis M. Ogden, a wise informant, told me that 'David' had become a 'wanderer' as a three-year-old, that he was averse from 'bunching' too closely in the larger fields, and, having speed, preferred to keep in the open—like a good sea-horse. Louis said that occasionally he won.

An early and welcome voyager in the *Transylvania* was Chris Morley, who sailed back to New York in her on the second west-bound voyage. In the *Tuscania* he had before sailed eastbound with me, and I had found him the most comradely of shipmates. Naturally, I gained much from that companionship, much that was tonic to the good reading the seafarer so often neglects. It was he who had then introduced me to the fine writing of John Burroughs, including a passage in *Fresh Fields* where the beauty of the Firth of Clyde is touched upon. And now I was eager to welcome him on board and show him the reality of Burroughs's observation. . . . I hoped he might contribute a similar appreciative essay to our newly-founded magazine *All Aboard*, which was largely written by members of the crew and passengers and printed and published in Glasgow by my brother John. Nor was I disappointed. He tells of the rail journey from Glasgow to join the ship which was anchored off Greenock ready to embark her passengers—this on account of the unsuitability of the tide. In part, his essay reads—

'For then, as the train wound among the green uplands of Renfrewshire, we had our first glimpse of her, far away down the Firth, with her three black funnels, dainty as a toy. So we saw her, larger and larger as we approached, until she towered steep above the Greenock tender. . . . During the voyage the Captain had on top of his desk a little model of the *Transylvania* in a glass box, skilfully fashioned by a sailor in Glasgow. He had this made for our small boy, and carried it off the ship himself to give it to the youngster, who was waiting on the pier. The brave little facsimile stands now on the boy's bookcase, his most honoured possession. And when I look at it there, it is exactly *Transylvania* as I first saw her, far and small, from the hills of Renfrew.'

On that memorable second voyage we did not have many passengers, for the westbound season was almost at an end, despite the mildness of a true Indian summer, and the employment of the new ship on the regular Glasgow–New York service could not be considered profitable. But I had learned before sailing that the ship had been chartered by a world-wide tourist agency to sail on cruises to the Mediterranean in the spring and summer. That programme had been much discussed between Chris and me on the voyage, and I had even put forward a suggestion for a 'Nomination' cruise in which the Three Hours for Lunch Club might be interested. Economy prevented us carrying this out and it was left to me to tell again how a retiring Vice-President of the Metropolitan Life Assurance Company, sailing with me on a cruise and noticing the preponderance of ladies on the passenger lists had his word on the inequality. 'Lot of our insurance money here, Captain,' he said, rubbing his clerkly hands!

Deprived of the company of my friend on the summer cruise, I had recourse to re-reading many books that he had quoted as informative for Mediterranean travellers, not guide-books, of which the High Seas Bookshop—now transferred to the *Transylvania*—had many in stock, but those of a classical standard. Among them I found a copy of Smart's translation of *Letters of Horace*. Its manner and phraseology, that I had idly glanced at before, became suddenly of compelling interest, with the locale of his correspondence so nearly within sight. The best I could contrive for Chris was a letter composed in what I thought the Horatian manner and that I posted as from Virgil's Cave at Naples. He used it in his *Bowling Green* column (a feature of the *Saturday Review* since the sale of the *N.Y. Evening Post*), offering a gift for the best translation into Latin (verse or prose). In part, my text was—

> O Christopher! Wherefor didst thou not cross with me the wild surges of the Atlantic, where northern storms and the rage of the south west winds roused the rolling monsters of the deep? What wonders have I seen since, braving tempests, I passed between the Pillars of Hercules and coasting the shores of barbarian Africa, anchored my ship where Carthage was. And, on the Athenian shore at Phalerum, did I not take chariot towards the fair Acropolis glistening purely white under the radiance of a swollen moon and bright stars?
>
> And now, Christopher, my heart cries out to thee. The days pass and here in tranquil zephyrs the Tyrrhenian seas sparkle at the approach of our ship and sportive dolphins, beloved of Aphrodite, rustle the smooth expanse and cast bright spray abroad.... But when the direful Ides no longer vex the Atlantic Sea I shall be with thee, and we shall bind garlands, and the Cæcuban, reserved for a festal occasion, shall be served by pleasant slaves.

A month later Mr Morgan Barnes of Ojai, California, was awarded the gift for translation into Latin of my Virgilian halloo.... Heaping Pelion on Ossa, he proceeded—

CARMEN OSSEUM

'Quare, Christophore, comes mihi magnos Atlantici fluctus Aquilone Africoque tergo manis monstrorum volventia e profundis excitantibus non est permensus? Eheu quid memorabile non vidi ex tempore quo, tempestati irridens, columnas superavi Herculaneas et, oris Africae barbarorum aridae nutricis post tergum relictis, litore quo olim fuit Carthago navem statui!

Ad portum Phalericum inde delatus in patriam Atheniensium celeriter vehiculo comparato ad castae Minervae templum fulgente sub luna luceque stellarum candentium sum vectus.

Nunc vero, O Christophore, desiderium tui me omnem habet. Dies et alter praeterlabitur, per tremulum aequor navi currimus, lenibus vela implentibus Zephyris, dum delphini lascivi Veneris deliciae spuma ludunt mareque coruscans tubant.

Veniet tamen dies cum tecum fuero, Atlanticum diris Idibus non jam vexantibus, cum serta nectemus Caecumbumque ad solennia reservatum pueri formosi profundent.

Morgan Barnes.'

A second exercise in ancientry was contrived by Chris Morley's brother Frank, who, with his friends Hamish and Sheila Miles and, as I seem to remember, Walter de la Mare, sailed out to New York in the *Transylvania* in 1926. It was expected that Chris would meet his brother at the pier on arrival, and Frank prepared for that. There had lately been a revival of interest in John Donne's *Sermons* in the *Bowling Green*, promoted by Logan Pearsall Smith's selections from them lately published, and before we arrived in port it was decided that the old cleric's strictures on prohibition were worthy of repetition. Envelopes 1 to 5 containing suitable quotation tracts were prepared for serial presentation to Christopher. In what manner and by whom the envelopes were delivered to him from the moment he arrived at the street entrance to the pier would take overlong to relate, but the shade of the reverend doctor of 1631 must have chuckled as the patrolman at the gate handed Chris No. 1 that read—

> '*Man hath a dram of poyson, originall Sin, in an invisible corner, we know not where.*'

No. 2, which reached him on the upper storey of Pier 54 had this reflection—

> '*As long as the glasse hath a gaspe, as long as I have one, I would breathe in the contemplation of this Joy.*'

No. 3, handed over at the gangway, read—

> '*But those Aquae, which the Prophet speaks of, they flow a magistro bono, from this good master Bone.*'

Upon entering my day cabin, the visitor's eye was taken by a prominent No. 4, tacked up on the face of the corner-cupboard which was fitted for cordial—

> *'He lieth in the covert of the reed.'*

No. 5 lay within beside a straw-covered receptacle and a glass—

> *'Behold now Behemoth.'*

Chapter XXIX

A HOLE IN THE ATLANTIC

'WATCH there, watch,' was the warning outcry of the seaman at one's forehand on the bulwark topgallant rail when his allotted coil of the deep-sea lead line slipped from his fingers at the taking of a cast. That would be in the old days, when I learned my business in square sail. Nowadays the deep-sea lead is stowed away in some obscure bos'n's locker and is only produced once yearly to prove to the Board of Trade inspector that the vessel is equipped in all respects with statutory essentials. Even Lord Kelvin's machine, by which soundings can be taken at almost any speed, is not often employed in deep water. By the use of radio bearings, positions far offshore can quickly be obtained and interest in the 100-fathom line, 'the edge of soundings', as we ancient mariners called it, has almost vanished. Almost, but not quite, for there are still a few old navigators who, when making the land, seek to establish themselves in position above that depth as a mark from which all subsequent dead reckoning can be measured. An old-fashioned but sensible routine, one might term it. It was by the practice of it that in 1929 we discovered a deep and unexpected 'hole in the Atlantic'.

Westbound in the *Transylvania* in November in a dense fog, and using the Kelvin electrically-operated sounding machine, repeated effort was made to find bottom on the edge of the continental shelf—the underwater plateau which extends 150 miles seaward from the North American coast—but without result, other than the loss of two sounding pieces and several hundred fathoms of fine wire doubtless parted under the strains of exceptional depth. Although puzzled, I did not agree that our navigations could be so greatly misleading and a subsequent bearing (by wireless) of Cape Cod and Nantucket supported that view.

When on passage from Glasgow towards New York we had received by wireless a 'Notice to Mariners' that had been broadcast to all ships. It reported the working positions of cable-repairing vessels off the northern coast of Nova Scotia—this as a result of the transatlantic cables being broken during a submarine earthquake some weeks previously. As we were far from the area, I had not paid much attention to the notice, but now the thought persisted that seismic distortions spread widely in any area and that the original survey upon which our British charts were engraved was very old. (It is said that James Cook charted the Straits of Belle Isle in 1756!) . . . At Gloucester, Mass., where seafaring men have long memories, I had heard the vagaries of the soundings on the George's Banks discussed, and one old-timer had affirmed that the charts were all wrong. But no one had suggested earthquakes as the cause of that.

It is well known that no reputable shipmaster is allowed to talk of the sea-serpents he has seen, and when we had made Nantucket Lightship without difficulty and arrived at New York, I decided to make no mention of my doubts. But one must have a reserve in equipment for the homeward voyage, and when Captain McConkey, the Marine Superintendent, called on board as customary, I asked him for replacements of the sounding gear I had lost. An inquiring reporter was within hearing and questioned me skilfully upon the experience. On the day following, I became the subject of many headlines. 'Liner Captain says bottom has dropped out of Atlantic' was the most amusing of many Press comments. I had a flutter of facetious telegrams from many friends and *Time* in its issue of 16th December said of me 'The earth was out of place, not he.'

When the mirth was at its height, I had other and less hilarious correspondence. The U.S. Coast and Geodetic Survey wrote to inquire if they might see a copy of my Log upon which I based my findings. I had no findings, I wrote, but Captain Cotton, the Superintendent of the Department of Survey, was welcome to the copy of observations and subsequent movements which I sent to him. I added that I understood Mr J. P. Morgan had given his Steam Yacht *Corsair* to the U.S. Government for service, when suitably converted and equipped, as a surveying vessel. I suggested that she could not be put to better use than on the George's Bank.

Throughout the spring and summer of 1930 there was much activity in these waters and, with all the latest sonic devices available, it took long to find the *Transylvania*'s 'hole in the Atlantic'. But it was located before the autumn hurricanes came roaring up the coast in September. The New York Field Station made the announcement at the end of the year—

> 'The remarkable submarine valley discovered during the course of the survey (on the George's Bank), is shown. . . . This valley extends across the steamer track along this edge of the continental shelf. The changes of depth across this valley are very abrupt—several hundred fathoms in a mile or more.
>
> 'This submarine valley and other configuration of the ocean bottom in this locality is of such a character as to lend itself admirably to the determination of the ship's position—when making a landfall on the transatlantic track.'

On the new U.S. chart of the George's Bank the 'hole' is given the name 'Corsair Gorge'. *Transylvania* has twelve letters, and would doubtless take up too much room on the plate when the chart was made, but I would like to have seen the name of my beautiful ship somewhere on the chart of the Atlantic, for she lies below its waters off Barra Head.

To one who had fisted sail in a windjammer when young it seems a far cry from probing the depths of the ocean to measuring the heights of the skies above it and finding himself in his later years having to do with overseas aviation. It is not that I ever adventured in flying hazards myself, for that requires a youthful spirit and a sense of levitation not easily acquired in later life. My interest was aroused by the airman's practice of navigation—if his position finding in the void above lonely seas can so be called. Sailing, as we did, on Great Circle courses between the north of Ireland and Cape Race in Newfoundland, the ships of the Anchor Line followed west- and eastbound routes that lay almost under the aviator's track on cross-Atlantic adventure. It is an area in which there is much fog and misty weather to cloud the mariner's dead reckoning. But he has instruments to assist or confirm his estimations, and when all else fails he can stop or lie-to, as the occasion may demand. Not so the airman, and it was often my privilege to help him from a position on the ocean surface—the *Transylvania* being well-equipped with direction-finding wireless instruments.

I cannot remember all dates and sequences, but Chamberlain in a

Bellanca monoplane—the *Columbia*—was found to be far off his projected course when we signalled a correction to him in his transatlantic flight of 1927. Then Commander Byrd in the *America* with his three companions (Noville, Acosta and Balchen) overhead in an enveloping dense fog east of Cape Race broadcast a request for position, and again we were able to meet his need—although unseen. Later, when I met him at a dinner to Van Lear Black—a notable passenger who honoured me by having a ship's bell specially cast for the *Transylvania* at Whitechapel Foundry in 1926—the distinguished aviator and explorer recalled our wireless voices in the fog. 'It is difficult to imagine,' he said, 'the relief and satisfaction one gets when surrounded by thousands of miles of water, two miles up in the air in a thick fog, suddenly to be told from a ship below just where you are!'

In this connection the estimation of imposing 'size' in a steamship (to which I have referred) becomes even more illusory. The frequent occasions on which at about this date ships and aeroplanes were in vital communication on the north Atlantic led to many photographs being taken from the air of ships in the sea below. Mistakes were often made in identification of the foreshortened vessels, and when the Fokker monoplane *Old Glory* was exercising off Long Island in preparation for a projected flight to Rome, a news photograph showed her flying over the mastheads of a three-funneled vessel described as the *Berengaria*; the ship was in fact the *Transylvania*, which measured only a third of her size.

Three weeks later the same photograph was reprinted in many newspapers, and in tragic circumstance. The *Old Glory*, on her way across the Atlantic, had been lost at sea, and the *Transylvania* was one of the three liners that had searched vainly for survivors. A halting wireless message, amateurishly sent—'S O S—5 Hours out of Newfoundland East'—was all we had to work upon in a full day's search of a rough sea in dismal cloudy weather. Then was silence. Nothing more. One had to guess what part of Newfoundland they were east of—on what course—and what speed the plane might have made in these vital five hours. A later message from the shore station at Chatham informed us of the projected course of the ill-fated plane with an estimation of her speed, and there was also reference to an area that might profitably be searched. But three hours had elapsed since the first alarming S O S, and although we were already on the southern fringe of that area, much precious daylight time had been lost as we swung, in wide tangential courses from one side to another searching for a spot of wreckage in the surly grey of a rising gale. During the black night that followed there seemed no sense in an aimless proceeding, and we lay to, using searchlights. But we were not idle, for there was always the possibility that a weak signal might come through, and our wireless listening was intent and continuous. (I had not forgotten the marvellous rescue of Hawker and Mackenzie Grieve in 1919.) When daylight came I persisted in searching the area until noon, when, in a moderate gale and with a harsh breaking sea running, I decided that there was no hope of survival in such weather and then turned to resume the voyage. . . . Upon the day following our arrival at New York the *Daily Mirror* printed my photograph in its columns reporting the disaster. A caption, accompanying the picture of a tired shipmaster, said that he was Captain Bone of the *Transylvania* who had 'given up the search' for survivors!

From such a tragic happening there is ever something to be learned. Through the whole anxious period a flood of wireless press messages—inexpedient, and irritating in such a stress—poured in on us to clutter up our sailorly affairs. In the *Transylvania* we had in Mr Davis and Mr Poustie as good a team of wireless officers as could anywhere be found at sea. But even they lost patience with such a flutter of irrational flimsies, when the need was all for wireless quiet to promote attentive listening.

We fared better on a later occasion when the measures agreed upon between me and Mr W. D. Davis, our Chief Wireless Officer, were suddenly brought into operation in the case of the British Seaplane *Southern Cross* (Captain-Major Kingsford Smith) in 1930. Some days after sailing from the Clyde, westbound, we were advised that a flying-boat was about to start out from the Shannon on a cross-Atlantic flight to Harbour Grace in Newfoundland, and it was no surprise when later, in dense fog and approaching the land, the *Southern Cross* asked for a position. In 1930 one ship alone could only give a 'line of bearing' from her known position; another ship, broad off, was needed to give a cut on that, and so an approximate position in the air could be assigned. But there were many ships in the area which had taken in the appeal of the *Southern Cross*, and the result was only confusion. At 0630 on the 25th June, Kingsford

Smith requested the *Transylvania* to assume charge of messages, and accordingly other ships and shore stations were asked to cease broadcasting, which they did.

Fortunately, we were in a good position to take that responsibility, for—in the prevailing fog—we had taken good soundings on the eastern edge of the Grand Banks, and we had, far south of us, the *American Merchant* co-operating in the plot. By this good system we guided the seaplane in dense fog to Harbour Grace when her compass had 'gone mad', and there was only one hour's fuel in her tanks. The last message we had was at 0930 (G.M.T.). 'Hooray. See land at last.' . . . The *Southern Cross* landed safely at Harbour Grace.

Chapter XXX

A CRUISE TO NOWHERE

TO be held up by fog is always a vexation to the shipmaster, but it is peculiarly exasperating when, after creeping cautiously in the last few miles of the voyage, one comes to an anchor in what would normally be a position within sight of the Chelsea piers in the Hudson. I can recall a notable fog in such a circumstance, three mean days of it, lying at anchor in New York's lower Bay after a lengthy passage from Glasgow. Even there, arrived in the harbour and at anchor, we were still endangered and, as the density persisted and vessels crept in from sea while nothing ventured out, the clamour of menaced shipping to make its individual presence known to an incomer became fearsomely insistent. . . . Roaring sirens from the ships under way; bells, bells, and bells again sounding out from those anchored, and the beating of copper gongs—*Rrr-oom! Room! Rrrr-oom!*—as the larger ships gave warning of their length.

But when the flood tide, on which we anchor, has exhausted its strength and the gentler yet purposeful ebb comes down to set the ships in line again, the alarming voices in the fog die down. . . . Then daylight breaks: not the glorious dawn that looks so well in shipping posters, but a growing of leaden light, wanly grey and depressing. The ebb tide is still running and scraps of flotsam set down in it—empty boxes, barrels, pieces of woodwork, tin cans, bits of timber, and pier fittings that the ice in the up-river reaches has dislodged. They loom large and out of proportion in the limited circle of vision, and the eye is drawn to them as the only moving objects in the fog.

But what is this that floats into sight, drifting down from ahead, bobbing jauntily in the stream, showing colours that even the drab grey of the fog cannot wholly dim? Paper hats? Gala hats—as I'm awake and gazing out at them from the navigation bridge of the

Transylvania. No doubt of it. Paper hats! The same that dignified men of substance, matrons, young men, and misses are inveigled into wearing at 'Get Together' dinners and farewell parties on the high seas aboard cruise liners. Rakish paper toppers that make every man over fifty look more and more like Mr W. C. Fields; mortar-boards for the clergy; Scots glengarrys and high conicals for the light of spirit; bell tippets for the jesters; and for the ladies, those jaunty little chips in every rainbow colour that can be set at a provocative angle atop the most elaborate coiffure.

There they come, whole fleets of them, in squadrons of six or seven and at timely intervals. It is now after 8 a.m., and I can guess the source whence they set out on this last adventure. I can envisage hard-working stewards in a ship turning-to for the day's work, clearing away the debris of a Gala Occasion and dumping the paper hats overboard to be investigated by the sheering seagulls. Yes. That will be their port of departure, from some liner anchored right ahead of us—her crew busily clearing up in anticipation of a quick turn around at the Piers.

That was in 1930, and the Eighteenth Amendment still in force; a period of hard times in the shipping industry. Emigration or immigration, whichever way one happens to look at the movement of a populace, had almost reached vanishing point. Cargo, both outwards and home, was sadly diminished. We were in the throes of a slump in seafaring, and many ships were laid-up to await better times. Our routine of scheduled sailings embraced a period of five or six days in port at New York. In normal times that stay in port was needed to unload and load the ship again, but with cargoes reduced to what could quite easily be handled in thirty hours, it became a period of idleness in the ship—a phenomenal ebb tide draining away and not a sign of the flood welling up to make things good.

It was certainly no ill wind that blew when, at this time, the head of a tourist agency in New York, doubtless in consideration of his own diminished returns, had a great idea. Mr Ralph Dellevie of National Tours came forward with a proposal to charter a ship for experiment in a 'Cruise to Nowhere', to employ her during three days of the period that would otherwise be spent in idleness in port. But it was to be no charter with restrictive clauses in it, clauses in keeping with the decorum of regular seafaring. The charterer was to be given a liberal hand in his conduct of the cruise and in such matters as advertising and that very colourful business of cruise literature. Mr Dellevie's proposals made something of a flutter in the board room. Certainly, cruises—generally to the Mediterranean or round the world—had become an established branch of our services, but they were quietly dignified affairs, entertainment being largely a matter of shore excursions. This three days' tripping was something quite different. And the party of the second part was to bring his own entertainers to sea with him—dancers, singers, fortune-tellers, teachers of contract bridge, jugglers. I surmised that there would be many shakings of head over the business, for ship management is a sober occupation. But it was an experiment, they said, and the ebb was still running.

I wonder if the 'great idea' did not come to our charterer as he sat in some good seat in the stalls, for there was much more than a hint of clever musical comedy in his operations, as I came to study them. Perhaps, in addition to his tourist agency, he had some experience of theatrical enterprise. I think he must have lived for a while within the glamour of the stage, seeing over and over again the grand finale, in which every swain in the cast was suitably matched, man and maid. Then there would be haunting melodies, glamorous lighting effects, and that indescribable something that comes at the end of a good performance—the feeling, as you step out into the cold and windy streets, that you would like to go back and see the show again.

I am probably all wrong in my conclusions, but that was the thought I had when looking at an example of exceptionally skilful window-dressing in a big department store in New York. One whole big window was set in semblance of a cruise liner's after-deck, the S.S. *Fantasia*, as indicated by the name painted on a lifebuoy prominently displayed. An incredibly blue sky and sunny background threw up the paint and pasteboard figures of young men and maidens sporting in a sunlit open-air swimming-pool. Slightly—very slightly—elderly people were playing quoits or shuffleboard on an immaculate deck. On an upper deck, leaning negligently on the rail, was a trim figure in uniform, maybe the Captain, but I did not recognize my prototype, who was much too handsome in face and figure. On each side of him a group of very personable passengers was smiling, with him, in approval of the scene below them. In an adjoining large window of the store the correct modes for 'cruise wear' were displayed, a riot of brilliant shapes and colours that made even the sunlit set-piece look dull by comparison. As I say, the thought occurred to me—how theatrical, for here were the stage properties and the wardrobe!

I suppose I have by now grown out of many of my conservative ideas in seafaring, and the gay midnight doings in my ship when we went gala on the main did not long give me the uneasy feeling that I had been miscast in the performance. I made haste to memorize my lines, but I do recall my dismay and misgivings when we were about to sail on that first 'Cruise to Nowhere' that was the prelude to this amazing vogue.

'Nowhere' requires explanation. When a ship is about to sail she is required to declare her intentions, and the master must attend at the Customs House in good time before departure to affirm the truth of his Manifest when stating the port to which his ship is bound. 'Clearing the ship' is the term for it. One cannot make oath to sail for no-whither; there are no charts for it as yet. When the charterer was told that some port must be named, he insisted that his advertising must stand, but agreed to 'clear' for a short visit to Halifax—the nearest 'foreign' port. But his aim was accomplished by keeping quiet about shore-going and stressing instead the entertainment to be found on board the ship out at sea on her lawful occasions—with no Eighteenth Amendment in force.

We were scheduled to sail at midnight. This was the 'Gala Sailing' as advertised.

> '*Bring your friends to see you off. Enjoy to the full the thrill that comes when you realise that you (Yes, you!) are sailing off to unimagined delights in a great ocean liner, whilst others less fortunate amongst your acquaintances have to return to the drudgery of desk and office.*'

That reiteration of the 'you'! The intimate appeal succeeded in crowding the upper floor-space of Pier 54 with a gay and stirring crowd, and as I stepped from the elevator, returning to join the ship some hours before sailing, I found the curtain up and the play in progress. Trebly lit by coloured bulbs, bedecked wherever a flag would hang, the floor from which our regular passengers had disembarked so lately was occupied by dancing tourists and visitors. A good jazz orchestra was sobbing and blaring right alongside the gangway, which seemed only incidentally to lead on to a ship prepared for sea. Elbowing my way through the press of happy strangers, I found that more people than were tripping it on the pier were stepping out in the ship. A second orchestra was busy making the same blare of trumpets and wail of saxophones that resounded from on shore. I had to do some kind of a step myself through the dancing couples to reach my quarters. The navigation bridge was also peopled, but by less boisterous passengers. It was evident that our gangway arrangements for a normal embarkation were ineffective on a Cruise to Nowhere, and there was a source of disquiet in the problem of how to get the visitors back on shore before sailing time came round.

But there is something salutory in what C. E. Montague once termed 'the drastic sanity of the sea' that makes people recognize their dependence on one another when cabined in a ship. I do not refer to the difficulty Mr Dellevie had in separating the voyagers from the friends who had come to see them off, when the orchestras had packed up and the coloured lights on the pier, string by string, were switched off. That was another story that ended, as so often it did, in a signal to the pilot-cutter at the Hook to send the big yawl to us when taking our branch pilot off, as, unfortunately, we had some ship visitors to send back to New York. That was another story that the *New Yorker* could fittingly relate. My reference is to how matters settled down when we got out to sea. Old Father Neptune did not impose his drastic purge, for we had calm weather all the way to Nova Scotia. '*Sit out on the sunlit deck in your chair and make friends to right and left*' was the injunction that gave us—of the ship—time to draw a deep breath and compose ourselves; later, to adapt the matters of entertainment on a cruise to a shipshape routine.

That was not so difficult. When I found opportunity to get around the decks, I learned that the vast majority of the Easter trippers had never been at sea in a ship before. Indeed, as many people told me, they had never had the prospect of sailing out in an ocean liner until our ingenious charterer in his compelling advertisements had quoted such moderate fares for what had hitherto been a luxury beyond their means.

Before we had been a full day at sea, I concluded that we had found a good crutch for our shipping infirmities. There was stout timber in it, even if the polish—not before employed on shipboard —was too shiny at first glance.

The *Tusitala*, New York

The cruising *Transylvania* in the Port of Venice

'Old Glory' flying over the *Transylvania*, 1927

Chapter XXXI

THE FREEDOM OF THE B.B. SEAS

IN those moderately priced pleasure cruises that were gradually extended from 'nowhere' off New York to greater distances, including the West Indies and, in the summer months, the littoral of the St Lawrence, we had found support for sea-going; but that was far from easing the Company's economic difficulties. With an excess of ship tonnage on the books, due in large measure to an over-bold building programme after the war of 1914–18, further retrenchment was called for, and it became necessary to limit the sailings in the North Atlantic service to meet what traffic remained. In that service the good name and reputation of a vessel are an asset of value and, to conserve that prestige, an alternation was made of the sailing schedules to ensure that each ship of large passenger size was employed in the regular routes from time to time. In this way the *Transylvania* was occasionally laid up in the dock at Glasgow for varying periods with only a small 'care and maintenance' party employed on board.

Such woeful periods of inaction were often lengthy, amounting to a month or two at times, and my attendance on board whilst the ship was thus safely in dock was not often required; but some of the Company's smaller vessels lay anchored in the Gareloch to ride out the world-wide slump at lesser cost. As my home was at Helensburgh, which lies at the entrance to the anchorage, I felt it my duty to keep a weather eye lifting in the direction of 'the owners' property'—as enjoined in the apprenticeship indentures I had signed when first I went to sea.

A pleasant practice in this leisured period was to take the train of a fine morning to Whistlefield, on the heights above the head of the Loch, and from there walk back towards the narrows at Rhu to observe the ships anchored there and idly swinging the tides until there was sign of freights improving. Red-rusted of outward appearance, for small funds were available in most cases to meet the expenses of upkeep, the empty ships provided an unexpected touch of colour to tint the scenery of a Highland Loch. But a few of the vessels, having retained their Indian crews on board, were using their labour to advantage and the diligent *tap-tap-tap* of chipping hammers on the high-sided hull of the eastern trader, anchored under a heather-browed promontory, broke the normal silence of the Loch on one day I made my rounds.

Whilst looking down at her from the hillside, remembering that I had last seen a ship like her loading a full cargo of cotton-bales at Alexandria, I heard a chatter of speech that once I used to know—*Lascari bat*, the language of the Malabar coast whence so many of the Indian seamen who man our eastern ships are drawn. . . . There they were—a dark-skinned, smiling group, on their way down the hill towards a ship's boat that lay on the beach below. With an unlawful joy, I noticed that one of the lascars was shouldering a gunny-sack plum full of wobbling creatures. In what little I could remember of their tongue I inquired what were they doing on the uplands. They grinned sheepishly, and one, apparently a headman of some sort, said, '*Arre, Sahib! Hum k-ya' carriga?*' which could be translated freely as, 'Oh, sir! What can a fellow do but catch rabbits on a fine Saturday?' . . . They looked well fed, too, and I have no doubt that some Highland laird would have rude words to say to his ghillies about the scarcity of rabbits on his Garelochside estate that year.

An essay on the shipping depression which I had written for the *Glasgow Evening News* included a relation of this incident, and apparently attracted the attention of the Talks Division of the B.B.C. I was invited to give a series of broadcasts on similar topics in the London programme, speaking from the studio in Glasgow. A request was made with the proposal, asking me to come to London for voice-tests and sundry instructions. As I had already done a little broadcasting from the Scottish studio then in Blyths-wood Square in Glasgow, and indeed had produced a little sketch there—'Bound Away', a description of sailing from the Clyde bound out to Melbourne in the *Loch Ness* in 1897—I thought the long journey unnecessary, even if my expenses were met by the Corporation. But I was wrong there, and when finally I did turn up at Portland Place for a contemporary vetting, I was surprised to learn how poorly my voice made out when the record was played back to me. I spoke too quickly at times, and had the fault of lowering my voice towards the end of a sentence. But I was an apt pupil, or so Mr Fielden said, even if I did refuse (*Scot scotorum*) to mute the letter 'h'.

There were six talks in the series called 'Waterfront and Open Sea', and I had to attend at the studio every Saturday at 9.15 p.m. to say my piece. I began the series by relating an incident that had occurred out abroad in the West Indies, from which my ship had just returned. I remarked to the Chief Steward on the poor and wilted condition of the potted plants on board, mostly palms and other semi-tropical varieties, saying that one would have expected them to flourish verdantly out there. He said, No, he thought that the fresh water we had taken on at the last cruising port was hard in chemical content and the plants were accustomed to our soft Glasgow water! This astonishing suggestion led me to think of the red-rusty sediment we had for drinking-water on long voyages in sail and to contrast that with the resources of seafaring to-day. On these lines, the talks seemed to interest the listener to the extent of stirring up a notable correspondence. I learned what 'fan mail' was.

In the sixth and last talk of the series I was anxious to end up with a dramatic incident, and recalled the menace of ice in the North Atlantic, saying that not great gales, but the combination of fog and ice, was the greatest danger in these waters, for icebergs have no foghorns mounted to warn a ship away. But then I remembered that icebergs sometimes do groan out a signal of their presence on the route, and I had heard it. That was in my sailing-ship days, and we were eastbound in the *City of Florence* rounding Cape Horn in about 1894. We were running in a light quarterly wind from north-west in misty weather, but not quite the dense impenetrable fog of the Newfoundland banks. The Mate had the watch, and early day-break was just lightening the eastern sky. We thought we heard another ship sounding his hand-horn somewhere near, and I, an apprentice then, was sent down to call the Captain. I can remember that he was angry when he came on deck and saw the state of the weather, and asked the Mate why he had not been called before.

Immediately after our own horn was sounded again, the stranger's note followed close upon it, and the Old Man, after looking fearfully around us, jumped towards the wheel, roaring—

'Down hellum, down! Haul th' yards forward!... Quick, Mister. Christ, what ye standing at?... Ice, ye bloody idiot! Th' echo! Let go and haul! Ice!'

The Mate stood aghast for an instant, then rushed to the brace-pins, roaring out hoarse orders as the yards swung forward. 'All hands! On deck there, men ... for your lives!'

Suddenly, the day growing, a glow appeared low down in the mist ahead and spread out on both bows, a luminous sheen in it, brightening the narrowed sea-line. The ice-blink, cold, white!

At the first glow, the Old Man started, his lips framed to shout an order. No order came, only a groan in his throat as he turned the palms of his great sailor hands upward. What was about to happen was plain—inevitable. The dazzling ice-blink warned him of a solid southern barrier, miles long perhaps, for the antarctic ice breaks away from the glaciers in long extended shelves. The ship lay to the wind at the mercy of the swell, drifting dead to leeward at every second. There was no sea-room to put the ship on the starboard tack, no room to wear or stay. There was nothing to be done, nothing but to get the boats out and leave her.

As we strove, utterly unnerved, at that task, we saw the now clear outline of a small and isolated berg shape out of the mist almost at our bows. It was a 'calf' of the main ice, but had weight enough in it to sink us when aided by the heaving swell. Madly, we knifed at the lashings and swung the two boats out.... Then, the ship struck on the lee bow, hammering and grinding at the sheer glistening wall of ice. The boom went first, then fore to'gallant mast—yards, sails, rigging, hurtling from aloft to drive the decks in. A shelf of solid ice, tons weight in it, crashed on board and shattered the fore hatchway. Then—the grind and scream of buckling iron as the heaving monster came at us again and again.

'Hold on all! 'Vast lowering th' boats!' The Old Man had seen more than the wrecking of the head as we struck, sidling, on the cheek of the berg. His voice had all the old confident ring in it again. 'Square main yards!... A hand t' th' wheel here!'

He had seen a chance for manœuvre. The power of gales long since blown out, but remembered in the heaving swell, had swept our stern around the berg. The 'calf' had put us about. We were head to wind, the foresail flat against the mast and straining us stern-ward. It was broad daylight now, and we could see the berg plainly as we drifted under sternway from it. A foot—a yard—an oar's length, and the canvas on the main now rustling as we swung the yards.

'Foreyards, let go and haul!' The ship brought up, then slowly gathered headway—the broken spars and tackle still tethered to the parent hull. 'Cut and clear away,' said the Old Man, speaking quietly to the Mate. 'We'll stand out to open sea again.'

'Ice, ye bloody idiot!' The Old Man used the word, the crimsoned adjective so much employed at sea, to rouse the startled Mate from stupefaction. It was the first time such an expletive had flown to mid-air when reporting Captain William Leask's alarm (although Shaw had used it in a suggestive sense in *Pygmalion* on the stage). I had no thought of affronting the listening public, and was astonished by the stir its use occasioned although my script had been approved by the B.B.C. 'The talk was about the sea,' they said later, 'and that was the language of the sea.' ... The newspapers made more of it, however, and I had many inquiries from reporters. One telephoned me from London to confirm his information. He said he had heard that my talk had been interrupted and that I had used an angry word in protest. I told him that nothing like that occurred, but that the adjective was in the passage I was reading from an old book. He asked what book? *The Brassbounder*, I replied. There was quiet for a moment. 'Brass*found*er,' he queried? 'No,' I answered. 'Brass-*bound*er. B—same as Bloody!' In the morning issue of a famous London Daily, a headline ran—

CAPTAIN BONE BLAMES AUTHOR

The slump in shipping continued throughout 1934, and brought about a serious situation for the Anchor Line, for the new tonnage had not all been paid for, and the shipbuilders were themselves in stress for clearance of their own accounts and with little prospect of new contracts. Matters did not improve, and in the spring of 1935 the Company changed hands. Messrs Runciman of London became the new owners and, to our great satisfaction, there was little if any revolution in the running of the ships.

Chapter XXXII

'1939'

ON the outbreak of war in September 1939, I was at sea in the *Transylvania*, homeward bound to Glasgow from New York, and immediately sought safety from attack by trying to embrace the one element I feared in North Atlantic weather. Zigzagging in the daylight hours, we steered far north, and found the fog and low visibility we were looking for. We arrived safely in the Clyde after a swift voyage. That was my last command in her, for she was quickly requisitioned by the Admiralty to serve as an armed merchant cruiser. Most of the officers and many of the men who had sailed with me continued in her as R.N.R., but I was up in years, and although I volunteered to serve as navigator, my application was not entertained. I was asked to stand by and assist Captain F. N. Miles, R.N., during the period of her conversion. Many changes were made in her, and when H.M.S. *Transylvania* sailed I hardly recognized her in her warlike guise. I did not feel the parting, as I had thought I might. I had not left her; it was she who had sailed away.... In August 1940, she was torpedoed and sunk off Barra Head.

It was a new sensation for me to be without a ship in the rush of tremendous events at sea following upon the outbreak of war, and I found it not easy to adjust myself to a situation in which, home on leave for a term, there was no date of departure to be planned for and no ship's gangway awaiting my hurried tread on sailing day. But I was fortunate to be at home on the rare occasion of a family reunion, rendered all the more precious by the menacing atmosphere of a bloody war in progress. My son David was also on leave from H.M.S. *Vega*, a destroyer engaged in convoy escort duties in the North Sea, and my daughter Freda, with two grandchildren, had returned home from London in the early stages of air attack. (Her husband's church and the Rectory were subsequently blitzed in the concentrated air attacks of 1940.)

Relating in an earlier chapter my success in passing the final examination for a master's certificate in 1902, I wrote of an important event in my life-story: my marriage to Ella Cameron at about the same date. I must have been a very confident candidate for both promotions, recalling that our banns were proclaimed at Leith at the time I was sitting for my examinations there. I have had a happy married life reaching on to the celebration of our Golden Wedding in 1952, always with comfort and support in the straitened circumstances of a modest household—for a merchant ship's officer was poorly paid in the years before the first World War. But it may well have been that the needs of the day impelled me to literary efforts that I might not otherwise have undertaken. Promotion to command relieved many of our financial problems, not the least being the opportunity to remove from a city tenement to the quiet of a country dwelling better suited to our children's upbringing. Of our son's career at sea, I have already written. Our daughter, Freda, showed early talent as an artist, and attended the Glasgow School of Art where her draughtsmanship was developed and her skill in wood-engraving quickly recognized. She has provided illustrations for several books I have written, and also has done woodcuts for my brother Alexander's *Bowsprit Ashore* among other commissions. She married the Rev. John Chapell Sprott in 1934.

In such a happy family circle, even if for a brief interlude only, one could escape from thought of the war at sea, but in wakeful hours as I pondered my situation I wondered what part, if any, I could take up in communal war effort on shore. Under the old ruling of the Anchor Line, I was due to retire at the end of the year in which my sixty-fifth birthday occurred—a month or two away. But the acquisition of the Company by the Runciman interests in 1935 had altered that, and in Mr Louis G. Carozzi—the new resident director of the re-established Anchor Line (1935)—I felt that I had found a strong supporter of medical opinion in matters of retirement. I was no sheer hulk at sixty-five and that being agreed, I was not long without a ship. I sailed in *Cameronia* (the second of that name), relieving an old shipmate—Captain George B. Kelly—on alternate voyages to and from New York. All the other large ships of the Company having been requisitioned by the Admiralty, it was by the *Cameronia* the Company's Atlantic service was maintained. We sailed without escort and not in convoy—a boastful-sounding way of sailing in the war—and one that often brought my heart to my throat when thinking of the many hundreds of evacuee children we carried out abroad on those perilous occasions. We were lucky in her and saw nothing of the ruthless enemy.

When Greece was invaded and overrun by the Germans in the closing months of 1940, all Greek shipping then abroad came under Allied control. In this arrangement the *Tuscania*—which had been sold to Goulandris Brothers of the Piraeus in 1939—was returned temporarily to the management of the Anchor Line and, with a British crew, I found myself again in command of her. Renamed the *Nea Hellas* and in outward appearance little changed from the ship I knew so well, I recalled her successes of earlier years and thought her almost a personal property miraculously returned at a time of stress. For she was closely associated with my home affairs at Helensburgh in earlier days. It was the assurance I derived from my appointment to her when the keel was laid that led me to purchase my home there: in the peaceful years it was often a treat for my wife and family to sail in her to Moville in Lough Foyle—a port of call in Eire—at the beginning of my Atlantic voyage, and my wife and daughter had both enjoyed a longer Mediterranean cruise in her. It was no wonder I was elated at my good fortune when I trod her well-remembered decks again.

But all was not quite as well below when Mr Spencer, the Chief Engineer, appointed with me, came to report his findings in stoke-hold and engine-room. While there was nothing seriously disturbing in the candid statement of the Greek engineer whom he was relieving, he had been warned that the state of the oil-fuel tanks and a condition of the boiler tubes caused an emission of dense volumes of smoke when under way—a major defect in convoy operations in wartime. There was no time to remedy such a state of affairs, for we were already embarking Australian troops in the Clyde and were due to sail in a large troop convoy almost immediately thereafter. But, at the convoy conference, there was opportunity for me to ask and obtain a rear position in its formation when we sailed from the Tail of the Bank in January, 1941, bound out to the Middle East by way of the Cape of Good Hope—a long voyage made necessary by enemy action in the Mediterranean.

It was as well I had done that, for no merchant ship in war-time can ever have advertised her presence at sea by a column of dense black smoke more effectively than the poor old *Tuscania*. On many occasions I feared that the irate Commodore would order us in to the nearest friendly port. It did not come to that crowning indignity. It may be that enemy submarines were concentrated in other waters, for the voyage was made without incident. Arrived at Suez, the old ship could voyage no further without repair, and we, in the only Greek ship in the convoy, had to suffer the humiliation of sending our troops forward by other ships and lying immobile and impotent at anchor in Suez Bay while others of our company swept on through the Canal to take part in momentous events at the Piraeus. When the tubes had been cleaned and the superheat system that (through former neglect) had caused our stupendous smoke emission had been removed, we sailed homeward as an independent ship, calling at Gibraltar to evacuate the greater part of its civilian population. I was sorry to leave the *Nea Hellas* in other hands on arrival in the United Kingdom, but had at least the satisfaction of knowing that she no longer blackened the skies above her and was as competent and inconspicuous as any vessel in fast convoy formations.

I fared no better in my next war appointment, which was to an even older and most certainly a more decrepit ship. The *George Washington* was already ten years old when seized by the authorities at New York in 1917, at the time the United States entered the first World War against Germany. I remembered that her German engineers had had opportunity to sabotage her engines (and possibly her boilers) effectively before the seizure. She was cleverly repaired in time to carry President Wilson to France when the Treaty of Versailles was signed in 1919, and was thereafter employed in transatlantic service, often interrupted by the need of repairs. Subsequently, she was taken over by the U.S. Navy and renamed *Catlin*, but saw little service at sea, and her distempers had been in no way improved by the long years she was laid up between the buoys in the Patuxent River in Maryland.

All this I learned when I returned to Glasgow in the *Nea Hellas*. The large ex-German ship (26,000 tons) had been acquired by the British Ministry of Shipping under the provisions of the Lend-Lease Act, and the business of management was given to the Anchor Line. I was appointed master and sent out to America with a large staff, mostly recruited from former officers of the *Transylvania*, to take her over. We found her far from ready for sea when we joined her in the Philadelphia Navy Yard. But her hull and engines were in good condition, the work of conversion to our needs was going on at a steady pace, and there seemed no reason why she should not be restored to sea condition for further service: it would take time, we thought.

There was a shaking of many heads over the condition of the boilers, which were the originals installed in her at Stettin in 1908. Immediately after our first survey I asked that they be renewed, as I could not see how any form of welding—which the Navy Yard advocated—could prove effective, the aged metal being fatigued beyond repair. My protest was dismissed and I was told bluntly by the British Shipping Mission at Washington that, had new boilers been included in the transfer, we should never have acquired the ship. But I had learned that a complete set of new boilers for her had actually been built and were, at the time, standing idle in the boiler shed.

The Japanese attacked Pearl Harbour on the 7th December, 1941, and the entry of the United States into the war had the effect of hastening the date of our departure from the Navy Yard; nor could we cavil at casual tests, hurriedly applied. We sailed on the 10th January, 1942, and proceeded to New York to coal and store ship in expectation of sailing ultimately from Nova Scotia with Canadian troops bound for the United Kingdom. Up to the last moments at Philadelphia, at New York, and again at Halifax, the boilers came under constant attention from the over-sanguine welders, but each time showed new weaknesses when put under test. Fully embarked and otherwise all ready for sea, we hauled off from the pier at Halifax and anchored offshore in a good position to sail at daybreak —but it was not long before the now-familiar thunder of escaping steam warned us that another boiler had proved unusable. A fully critical Canadian Naval survey was then held, and as a result the voyage was abandoned. We landed the troops and, a month later, sailed back to New York and returned the ship to the United States Commission.

About a year after that bitter experience I saw the *George Washington* at the Ballard Pier in Bombay. She looked spick and span under her own Star-spangled Banner. I learned that the new boilers were working well.

In contrast with that long and vexatious term of trial and error, my appointment to the motorship *Circassia* in 1943 was a matter of straight sailing for me, although unfortunate for the ailing Captain whom I was sent hurriedly to relieve. The ship lay anchored off Greenock when I joined her and was fully embarked with troops and in readiness to join convoy on the day following. There was just time for me to get my name on the Register and attend a Convoy Conference ashore before darkness fell and I had leisure to collect my thoughts. Recalling the sequence of events in my hurried transfer from the *Tuscania* to the *Transylvania* in 1925, I saw a resemblance in the haste of this quick movement and hoped for the better days that followed in that well-remembered ship. Nor was I unfortunate in that expectation. I sailed nearly three years in the *Circassia* throughout the final years of our victorious effort in which she took part. Built by Fairfield in 1937, after the Runciman interests had acquired control of the Anchor Line, she was a diesel motor-ship of 11,170 tons and—in peaceful days—was a great favourite in the Indian trade. On the outbreak of war she had been requisitioned by the Admiralty and armed to become a merchant cruiser. In that capacity she did all that was required of her. But in 1942 merchant cruisers had served their day, and she was handed back to the Company to be reconverted as a troop transport. When I took over from Captain Henderson she had just come from the dockyard at Belfast, where she had been refitted and fully equipped. I was happy to be afloat again in such a fine and seaworthy ship.

We sailed at daybreak on the 28th July and joined company with a large group of troop transports from Liverpool and the South when heading through the North Channel. In all, we made a heavily escorted convoy of twenty-four troopships carrying probably 60,000 men to reinforce the Eighth Army in the Western Desert. In the *Circassia* I had no need to seek a rear position and found station-keeping in her a rewarding exercise. In general, the convoy averaged fourteen knots, and with calls at Freetown and Durban for refuelling, we reached Suez on the morning of 5th September. The troops our convoy landed there would be seasoned in time to take part in the glorious victory at El Alamein. . . . On the return voyage from Suez, sailing independently, we were ordered in to Durban to embark Italian prisoners taken in the collapse of the Italian campaign in Ethiopia. Strangely enough, we had Polish troops as ship guards. We made a fast passage home, and arrived in the Clyde early in October—to find a great overseas adventure impending—'Operation Torch', in which the *Circassia* took part as a unit of the huge merchant tonnage employed to land troops at some point unknown.

At that date—mid-October of 1942—not much war information was confided to the masters of troop transports. It was enough that we should obey orders with intelligence. Doubtless there was much to be said for keeping things dark in war time, but the seeming indecisions of our Commodore when in Latitude 38° North and about 120 miles west of the Straits of Gibraltar did nothing to urge us on to whatever port was detailed in his secret orders. Again and again the ships were turned in their tracks to engage in odd formations largely devised for marking time. We did not know for what decision the convoy was thus hove-to, but from the composition of the personnel embarked with us we could guess that this could be no ordinary entry into a friendly seaport, but an opposed landing. Common rumour in the ship gave Genoa or Civitaveccia or even Dakar as a port to be attacked. But when, on November 11th, we steered easterly again and increased speed, it seemed that everyone in the ship but the master knew we were heading in towards Algiers, and that 'Operation Torch' was on.

All was quiet at Algiers when we, the 'follow-up' troop convoy, entered the Bay and the ships in turn were called in to disembark their contingents at the *quais*. The only sign of warfare to be remarked was a spiral of black smoke arising from the summit of Cape Matifu at the harbour entrance, where a fortress had been bombed out of action, as was said, by the Fleet Air Arm. In the bright morning air there was an acrid scent diffused. We were to recognize it soon as the merchantman's defence against air attack— the pungent odour of a smoke-screen.

The landings in North Africa required constant troop and material reinforcement, and the *Circassia* was busily employed in that service throughout the winter of 1942. That was the most bitter period of storm in the eastern Atlantic that I have ever known, and the urgency of the service precluded any measures to ease the violent labouring of a ship in convoy. Reasonably laden in the trade for which she was designed, the *Circassia* could be sea-kindly, but war shipments untimely stowed gave her an excess of buoyancy that threw her every-whither in high tempestuous seas. But if, in an 11,000-ton ship, we had our moments of ill content with the foul weather and high seas, what can have been the situation in the little vessels—the destroyers, frigates, and corvettes of small tonnage—who so gallantly kept with us throughout the worst of the weather.

On our second trooping voyage to North Africa we were ordered on to Bone, the advanced seaport base of the British First Army, about 220 miles eastward of Algiers, and unpleasantly close to the enemy's airfields in Sardinia, now manned by the Germans. When, at about sunset, we anchored with the other ships of the convoy in the Bay of Algiers, a heavy air raid was in progress, and we had to grope through a dense smoke-screen the ships in harbour had quickly put up. We knew before arrival of the change in our destination, but it was nearly midnight when our new orders to weigh and proceed reached us where we lay. With the *Cameronia*, in which Captain G. B. Kelly was acting Commodore, and the *Clan Lamont* (bound for Bougie), we crept cautiously through the swept channel and came to clear and open sea again.

It was a relief to breathe freely again after inhaling the fumes of a smoke-screen, and a comfort to the eyes to be able to scan once more the route to the east, which was bright under moonlight. But we were not left long to enjoy that brief refreshing moment, for we were attacked by torpedo bombers almost before we had cleared the harbour limits. But there was sea room, and by alterations of helm when, in the moonlight, we saw the torpedo racing towards us, an evasive turn to or from the weapon's track could be made. Even the moonlight was fugitive, for rain-squalls came, and in these no one could foretell from what position a torpedo would run. . . . What information Captain Kelly's orders contained I never learned, but mine had not the usual detail of an escort being provided, and I thought the inshore courses we were instructed to steer had some bearing on that situation. When the squall had cleared, that question was answered—or forgotten—in the stresses of taking up position in a fleet of ships which later we found to be Force 'Q'—a British light-cruiser squadron.

Throughout the night the squadron, covering the three speeding merchantmen, was almost continuously attacked and, with sea room restricted by the close formation of such a large number of ships, many cases occurred where collision was narrowly avoided. In the dim half-light of the morning, the moon low and the sky in part obscured, the *Cameronia* was torpedoed. We did not see the Heinkel coming in from a southerly direction, for the dawn was breaking high and the bombers attacked at very low altitudes. I saw two, but there may have been more, taking advantage of the dark in distant mountain ranges behind them. The *Cameronia* was hit on the starboard quarter—on the side away from us—and the explosion, which was not great, did not cause her to heel over. A second torpedo raced across her stern and seemed to endanger us, but a quick turn away evaded it. The second Heinkel roared closely overhead, exposing his great dark shape to our fire and that of the nearest warship. This enemy had been hit, and thick smoke was pouring from one wing. After passing us, he endeavoured to gain height, but was obviously in difficulty. . . . When immediate action was no longer required, and I turned to focus my binoculars on the *Cameronia* far astern, I heard what I thought the tinkling of innumerable small bells—a curious salute to the disabled ship. The *Circassia* had heeled sharply under helm when the course was resumed, and her curtsey had brought down the night's accumulation of empty shell-cases from the Oerlikon emplacements on the deck overhead.

The stricken *Cameronia* was not sunk. Under her own steam, limping slowly on one engine and seriously flooded with sea-water, she made port at Bougie: seventeen of her men were killed and many wounded, for the torpedo struck in a troop-deck. She was subsequently repaired and returned to further service. Captain Kelly, who had already been decorated for gallant service in the evacuation of Greece, was promoted C.B.E. for the fine seamanship he displayed in damage control on this occasion.

In the New Year's honours of 1943 I was made a C.B.E., and when later I was commanded to Buckingham Palace to receive that decoration from King George VI, feeling somewhat distracted by the high honour thus conferred, I did not hear all the Lord Chamberlain read out from the citation that referred to me. But my dear wife and eldest grandson, seated not far away, were agreed that the important words Lord Clarendon included were—'for services at sea'.

Chapter XXXIII

L.S.I. CIRCASSIA

AFTER 'Operation Torch', and when the planning of sea-borne landings on enemy-held Europe had grown to for-midable proportions, it became necessary to employ more and larger merchant ships in Combined Operations. The practice of requisitioning and commissioning such vessels as units of the Royal Navy was discontinued, and those converted to L.S.I. (Landing Ships, Infantry) remained under the Red Ensign with their mer-cantile masters in command. In addition to merchant crews, each carried a substantial contingent of naval officers and men whose duties were to control beach-head operations and man the L.C.A. (Landing Craft, Assault) with which the landing ships were equipped.

In the spring of 1943, the *Circassia* was taken from trooping services in the Mediterranean and sent to her home port to be con-verted as a landing ship. We were re-armed, largely with a view to anti-aircraft defence, and many new devices were installed. I had to go to naval school again, at seventy, to learn something about these. A special range of electrical winches was fitted in her to serve the double banks of landing craft that we carried strapped outboard and ready to be manned and lowered for instant service. As senior ship of the group of merchant vessels thus employed in Force 'V' we embarked also an S.N.O.L. (Senior Naval Officer, Landings) with his large staff of specialist signalmen and boatmen for duty on the beach.

Thus manned and equipped, the ship was inspected by Rear-Admiral Lord Louis Mountbatten, then Chief of Combined Opera-tions, and sent off to practise commando landings on the rocky beaches of Loch Fyne and the smoother sandbanks of the Ayrshire coast. We became reasonably expert in the duties required, and I learned a new technique in 'picking up' an anchorage in shallow waters during hours of darkness. Towards the end of June 1943 we embarked troops of the First Canadian Division, together with a large proportion of its Headquarters Staff and, with the other merchant L.S.I., anchored in the Gareloch to await departure on 'Operation Husky'—the assault on Sicily.

Force 'V', to which we were assigned in it, was commanded by Rear-Admiral Sir Philip Vian. There was no Commodore in the group of merchant ships attached to the force. Commodore England had sailed in the larger convoy of supporting troopships and munitions carriers some days before us, and the Rear-Admiral in H.M.S. *Hilary* (a converted Booth liner) led the vessels of all classes in the faster convoy, in which I was appointed Vice Commodore.

Although the utmost secrecy shrouded all preparations and movements, we in the landing ships were fully briefed for the operation. We knew our destination and the measures to be taken to land the combat troops on the beach westward of Cape Passero in the small and slightly sheltered Bay of Chiappa. It seemed inconceivable to me at the time that no word of our purpose leaked out, for the enormous concentration of grey shipping in the harbours, lochs, and inlets of the Firth of Clyde lay under the public eye, but even the most friendly curiosity apparently failed everywhere to be reliably informed. Force 'V' sailed before dawn on the 28th June, 1943.

The convoy steered wide in the Atlantic, probably to avoid air observation by the enemy, then approached the Straits of Gibraltar on an unusual course. Upon entering the Mediterranean we all came under the command of Admiral of the Fleet Sir Andrew Cunningham, and a message was addressed by him to every master of a ship engaged in the operation. Every one of us was stirred and encouraged by this letter from an invincible sailor—

'The operation you are being called upon to undertake has as its object the assault and capture of the Island of Sicily as a base for future operations against the Axis powers. . . . This is a great operation, the greatest seaborne attack that has so far taken place in history. It may have a decisive influence upon the course of the war. A great part of its success is entrusted to the well-proved steadfastness and seamanlike skill of the Merchant Navies of the Allies, whom I am proud to have under my command in this momentous task.'

An inspiring message on this threshold of great events!

Landing Ship, Infantry, *Circassia*, 1944

Author with Lady Bone

David Bone, jr.
Lieut.-Commander David D. Bone,
D.S.C., R.N.

Freda Bone
(Mrs John Chappell Sprott)

For the greater part of the voyage the weather was fine, but on the 9th July (D-Day minus 1) a Mediterranean 'snorter' blew up out of the W.N.W., and roused an unusually high sea. It came up quickly and at daybreak, which is often taken as a sign of limited duration. 'Long foretold, long last: short notice, soon past,' is usually the feature of a 'snorter', but as the day wore on there was little indication of its blowing out and its long continuance aroused much misgiving. To us in the full-powered ships of the assault convoy, the rough and rising sea made little difference, but when we had rounded the western point of Gozo and entered upon the last sea stretch across the Malta Channel, the plight of the small craft of the landing flotillas—who by then had been released from Malta's creeks and inlets to accompany us—was perilous in the extreme. In the long twilight we saw the smaller craft plunging and labouring—bows under at times, and doubtless all hands to the pumps—in highly dangerous seas, and steering perilously close to the tracks we and they both followed, and from which we could not diverge because of suspected minefields. It was, I think, the most anxious moment of the landing as I took stock of the situation. Even if, as I predicted, the wind would fall with darkness, there would still be a dangerously confused sea running on the beaches to imperil the landing craft. . . . If? If? Poring through the two weighty volumes that contained the rules for 'Operation Husky', I could find no instruction concerning withdrawal should the weather defeat us. . . . The prediction that the wind would decrease before darkness came was fulfilled, and even its direction hauled northerly as it fell away, thus helping to shelter the craft should the seas be still running on the sands of the Bay.

To the seaman there is often a strange and almost mystical assurance in the rightness of his sea sense when, after doubts and hesitations, his early intuitions are confirmed and the course he has pursued is justified by the event. Something of this conviction must have dwelt with me on the navigation bridge of the *Circassia* as she was steered into the darkened loom of a hostile Europe on that historic night. We had the moon at first quarter, and after it had set the northern sky remained clear. 'H'-Hour, the date for the first 'wave' of commandos to break upon the beach, was at 0245, less than two hours away, and the film of storm-cloud that we thought might help to obscure our approach, like the strong winds that had caused it, had lessened. A quick scribble on the chart showed me that we were now within the range of hostile gunfire, for it was known that some heavy batteries were mounted on the coastline we were nearing. I could not understand why there was no opposition to our steady approach, and the silence of it all seemed pregnant of alarm. . . . The high wind had abated and the cross seas, as we came under the shelter of the land, had subsided. But we had seen and heard little from outboard in the hours of furtive approach to the coast; there had been no signals from the flagship leading silently ahead. Some hint of action was needed, or so I thought, to break the dread expectancy.

It came. Exactly in its sequence and at its time in the big book of 'Husky', I heard the drone of burdened airplane engines. The R.A.F. from Malta was on the wing overhead to set alight a torch of freedom in Europe after its long enslavement.

It seemed only minutes after the flights had passed over us when a glow in the north-eastern sky and the flickering of nervous search-lights showed us where Paccino lay. Over-distant for the sounds of air attack and indifferent defence to reach out to us, we watched the furious bombardment of the aerodrome go on until the flames died down and resistance had apparently ceased. But on the line of the foreshore fugitive lights appeared, and one could guess that the countryside was widely alerted as we in the convoys slowed down and stopped to anchor just where, some weeks ago at the conference in the *Hilary* anchored in the Firth of Clyde, the Staff Commander's scholastic pointer had tapped the wall-chart of Chiappa Bay.

For long I had tried to visualize the scene at the landing of our first waves of attack, constructing my picture by recollection of exercises in dark Loch Fyne, where there was some minor simulation of enemy resistance. But the event—as we took part in it— was curiously quiet and orderly when, just as we came to an anchor the L.C.A. were manned, lowered, and sent away and a tense period of silent watch dragged on. . . . The dimmed lights that we had observed on shore as we crept in to our anchorage seemed to have been extinguished or obscured: Sicily had apparently turned over in its sleep.

'H'-Hour had come and gone, and the leaden moments of suspense were long of passing as from the bridge we peered into the loom of the high land, wondering which would come first—the flash of heavy gunfire against us or the mounting green Verey Lights that would signal success? . . . It was 'success'—and no time was lost in sending away the supporting battalions. . . . Almost at the moment the green lights on a point we thought Castellazzo had been displayed, the lions of the Fleet woke up and roared. The stillness of the night was shattered by a first salvo from H.M.S. *Roberts*, a monitor that lay about three cables from us, and although her guns had high elevation, the din and disturbance of her 15-inch guns were perilously near. Other warships joined action, firing at some position on the heights and apparently extending the ranges; destroyers, in rear of the anchored troopships, commenced to throw a smoke-screen around us in anticipation of a full-red enemy air attack that could be expected at dawn. It did not come, and when daylight broke we were signalled to weigh and follow the flagship into an inshore berth in the anchorage that had now been swept for mines by the *Cadmus* and *Circe*. In that position we were able quickly to disembark the remaining troops and material loaded in the ship.

Having 'rung the bell' to such good purpose, it was now in the scheme of operations to recover our L.C.A. and their crews—fortunately, all without serious casualty—and sail elsewhere, leaving further action to the great 'follow-up' convoys that we passed at sea on our way to Malta for further orders.

With the completion of our part in 'Husky' we were ordered east to Bombay to prepare for some movement against the Japanese in the Andamans or Nicobar Islands. For these operations, troops of the Indian Army would largely be employed, and we exercised the sepoys in landing from the sea on the Malabar coast at Ratnaghiri. But the weather was too unsettled for an assault on the Islands, and later (doubtless as a minor decision of the Conference at Teheran) the operation was negatived. In the group of landing ships we were now 'Force P', under the command of Rear-Admiral T. Troubridge in H.M.S. *Bulolo*. In late December of 1943 we left Bombay and sailed for Naples at our best speed. The Italian front was beckoning with urgency. Adverse weather there had arrested the promising advance at Cassino, and it was thought that another assault from the sea must be made to break the deadlock. We arrived at Naples on the 6th January, 1944.

Operation 'Shingle' directed against Anzio and the road to Rome itself was mounted by the American forces, and that involved a separation of the units of Force 'P'. With the *Winchester Castle* and the *Ascania*, the *Circassia* was detached and placed under the orders of Admiral F. J. Lowry, U.S.N., the other ships *Derbyshire* and *Batory* being retained by Admiral Troubridge to act with his naval force in a coincident attack west of Anzio. Operation 'Shingle' differed from the landings in North Africa and in Sicily, for no long sea voyage was involved, and the many harbours and inlets under Allied control in the area provided convenient anchorage for the vast assemblage of small craft employed. In keeping with the lesser size and tonnage of these 'hornets', the command of each was entrusted to very young officers, and at conference before sailing the bald or greying heads of the masters of the 'Trojan Horses', as the youngsters called our ships, were embarrassingly conspicuous. . . . A sinister feature of the short distance between attacker and attacked on this coastal strip was the opportunity given to the enemy to mine his waters heavily, and I spent the night of passage between our anchorage off Nisida and arrival in the combat area in dreaming about the efficiency or otherwise of our mine-cutting paravanes. . . . The operation was successful in landing a great army on the Pontine littoral, but its support there entailed difficulties and long-continued exertions before victory in Italy was finally achieved. We were not needed after the first beach landing. On returning to Naples the *Circassia* was engaged in troop movements between that port and Alexandria or Algiers until the summer of 1944.

In the early spring of that year Force 'P' did not seem to belong to any special framework in either movement control or combined operations. Troop transport in the Mediterranean had assumed a fairly stable pattern, and while busied in that we were often separated from the landing ships that had sailed with us from the Gareloch in 1943. But we were not quite forgotten, and there seemed some significance in the retention of the L.C.A. and the berthing of the naval crews to man them throughout our normal trooping voyages. There was rumour, too, of the great invasion on the northern coast of France in which shipping such as ours would certainly be used. High hopes! But, one by one, we lost touch with the ships we had joined up with in convoy for so long as they left for home on a special assignment which, as we guessed, had to do with the greatest landing of all—in Normandy.

For that D Day, the *Circassia* was not enlisted. A lesser task was assigned to us when, in August 1944, we embarked French troops at Taranto and sailed in a large and well-equipped international convoy to the liberation of southern France. I was made Commodore of a section of the convoy detailed to enter the Gulf of St Tropez and land the Headquarters Staff of the First French Army. Its commander was General de Lattre de Tassigny, who was embarked in the Polish ship *Batory*; his Chief of Staff, General Montshabert, who subsequently was killed, sailed with us, and two battalions of Colonial troops. The first casualties of which I had experience occurred at this landing, a German bomber succeeding in destroying a landing craft fully embarked with troops that had just left the ship's side. The air raid in which this happened set alight the dense forest on the southern shores of the Gulf, and when darkness fell the scene was one of flaming grandeur. A heavy smoke-screen from the anchored ships added to the spectacle, and its eddies and whirls in the upper air, lit up by the inferno of the forest fires, made a conventional scene of raging battle; but when action had ceased and the smoke-screen had dissolved in thin air, it was seen that the ships in the Bay Gulf, crowded together as they were, had not suffered great damage. One American 'Victory' ship had been sunk at her moorings and two set afire. None of the vessels comprised in our Taranto convoy had been hit, and the casualties in one of *Circassia*'s landing craft—which was at the jetty when hit by an aerial bomb— were not great, considering its crowded state. The wounded French *tirailleurs* were returned to the ship, and I was prepared to bury the dead at sea or carry the remains on to Mers-el-Kebir, whither the ship was bound when 'Operation Bigot' was concluded. But General Montshabert preferred to have them buried ashore on the soil of France they had vowed to liberate.

After the landing in the South of France there seemed to be no further trooping services required of us, but the ship was busily employed in migration movements of people displaced by the wars in Europe. The *Circassia* was hurried home to Glasgow, where we embarked a large body of Russian ex-prisoners. These had been liberated in the British advances on the Continent. We sailed to Odessa with them, and returned with British ex-prisoners of war, similarly released by the Russians. Civilian refugees from many war-torn lands were transported temporarily to Egypt, and an exceptional service was to relieve an embarrassment that befell the American military authorities in Brittany by evacuating from the district of Morlaix many hundreds of destitute and demoralized Senegalese troops.

*   *   *   *   *

The *Circassia*, in company with a large assembly of warships, troop transports and auxiliaries, was at anchor in Bombay harbour awaiting orders to sail towards an assault landing in the east when the first atomic bomb had fallen on Hiroshima. When we heard the awesome news of it by wireless the futility of any comment imposed a silence on us all. It was as though we realized the fruitless character of all our war efforts. . . . But when the time came for the great convoy to 'weigh and proceed in accordance with previous instruction' Operation 'Zipper'—the last seaborne assault landing of the war—was carried out and the Indian troops we had embarked for it were duly landed in war array on a muddy beach-head at Morib in the Straits of Malacca.

It was in that last war effort I served together with my son in a seaborne operation. At Bombay I learned that David had been detailed to act as P.B.M. (Principal naval Beachmaster) on a long strip of mangrove front not far from the position where the *Circassia* would lie at anchor offshore. I had hopes that we would join company somewhere thereabouts.

Except for an occasional meeting at home when our 'leave' coincided, I had seen little of him throughout the years of war. A Sub-Lieutenant, R.N.R., in 1937—when he was a navigator in the R.R.S. *Discovery* on an Antarctic expedition—he had transferred to the Royal Navy a year later, and when the war broke out he was a Lieutenant in the destroyer H.M.S. *Vega* in the North Sea, almost on the German doorstep. From time to time we enjoyed brief reunions at Glasgow, and I recall that when I returned from 'Torch' voyaging and told him of the *Cameronia*'s ordeal, he was an excited listener, for he had served in her when he was apprenticed to the sea in the Anchor Line. He had just been appointed to his first command in H.M.S. *Wells*, an American lend-lease destroyer then refitting at Glasgow, and the news that the staunch old ship had survived a torpedo attack could not be other than stimulating at such a juncture. . . . From time to time I heard of him from naval friends who had informations we merchantmen could not easily decipher. (I was at my ease in the Union Club at Valetta when I heard, almost by accident, that he had been awarded the D.S.C. for sinking an enemy submarine in the Georges' Channel—he being then in command of H.M.S. *Icarus*, attached to Captain Walker's notable anti-submarine flotilla.) . . . At Bombay we had a brief exchange of signals, but where he was when we all sailed out I did not know. . . . And now, my best reward for staying the course with him was when, his task on the beach completed, he hurried to join me on board my ship in the offing and he and his friends from the frigate H.M.S. *Nith*—which was taking him on to new duties in the East—celebrated with me the ending of the war.

On the following morning, when 'heaving up' to proceed to Singapore, I noticed that the *Nith* was also getting under way, and thought the similarity of manœuvre had a Kiplingesque (or would it be Conrad-like?) ending to my story of sea service—the younger sailor in the frigate steaming off northward towards further adventure and the elder turning south 'in execution of previous orders' when his anchor came aweigh!

Chapter XXXIV

LANDFALL

JAPAN had surrendered before the landing on the Malayan beach at Morib was carried through, but with its completion there was still the *hara-kiri* tradition to be reckoned with in the islands of the China seas which the enemy had occupied in the early days of his seeming success. After the British re-entry into Singapore, the *Circassia* was employed in retrieving prisoners and displaced people from little-known outports where the cunning 'Nips' had forgotten them. Not all the inhabitants of the ports we entered were friendly to us and it was not easy to separate the aspiring sects and nationals. A longer voyage to Australia with convalescents took us away from these unsettled areas. Upon return to Singapore I was met by the amazing news of a high distinction conferred on me in the New Year's Honours List of 1946. I was to be created a Knight Bachelor for services at sea and was commanded to attend at Buckingham Palace for conferment of the accolade. . . . The ship was ordered home in the Spring of that year and, after an uneventful voyage, I made my last landfall in the United Kingdom.

Landfall, or 'falling in with the land' after a long and perhaps hazardous voyage at sea, is a pleasant word to the sailor. It is a word only appreciated to its full flavour by one trained in a sailing-ship, for then he will remember and enjoy again the 'feel' of the brave day when he came in from sea.

Homeward bound under sail, our only outlook for days and months perhaps had been the sea: a calm sea, a stormy sea, the sea shrouded under fog, in darkness, in moonlight or sunshine, but always the sea. The routines of shipwork—as against the excitements of handing sail aloft—had become a drudgery. Food, poor in quality in any case, was by now doubly distasteful. Fresh water had run out and the red dirty sediment of the tank lees had bad effects.

Tempers had run out, too, for shipmates had told and retold their yarns, and discussions now verged on a bout of fisticuffs. We were sea-weary, yearning for a breath of the land towards which we had been sailing for so long. It seemed as far away as ever it was, and we were sailing, sailing, sailing on, apparently towards nowhere. We did not know the ship's position, for of course the Old Man and the Mate kept that a cabin secret (it was said in the old days that that reserve was in fear of mutiny), and we could only guess our nearness to the land by counting up the length of days since departure from a port abroad.

Then came the day when we were given hint that landfall was imminent. The deep-sea lead was often used, and I can recall the interest aroused in a wonder-stricken apprentice by sight of the few grains of sand brought up in the 'arming' of a cast when making the channel in misty weather. But the real day of enlightenment was when we were ordered to heave the anchor cables up on deck after their voyage-long rest in the chain locker, shackle the big links to their anchors, and make all ready for immediate use. That task completed, another confirmed the promise it had aroused. The teak-wood gangway would be brought on deck, and we would know without a doubt that the land lay just under the rim of the horizon when we first-voyagers were set to scrubbing the ship's front steps with sand and canvas.

Sailormen prefer to make port at daybreak, for then there is the whole of the day before them to renew their contacts with the land; but it is not always possible to choose the moment for landfall when the vagaries of the winds or the accumulating error in the ship's chronometer make calculation difficult. When the reckoning is thus upset, it is best to take in sail or heave-to and wait for daylight. That was our case when, in the ship *City of Florence*, I made a first landfall in home waters. It was winter time, but mild weather prevailed when sail was taken in at about midnight. As we swarmed aloft to furl the lighter canvas, a hail from the fore cross-trees, where a look-out was posted, made us pause in the rigging. Landfall! The brightly flashing light broad off on the port beam could be no other than the Lizard. . . . From then on we made slow progress, and daybreak found us lying-to off St Anthony's Head, waiting for the Falmouth pilot to board us. How eagerly then, we lean sea-wanderers would gaze and gaze again at this new Palinurus come among us to say 'good marnin' to the Old Man in almost the same breath he used to order the trimming of the yards anew! How well we responded, and later showed how active we could be in clewing up and furling sail when at length harbour was made and the anchor took firm grip in English ground!

When I reflect upon these bygone days, remembering all the thrills of juvenile action and reaction in moments of stress when serving under sail, and contrast them with the times that now prevail in the steamship, I feel that I have been a seaman in two differing worlds. But the sea is ever the same in both—only the ships and perhaps we sailormen have changed.

How quickly the old ships I knew in that earlier sea world passed over their last horizon when once the steamship owners had solved the problem of serving coal fuel to their vessels from bunker stocks at ports abroad! That was before coal was found in so many foreign lands. It was even thought at one time that the steamer could not profitably be employed in other than short cross-channel coastal trades. In my young days, almost the only charter obtainable to the sailing-ship owner was to carry coal abroad for delivery at coaling stations set up on the steamship routes. The solution of the bunker problem—which so greatly delayed the full overseas development of the steamship—relied upon the services of the windjammer which the steamer was designed to conquer and displace.

There are few sailing-ships now engaged in any trade at sea, although sometimes a fleeting vision of the past sails like the Flying Dutchman across the bows. I sighted such a ghostly bark when, in the *Circassia* leaving Colombo in 1946, we had to alter course to keep clear of a 'country' craft standing in under rags and patches to make harbour behind the breakwater. Something about her made me train the telescope on the oddly fashioned square-sail set lubberly above a graceful composite hull. Rigged as a barquentine of sorts, and probably hailing from the Maldives, she showed in her ragged sails and spars and rigging little trace of noble ancestry as one of the China tea-clippers that she may well have been, but as the object lens of the big bridge telescope dipped to her waterline, I saw the beauty of her clipper lines and could guess at a master shipwright's art in her design.

While I would admit myself a nostalgic remembrancer where the old ships are concerned, I am not so brimful of sentiment as to

discern in them any special virtue as a training factor in modern seamanship. No! I am glad that my good fortune was to have known
and served in them at sea in the last great days of harnessing the un-
bought winds for progress. I accepted their passing with regret
when it came to that decision, then 'turned to' with energy to learn a
new trade in the modern steamship. But was it the different and
divergent new trade that then I thought it was, or did not the old
excitements of meeting the emergencies of handing and trimming
sail in great winds fit me the better for the no less urgent tasks in this
new world of steam and motor power and the mechanical contri-
vances it brought about? Thinking the more of these, it seems
almost inconceivable to me that once I sailed in a ship whose only
mechanical device was the Archimedean screw in her old-fashioned
windlass which we applied to raise the anchors in many far harbours!
. . . The new world at sea has had many and diverse instruments
designed for the swifter employment of its ships and the greater
security of its mariners, and in their operation there is little of an
earlier seamanship required. In swift succession, and as the size
and value of the ships increased, the new appliances came into our
hands—wireless and its development in position-finding at sea, the
gyro compass, hydrophones and echo-sounding devices, radar, were
all planned to aid us on a trackless journey. In this new schooling
the master himself had much to learn, and it may well be that with it
he discarded many rough methods that had been found necessary in
the harsher discipline of the old days.

The hands employed on shipboard (seamen 'under the Act', be
they deckhands or stokers, stewards and cooks and bakers, hair-
dressers or laundry workers) changed quickly in the changing times
at sea. That was to be expected of the strangers—the men and
women from other longshore trades now come to sea—but it
seemed almost no time before the ratings employed on deck had
adopted landward views in keeping with the shorter and more predictable voyages on which they were now engaged. Much of the
old tradition was lost in them, and as the elder men who had known
the days of sail became fewer, the survivors of that age at sea were
not held in great esteem in the modern liner. Indeed, old Bartimeus
was wise to hold his tongue in the fo'c'sle and let the youngsters
prate of longshore diversions.

I am led to this by thought of Old Sloan, who signed with me for

many years in the *Transylvania*. An old shipmate in sailing days,
I had found a post for him in our manning where his years—and
they were many—would not burden him unduly. He was yeoman
of stores in the deck department and, in the intervals of serving out
gear for work in progress, he made a model of the wool-clipper
Loch Ness, in which he and I had served together. I do not think
the model was ever finished. I doubt if it was ever intended to be,
for it became almost a ritual at master's inspection time that it
should be brought out from his 'cubby hole', and some matter about
the lead of the rigging or sailing gear would be referred to me, the
while a group of the ship's officers might be stiffly standing by and
wondering why the Old Man put up with such a notoriously cranky
old shellback. They did not know that when I was a very junior and
inexperienced second mate in the *Loch Ness* of Glasgow under
Captain 'Bully' Martin, the old 'growse' was leading hand in my
watch. It was my first voyage in her. I did not know much about
trimming sail in the early stages, and Sloan guessed that. He would
come up on the lee side of the poop just as day was breaking in the
morning watch and find some quite unnecessary job to do. Then,
out of earshot of the man at the wheel, he might whisper, 'Ye better
get them head yards trimmed a bit, young feller me lad, afore the
skipper comes roarin' up to see what the hell ye're doin' with her!'
. . . Old Sloan! And he used to ask *me* about the lead of the gear in
the *Loch Ness*! Personal relations are rarely as shipmately as that
nowadays, in steam.

I have tried to convey something of the joyous emotions of
making the land after a long voyage in a sailing-ship. How different,
nearly fifty years later, was the landfall made by the same narrator,
who as a boy exulted in helping to furl his ship's white wings as she
anchored in Falmouth Roads on his first arrival home from far
abroad!

This time, I am peering from the bridge of a large steamship in a
dense fog somewhere north of Rathlin Island, of whose bearing I am
at the moment uncertain. The fog has persisted for some days and
the *Cameronia*, inward bound from New York towards the Clyde, is
moving through it at reduced speed. The ship's fog siren is not
being sounded, for it is 1940, and furtive sailing is advised in war-
time in waters where enemy submarines are known to be active.
We have seen nothing of the land and our course has been set only

by 'dead reckoning'. Added to anxieties about the ship's position we have no assurance that the fog gun on Rathlin is being sounded at its regular explosive intervals, for war measures include the summary extinction or dimming of guiding coastal lights and disuse of fog signals when the enemy is about.

In such a situation most of the ship's position-finding devices requiring co-operation from a fixed point ashore cannot be used. Only the ancient practice that St Paul remarked in the Acts was available to us, and it is by constant use of the lead that we have edged in towards the land in the Western Approaches. But the sea bottom thereabouts is notoriously irregular, and a confirmation of our reckoning is sorely needed. In the Atlantic we had been steering far from our normal courses and were approaching the land on an unaccustomed angle from northward; there was in that all the more reason for caution, and speed was further reduced. We have passed an anxious half-hour making small progress (often turning on our tracks) with all hands on the bridge listening intently for the crack of Altacarry's signal gun that, as we thought, might possibly be put in use, for such an explosive report would be difficult to capture by the enemy's hearing devices. At length we heard it—sounding faint and on an unexpected bearing—and our course had quickly to be rectified. We saw nothing of the Island, but we had heard and identified our landfall sufficiently to proceed with caution.

Chapter XXXV

AT SUNSET

IN a ship at sea, as elsewhere in the working scene, dawn brings with it a summons to bestir and attend to the duties of the day, and often its growing radiance is disregarded by the sailor as he strives to overtake the tasks of the morning. But the waning beauty of the sun's setting in quiet weather is more thoughtfully observed, for the duties of the day have by then been accomplished, and the lingering twilight arouses a vein of reflection upon what has been done and what yet remains to do.

Something of this was in my thoughts when, on my last arrival in the Clyde, I conned my ship in the Firth, coming in from southward to skirt the shores of Ailsa Craig and the familiar coastline of the Isles of Arran and the Cumbraes, then entering the upper reaches just as the setting sun tinted with golden radiance the surrounding uplands and the distant peaks of Argyll. . . . Never, I thought, did the hills of home seem more grateful to me as I gazed longingly at their endearing prospect in that brilliant sunset glow, for I knew that I would not view them in such a circumstance again. My days at sea were done.

But it was in no mood of repining that I adjusted the ship's course to steer in towards the anchorage off Greenock in that mellow dusk, for the dimming of my sea horizon (whose many aspects I had come to know so well) was a not unenviable prospect for an old man returned from far adventure. Retirement after nearly sixty years of seafaring was something Jack Yeats's old 'Sylvanus' would be thinking of when he spoke of a secret understanding with the sea. 'I had been long enough in it,' he said! . . . I had served in two ship worlds separately enrolled under sail and steam—and had even lasted out to toy with the matters of air navigation in transatlantic flight in so far as that was concerned with surface contact through a ship on the sea. And now a third field of effort was opening out to me—a world on shore in which I might find a place and perhaps the occasion to extend my writing beyond the short essays and brief descriptive articles I had latterly contributed to a few magazines and newspapers. I had still a fund of seafaring incident upon which to draw and had the ambition to write one more book about sea life before the mists closed in and memory forsook me. Already, I was in touch with the publishers of *Merchantmen-at-Arms* (which I had written in 1918–19 concerning the war at sea as a merchant sailor saw it then), and had made arrangements to proceed with a second volume of reminiscences of service in the greater conflict of 1939–45. In working on it, I looked forward with happiness to renewed co-operation with my artist brother who had made the splendid illustrations for the earlier book. In the second Great War, Muirhead had again been commissioned as the Official Artist at Admiralty and with the ships at sea. As before, he had agreed to the inclusion of a number of his drawings in the new volume. . . . That I would have no lack of congenial occupation in the twilight when I settled down ashore was amongst my pleasant anticipations as I brought the *Circassia* to anchor at the Tail of the Bank.

Daylight was fading then and the steep hillsides above Greenock and Port Glasgow were becoming brightened by the glow from street-lamps and houselights in the high tenements as the twilight deepened. With a newly revived interest in the manners of life on shore, I noted the homeward-hurrying traffic on the nearby water-front, the townsfolk streaming westward towards the neat housing districts in relief from working hours at sunset. My thoughts were in keeping with theirs for I too was on my way home at the close of a long day.

THE END